Pedro de la Cruz

Richard Cocks

Diogo de Mesquita

Organtino Gnecchi-Soldo

Juan Fernandez

Carlo Spinola

Francisco Calderon

Francisco Cabral

St. Francis Xavier

Mancio Itō

John Saris

-rois

Cosme de Torres

Bishop of Japan
(Luis de Cerqueira)

The
SOUTHERN BARBARIANS

The First Europeans in Japan

The SOUTHERN

MICHAEL COOPER, S.J.

ARIMICHI EBISAWA

FERNANDO G. GUTIÉRREZ, S.J.

DIEGO PACHECO, S.J.

BARBARIANS

THE FIRST EUROPEANS
IN JAPAN

Edited by Michael Cooper, S.J.

Published by
KODANSHA INTERNATIONAL LTD., Tokyo, Japan and Palo Alto, Calif., USA,
in cooperation with SOPHIA UNIVERSITY, Tokyo, Japan.

Distributed in the British Commonwealth (excluding Canada and the Far East) by Ward Lock Ltd., London and Sydney; in Continental Europe by Boxerbooks, Inc., Zurich; and in the Far East by Japan Publications Trading Co., C.P.O. Box 722, Tokyo. Published by Kodansha International Ltd., 2-12-21, Otowa, Bunkyo-ku, Tokyo 112, Japan and Kodansha International/USA, Ltd., 599 College Avenue, Palo Alto, California 94306. Copyright © 1971, by Kodansha International Ltd. All rights reserved. Printed in Japan.

Library of Congress Catalogue Card No. 74-128689
SBN 87011-138-8
JCB 0021-782852-2361
First edition, 1971

Contents

LIST OF PLATES

8

INTRODUCTION

IT WAS ONLY at the beginning of the present century that Japanese scholars first turned their attention to the work of the Christian missionaries in Japan during the sixteenth and seventeenth centuries. But several decades elapsed before experts in history, religion, linguistics and other disciplines began to delve deeper into this subject and to make investigations from their own specialized standpoints. In the course of this research further primary materials were discovered, and interest in *Kirishitan* (or early Japanese Christian) studies increased and diversified. As a result, a new field of scholarship was inaugurated and duly recognized in academic circles.

There are, I believe, various reasons why the study of early Christianity in Japan has attracted so much scholarly attention. The Europeans who arrived here at that time came into contact with a totally new and unfamiliar country. Many of them sent back reports that show a deep interest in Japan, and these foreign observers clearly went to considerable trouble in their attempts to understand the people and the country. They faithfully recorded matters that the Japanese themselves either disregarded or failed to note. What to the Japanese was merely routine and commonplace appeared as novel and strange to the Europeans. Thus the accounts of the visitors often supplement Japanese historical records and help to fill in our knowledge of those times.

This is particularly true of the countless letters, annual reports and other materials of the early Jesuit missionaries. There were, of course, some limitations both as regards knowledge and understanding on the part of many Europeans who visited or lived in Japan at that time; some of these men lacked both insight and experience to make a lasting contribution. Nevertheless, it remains true that much information not to be found in Japanese records was first brought to light through a study of the reports written by the men from the West.

For example, in order to study the colloquial language of that age it is necessary to turn to the *Vocabulario da Lingoa de Iapam*, the Japanese-Portuguese dictionary published by the Jesuits at Nagasaki in 1603–4. The Japanese have always attached an overwhelming importance to their classical and written language, but a study of the way in which ordinary people spoke was almost entirely ignored until recent times.

Thus this dictionary is greatly esteemed as a valuable historical source in the study of Japanese linguistics. In addition to giving the exact meaning of a particular word, it also records the region and social class in which it was used. It points out its degree of social politeness; it indicates by examples the way in which it was used; it explains its various particles and inflections. It goes without saying that this dictionary was of the greatest use in missionary activity, for it enabled the Europeans to understand and be understood no matter where or in which social class they were working. It helped them to obtain a command of elegant and refined Japanese so that they could converse freely with the intelligentsia.

About the same time a grammar entitled *Arte da Lingoa de Iapam* was compiled by the Jesuit João Rodrigues and published at Nagasaki in 1608; a revised edition was produced at Macao in 1620. This work is equally indispensable to a historical study of the Japanese language. While a dictionary lists words in alphabetical order, a grammar book is organized according to a definite system of linguistic structure. But during the Middle Ages knowledge of the structure of the Japanese language was extremely vague and fragmentary and could not be compared with the European study of the grammar and syntax of Latin. Consequently Rodrigues was obliged to base his Japanese grammar on the pattern of contemporary textbooks of the Latin language.

But when trying to fit the Japanese language into the linguistic structures of Latin, Rodrigues met with various patterns that could not be adequately explained in such a system. He did not disregard these constructions peculiar to the Japanese language but did his best to illustrate their meaning and use. While he admittedly worked from a European standpoint, he attempted to produce a grammar in conformity with the peculiar structure of the Japanese language. For the sake of convenience his methodology was European; the work, after all, was primarily intended for the use of European missionaries arriving in Japan. Nevertheless, the author went out of his way to adapt his text in order to conform to the Japanese way of speaking and thinking.

Rodrigues, incidentally, had a great deal of experience as an interpreter in Japan and was well qualified to compile his *Arte*. But his interest was not confined to the study of the language, for in the introduction to his unfinished *História da Igreja do Japão* he gives lengthy accounts of the geography, history and culture of Japan. Here again he was in a good position to write on these topics, because the book is based on the experience of more than thirty years' residence in the country.

We owe much to Rodrigues for making this knowledge available, for his reports are highly perceptive and completely differ from the superficial observations of a transient visitor. The zeal with which he describes in detail various aspects of Japanese culture stands in marked contrast to the accepted Japanese tradition of transmitting arcane information only by word of mouth. As a result, matters that were seldom committed to writing are sometimes minutely described and explained in the literature of the early Europeans in Japan.

There are a great many other points of interest to be found in the study of the first encounter between the Japanese and Westerners. So I welcome the publication of this book in the hope that readers abroad will come to a greater knowledge and appreciation of this subject. As far as I know, no other illustrated account has ever appeared in English, and I am confident that reading about the Europeans in Japan during the sixteenth and seventeenth centuries will give a deeper insight into Japan of the twentieth century.

Hiroshima,   TADAO DOI
August, 1970

[Professor Tadao Doi is the president of Hiroshima Women's University and an honorary member of the faculty of Hiroshima University. He has made a special study of the early Christian literature of Japan and is the author of various books on this subject. He has edited and translated into Japanese the *Arte* and *História* of João Rodrigues.]

JAPAN AND THE WAY THITHER

JAPAN
AND
THE WAY THITHER

"INDEED IT SEEMS Nature purposely design'd these Islands to be a sort of a little world, separate and independent of the rest, by making them of so difficult an access, and by endowing them plentifully, with whatever is requisite to make the lives of their Inhabitants both delightful and pleasant, and to enable them to subsist without a commerce with foreign Nations."[1] Thus wrote Engelbert Kaempfer on his return to Europe after his two-year residence in Japan, 1690–92, as physician at the trading post of the Dutch East India Company at Nagasaki, and like so many of the genial Westphalian doctor's observations the statement contains a good deal of truth. For whether or not purposely designed thus by nature, Japan was an island nation that enjoyed complete independence from the outside world.

To say that Japan was an island nation is, of course, to state the obvious, but this insularity, in both the geographical and psychological senses of the term, must be constantly borne in mind for a proper understanding of Japanese history. For on account of its relatively remote and inaccessible position, Japan remained outside the mainstream of Asian history and development; it was, so to speak, in Asia, but not of it. This situation doubtless involved some drawbacks for the Japanese people, but on the other hand its advantages are evident. When circumstances were favorable, as in the seventh century, Japan opened wide its doors to foreign influence and culture; when circumstances became less favorable, as in the ninth century during the decline of the T'ang dynasty in China, the doors were closed again and the Japanese subsisted quite happily by themselves in their island fastness, awaiting more propitious times. Their national sovereignty was threatened only briefly when the Mongols unsuccessfully tried to invade the country in 1274 and 1281; apart from these abortive attempts the Japanese had little cause to worry about foreign interference and were largely unaffected by events on the Asian mainland. It was this isolation that gave rise to a sturdy spirit of independence, a distinctive culture and an insatiable curiosity when foreign visitors finally reached their shores.

Although, according to Kaempfer, the country possessed everything to make the lives of its inhabitants both delightful and pleasant,

Michael Cooper, S.J.

---

[1] Engelbert Kaempfer, *The History of Japan* (Glasgow: 1906), I, p.102.

this somewhat idyllic state was seldom realized, and the history of Japan is far from being an unbroken record of peace and prosperity. For if its history is notable for the lack of contacts and conflicts with other nations, it includes its fair share, perhaps more than its fair share, of civil wars and internal strife as various factions struggled to obtain political power. It is as if, lacking a foreign adversary to combat, the Japanese were obliged to turn their aggression in on themselves. The absence of any threat from the outside may well have contributed to the delay in forming a stronger and more cohesive national unity. Had there been an enemy on the borders waiting to take advantage of any weakness and disunity, Japanese history might have recorded far less internal dissent and upheaval. In this context it may be recalled that one of the reasons traditionally advanced to explain Toyotomi Hideyoshi's invasion of Korea in the late sixteenth century was his desire to preserve thereby peace on the home front.

The waves of immigrants who populated the Japanese islands from the Asian mainland in remote times (if we may believe Engelbert Kaempfer, they had set out from the Tower of Babel) found a pleasant and hospitable land of wooded hills and fertile valleys, blessed with great scenic beauty. Although subject to both earthquake and typhoon, the islands were spared the extremes of heat and cold, of drought and flood. The various legendary names given to the country—the Luxuriant Reed Plain, the Land of a Thousand Autumns and other such splendid titles—were probably meant to express these favored conditions in contrast to some of the harsher extremes to be found on the mainland. The oldest written chronicles that have survived to the present day date back to the first half of the eighth century, but are obviously based on far earlier oral tradition. A description of the foundation and development of the Japanese state is given in mythological form, and at least one sixteenth-century European visitor was sufficiently perceptive to recognize the historical basis of these fables. They narrate the eastward migration of one particular clan as it crossed over from Kyushu to the main island and traveled along the north coast of the Inland Sea until it eventually settled in the fertile Kinai region. This is the second largest plain in the archipelago, and it was here that the Japanese state was founded. The ancient chronicles assign a definite date, February 11, 660 B.C., to this event but obviously exaggerate on this point in order to attribute an aura of greater venerability to the reigning house. Modern historians agree that this date is much too early but are generally reluctant to commit themselves to a definite alternative; probably few, however, would object to assigning the event to the beginning of the Christian era in the West. In due time this clan, whose rulers claimed descent from the mighty sun goddess Amaterasu-o-mikami, grew in power and occupied a dominant position in central Japan.

As early as the fourth century A.D. the Japanese had established a small colony at the southern tip of the Korean peninsula and were actively involved in the struggle for power among the rival kingdoms of that region. But if the Japanese later withdrew from Korean affairs, they were to receive inestimable benefits from the Land of the Morning Calm, for it was through Korea that much Chinese thought and culture were first imported. The generally accepted date for the introduction of Chinese script (a mixed blessing, for the use of myriads of ideographs is not suitable for the agglutinative language of Japan) is A.D. 405, and Chinese scholarship made an immense contribution to the political and cultural development of the Japanese nation. But it should not be overlooked that, as in the case of their writing, the Japanese not only adopted but also adapted this foreign learning to suit their own particular needs and inclination, and in the process they produced their own distinctive culture.

Buddhism was introduced from Korea in the middle of the sixth century A.D., and with its profound metaphysic and colorful ritual it soon displaced the cult of clan deities and the veneration of the powers of nature. But if it is difficult to overestimate the role of Buddhism in the religious life of the Japanese, it is at the same time easy to understimate the resilience and deep-rooted influence of the indigenous cult. Although logically (according to Western logic, that is) the two creeds were doctrinally at variance and quite incompatible, both were assimilated and practiced in harmonious accord. Nothing perhaps better illustrates the joint influence of these two religions than the standard theme of traditional Japanese poetry, which expresses a delicate awareness of the seasonal beauty of nature and laments the inexorable transience of human existence. This sense of compromise, this preference for avoiding conflicting extremes to achieve a harmonious settlement may be found in various inherent aspects of Japanese life and was a source of considerable puzzlement for the early European visitors, whose cultural and religious tradition dealt in terms of more absolute values.

The first permanent capital was the city of Nara, which was founded in the year 710 and served as the political and religious center for most of the eighth century. In 794 Heian-kyō, now known as Kyoto, was laid out in symmetrical design on the pattern of Ch'ang-an, the metropolis of the Chinese Sui dynasty, and with its numerous palaces and monasteries this great city remained the capital of Japan for more than a thousand years. It was here that the ruler, or emperor, held his court, and the political authority of the monarchy reached its apogee soon after the founding of the city. Shortly thereafter the power of the throne began to decline as the emperor was gradually reduced to being a ruler in name but not in fact. With the rise of the influential Fujiwara family, the political regents controlled the court and effectively governed the country. The Fujiwara never attempted to seize the throne for themselves, but then it was not in their best interests to do so, for by skillful intrigue and intermarriage they were able to obtain complete control and exercise their authority in the name of the emperor. Thus the emperor and his court were left free to indulge in ceremonial ritual and aesthetic pastimes. It was the age of elegance, the age of taste—for the few and favored members of the aristocracy but certainly not for the uncouth and illiterate peasantry. It was the age so brilliantly depicted in the contemporary novel *The Tale of Genji*, and the English reading public is fortunate in possessing such a superb translation of this literary classic.[1]

Even after the eclipse of Fujiwara power in the second half of the eleventh century, political authority was not directly exercised by the throne, for in the interval between the decline of one dominant family and the rise of another the country was governed by emperors who had retired to the cloister. The emperor Shirakawa, for example, after abdicating in favor of his nine-year-old son, continued to rule for the following forty-three years during the nominal reigns of his son, grandson and great-grandson until his death in 1129. In his religious zeal Shirakawa raised temples and monasteries on a grand scale and, to finance these operations, he allowed provincial governorships to be purchased for life or even to become hereditary, thus eventually weakening the power of the central government. The struggle between the Taira and Minamoto families in the twelfth century was succeeded in due course by the military administration of the Hōjō regents and once more the throne was deprived of effective authority. Emperors who felt inclined to exert their hereditary rights were persuaded or obliged to abdicate in favor of more docile candidates, and at one point at the beginning of the fourteenth century there were no less than five former emperors living in retirement.

The downfall of the Hōjō took place in dramatic fashion at Kamakura in 1333, but imperial independence was short-lived, for within a matter of a few years political power had been taken over by the Ashikaga clan, which had conveniently helped to bring down the Hōjō. But, in accordance with the apparently inevitable fate of dynastic families, the authority of the Ashikaga began to decline in the following century, and effective control was lost with the assassination of the sixth shogun, or military commander, Yoshinori, in 1441. The office was then occupied by his eight-year-old son, Yoshikatsu, who was succeeded on his death, two years later, by his younger brother, Yoshimasa. It was a sign of the troubled times that of the fifteen Ashikaga shoguns more than half met their deaths either violently or in exile.

During Yoshimasa's long term of office, lasting some thirty years, the situation deteriorated

---

[1] Murasaki Shikibu, *The Tale of Genji*, trans. Arthur Waley (New York: Modern Library).

and unrest steadily increased. A famine in 1461 caused incredible suffering, and contemporary records vividly describe the scenes of anguish and misery in the capital. In an attempt to quell social agitation, Yoshimasa had recourse more than a dozen times to the stopgap measure of *tokusei* (the literal and inappropriately gracious meaning of the term is "virtuous government"), by which outstanding debts were either reduced or canceled by proclamation. This policy may have provided a temporary respite and staved off peasant uprisings for a time, but in the long run it produced only more fiscal chaos. In view of the practically uncontrollable situation, Yoshimasa neglected his official duties and abandoned himself to aesthetic pursuits, allowing his corrupt court to make fortunes from bribes and peculation. It was during his shogunate that the Ōnin War, which was as complex as it was savage and futile, broke out between rival barons in 1467, and Kyoto was the scene of the prolonged conflict. In the first year of the struggle the capital was reduced to ruins, and in the words of an anguished eyewitness, the once glorious city of Heian-kyō became a desolate "lair of wolves and foxes." Even after the rebellion had petered out inconclusively eleven years later, the authorities were unable to restore law and order in Kyoto, let alone the rest of the country, and for some time citizens were terrorized by gangs of armed men who roamed the capital at will. But if the house of Ashikaga had fallen low, the plight of the imperial family was even worse. At the death of the one-hundred-and-third emperor, Go-Tsuchimikado, in 1500, burial had to be postponed for more than a month because of insufficient funds, while .the coronation of his successor, Go-Kashiwabara, was delayed for twenty years for the same reason.

The collapse of central authority led to the *sengoku jidai*, "the era of civil wars," a somewhat vaguely delimited period starting in the last decade of the fifteenth century (some historians not unreasonably date its beginning back to the Ōnin War twenty years earlier) and lasting until national government was once more restored, with the Europeans as interested onlookers, towards the end of the sixteenth century. It was an anarchical period when landed barons, or daimyo, recognizing no effective central authority and enjoying absolute power in their own domains, squabbled and fought among themselves to increase their wealth and territory. According to João Rodrigues, a Portuguese who reached Japan towards the end of this period, "Men chastised and killed each other, banished people and confiscated their property as they saw fit, in such fashion that treachery was rampant and nobody trusted his neighbor." Small wonder that the early Europeans in Japan referred incorrectly but realistically to the daimyo as kings, as the true emperor resided poorly and obscurely in his half-ruined capital. In marked contrast to former ages, the imperial title passed in direct succession from father to son for more than a hundred years, during which period there were exceptionally long reigns and no abdications. At first sight this might appear to indicate the flourishing state of the royal house; the reality, in fact, was quite the reverse. As far as the warring barons were concerned, it hardly mattered who was on the throne, and there was no need for them to interfere with the imperial line.

Accustomed to strong monarchical government, the visiting Europeans, and especially the Iberians, found it difficult to comprehend and impossible to appreciate a system that in at least some respects—although the comparison should obviously not be pushed too far— resembled a constitutional monarchy in which the king reigns but does not rule. The Jesuit Luis Frois described the situation succinctly when he observed, "The *Dairi* is the true king or emperor of all these 66 kingdoms but is obeyed by none."[1] Here he was speaking from personal experience, for when the emperor Ōgimachi issued a rescript in 1569 ordering the missionary to leave the capital, Frois was advised that he could safely ignore the decree. To add to the confusion the shogun was also powerless, and there were frequent letters sent back to Europe commenting on the bewildering lack of political stability.

---

[1] *Cartas que los Padres y Hermanos de la Compañía de Jesus que andan en los Reynos de Japon escrivieron . . . .* (Alcalá: 1575), f. 293.

Yet it would be misleading to paint a picture of complete gloom when describing this period. Although the country as a whole had no central government, there were still territories where the undisputed authority of the local daimyo ensured that peace and relative prosperity could be enjoyed for considerable lengths of time. Even when cities and towns were destroyed in the intermittent fighting, such was the style of native architecture and the skill of Japanese carpenters that the wooden houses could be quickly rebuilt and the life of the community restored to normal. Not all of the daimyo callously exploited the peasants by imposing inhuman taxes. Many encouraged the development of industry, mining and agriculture, and if this was done primarily to boost their own revenues, the increased production nevertheless also benefited the common people. Buddhism was undeniably in a state of decline, and clashes took place between the armed retainers of rival sects. But just as Christian monasteries helped to preserve Europe's intellectual heritage during the Dark Ages, so the great Zen foundations in Japan provided facilities for scholarship and art. Nor were the ordinary people forgotten, and the monks organized numerous *teragoya*, or small temple schools, which provided elementary instruction for the local children.

As a result of the unsettled conditions in the cultural center of Kyoto, provincial cities received an influx of artists and craftsmen, who were welcomed by wealthy barons eager to acquire social grace and credit. The Ōuchi family at Yamaguchi was notable in this respect, and it was they who patronized the great Sesshū (1420–1506), considered one of Japan's most outstanding artists. It was also the age of Kanō Motonobu (1476–1559), son of the founder of the school bearing his name and one of the finest exponents of its characteristic style; of Tosa Mitsunobu (1434–1525), the most renowned member of his school of painting; of Sōami (d. 1525), painter, tea master and art connoisseur. Whatever his shortcomings as a political ruler, Ashikaga Yoshimasa built the Ginkaku-ji in Kyoto, encouraged the arts and stimulated aesthetic appreciation. His influence was largely instrumental in forming the simple and frugal spirit of the ritual tea ceremony. During the century of unrest, this pastime became increasingly popular among people who wished to enjoy the beauty and serenity of nature and withdraw, if only for a few hours, from the turmoil of life in the *sengoku jidai*.

It was at this unpromising juncture in Japanese history that the first Europeans accidentally arrived on the scene in 1543. Although the political and social instability to a certain extent hampered the activities of the foreign visitors, it must be admitted that, on balance, the unsettled state of the country initially worked to their advantage. There was no central authority that could effectively order their expulsion; if one particular daimyo did not care to have the foreign merchants and missionaries in his domains, then they could always move off to another district where a more cordial reception would be extended. Moreover, the competition between rival barons considerably benefited the European merchants, for foreign trade was in great demand since it produced the wealth needed to maintain and expand territorial boundaries. The missionaries, too, were able to use this desire for commerce as a means of firmly establishing themselves in western Japan. It should also be noted that the foreign merchants brought with them not European goods but mainly Chinese silk. Here again the political instability worked in their favor, because there was no central authority sufficiently strong to suppress the *wakō* pirates, whose depredations had helped to cause a rupture in Sino-Japanese relations and necessitated the employment of neutral intermediaries to conduct trade between the two countries. The Chinese wanted Japanese silver; the Japanese wanted Chinese silk. As both sides were prepared to pay good prices, the Portuguese, sailing in their spacious carracks between Macao and Nagasaki, could take advantage of the situation and make a handsome profit.

But at this point it may be pertinently asked what the Portuguese were doing so far from home and how they had made the long journey to the Far East. The Japanese occupy a chain of islands off the eastern rim of Asia but were not a great seafaring race, although it is true that they traveled further abroad than is generally realized. Portugal, on the other hand, is situated at the western limit of the Euro-Asian landmass, and the maritime expansion of this small nation, whose population at the time probably did not exceed one and a half million people, is a remarkable story. For the Portuguese intervention overseas was to affect, for better or worse countless peoples and nations throughout Asia.

It has been suggested above that the record of internal strife and dissent in Japan was partially due to the absence of a foreign enemy against whom the Japanese could have united their forces and expended their martial energy. The same could not be said of the Portuguese, for they were occupied during the thirteenth century in finally expelling the Moors from their territory (the last Moorish stronghold, Silves, was captured in 1249), and during the following century in defending their national sovereignty against the claims of Castile. After establishing their independence, the Portuguese were left free to take an interest in foreign affairs, and, as their geographical position precluded an active role in Europe, they started to turn their attention overseas. Taking advantage of their internal unity and their lack of involvement with other nations, they carried the war to their traditional enemies, capturing the Moorish port of Ceuta on the coast of North Africa in 1415. Thus began, in this modest way, the expansionist policy that would eventually take the Portuguese to India and the Far East.

Their general plan was to outflank the Mohammedan power of North Africa by sailing down the west coast of the continent, and their reasons for wanting to do this were various. In the first place they sought the gold that was known to exist to the south of the Arab regions. Then they were anxious to contact the mythical Christian monarch Prester John, about whose kingdom so many legends had risen; they also recognized their duty of spreading Christianity throughout the pagan areas that might come under their control. Later, in the second half of the fifteenth century, the Portuguese began thinking of reaching India and the spice-producing regions by sea. If they could break into and take over the valuable spice trade, they would not only win large profits but would also deal a damaging blow against the Mohammedan merchants who enjoyed a virtual monopoly in supplying spices to Europe. Cloves, ginger and cinnamon are not generally considered today a very exotic or important item of international commerce, but in the fifteenth century the demand for oriental spices, especially pepper, was very great, and trade in this commodity realized profits that, in the words of one historian, were not to be sneezed at.

During the course of the century, the Portuguese ships commissioned by the crown gradually edged their way down the west coast of Africa. The explorers showed considerable courage in undertaking these voyages, for they were sailing into completely unknown waters. Weird tales of the dangers to be encountered in the uncharted ocean were commonly recounted and often believed. It was said that no ship could ever negotiate Cape Bojador at 26° north, and that even if this obstacle were successfully overcome adverse currents and winds would prevent a safe return. Had not the great Ptolemy declared that human life was impossible in the equatorial zones and that ships would inevitably be becalmed there permanently? But despite these forebodings the Portuguese passed Bojador in 1434, duly crossed the equator, and reached the mouth of the River Congo in 1482. Finally the most formidable barrier of all, the turbulent Cape of Good Hope, was rounded by Bartholomeu Dias in 1488 and the sea route to India lay open.

It is ironic to note that Christopher Columbus had applied to the Portuguese court for patronage only a few years earlier. But because of the preoccupation with the exciting progress towards establishing the eastern sea route to India, his alternative plan of opening the western route had not found favor, and he had retired to Spain where his services were eventually retained. Columbus, incidentally, was well acquainted with the writings of the thirteenth-century Venetian Marco Polo, and his copy of the 1485 edition of the merchant's travels, liberally scored with many marginal notes in his own hand, is still preserved. While living in

Pl. 9

China, Polo had heard of the Japanese islands (which he called Cipangu) and their alleged wealth in gold, and one of the aims of Columbus' exploration was undoubtedly to find these fabled islands. He believed that he had in fact discovered Cipangu when he first reached Cuba in 1492. Had Columbus' services been accepted and financed by John II, the Portuguese would have won an empire of enormous, albeit unmanageable, size. As it was, their Asian empire consisted more of a long, over-extended line of supply depots and military bases than of large colonies, for the Portuguese realized that they possessed neither the men nor the means to control and administer extensive territories in Asia.

Once it had been proved that Africa's southernmost cape could be rounded, the Portuguese began to reach out towards India. Vasco da Gama reached Calicut on the west coast of India in 1498 and Portuguese investment in the spice trade began paying high dividends. A hundred-weight of pepper could be bought in India for three ducats and sold at Lisbon for twenty-two, while nutmeg costing four ducats realized no less than three hundred. An important prize was won in 1510 when Afonso de Albuquerque, taking advantage of the disunity of the Indian states, captured Goa and set up the commercial and military base that was to remain the center of the Portuguese empire in Asia for more than four centuries. Malacca was taken in the following year and served as an entrepot for the spice trade and as a base for Portuguese shipping passing from the Indian Ocean into the South China Sea. It was this string of strategically positioned bases—Mozambique, Ormuz, Goa, Malacca and, later, Macao—that enabled the Portuguese to trade from one end of the world to another and dominate their commercial rivals for a century.

Today, when the Far East can be reached from Europe in a day with all comfort and security, it is difficult to appreciate exactly what the voyage to the Indies entailed in the sixteenth and seventeenth centuries. Depending on prevailing winds and currents, the Portuguese carrack, or *nao*, took two or more years to complete the voyage from Lisbon to Nagasaki. The ship sailed from Lisbon in March or April and followed the African coast until reaching the latitude of Sierra Leone, where it made a wide southwestern sweep towards Brazil to avoid the southeast trade winds. The Cape was rounded in June or July, and the ship then continued through the Mozambique Channel or, if it was after July, to the east of Madagascar. If at all possible, no stop would be made at the fever-ridden base of Mozambique, but ships starting out late from Lisbon were sometimes obliged to pass the winter there. Goa was reached about the beginning of September, and there the winter was spent before the voyage was resumed in April or May of the following year. The *nao* generally called in at Malacca and eventually reached Macao about July or August. Here she would winter once more for the loading of Chinese silk obtained at the Canton Fair, but with luck some of the passengers might be able to transfer onto a large junk and continue their journey without undue delay. In the following year the great ship left Macao about July to catch the southwest monsoon and reached Nagasaki in anything from two to four weeks.

If all went well, that is, and only too often things did not go at all well. Travel by sea in the sixteenth century was a distinctly hazardous venture, and the number of misfortunes that could befall a ship, crew, and passengers was legion. Ships were liable to be becalmed for weeks on end in the insufferable heat of the tropics, or else buffeted by storms and blown miles off course, presuming that they were on course in the first place. The art of navigation had made much progress but still left something to be desired. Pilots relied not so much on sea charts as on their "rutters," or navigational manuals describing in some detail earlier voyages made along the same route. These directions were in fact more useful and practical for determining the position of a ship than might at first appear to modern eyes. But the passenger reading in the rutter that the proximity of the dangerous Cape of Good Hope could be known by the color of the seaweed floating in the water and of the gulls and albatrosses flying in the sky might well be forgiven for feeling a little uneasy.

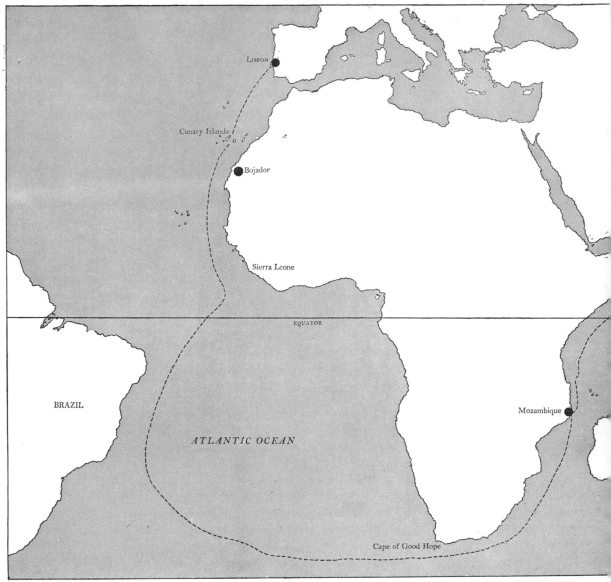

In the map: LISBON, Canary Islands, Bojador, Sierra Leone, EQUATOR, BRAZIL, ATLANTIC OCEAN, Mozambique, Cape of Good Hope

In addition to the unpredictable storms another danger to be feared was the possibility of running onto shoals, such as the notorious *baixos da India* in the Mozambique Channel, which claimed the *Santiago* in 1585. The number of wrecks, especially on the return journey to Lisbon, when the ships were often grossly overladen, was pitifully high. In the dozen years between 1579 and 1591, some twenty-two ships were lost between Portugal and India, while, over the longer period between 1550 and 1650, 112 vessels are estimated to have foundered with great loss of life and cargo. Often enough there were no survivors from these disasters, but, from those who lived to tell the tale, the Portuguese appear to have had a morbid fascination to learn the details, and numerous accounts of these tragic histories were published.

These external dangers were matched, perhaps surpassed, by the hazards encountered on board. The ships were generally so packed with cargo and luggage that the crew and poorer passengers barely had room on deck to lie down and sleep. The crews were often untrained and incompetent; discipline among the soldiers being shipped out to man the garrisons in the Indies was liable to break down in moments of crisis; and some of the emigrants carried with them no provisions for the long voyage. The observance of hygiene was minimal, and diseases such as scurvy and dysentery spread rapidly in the crowded and squalid conditions. Medical facilities were practically nonexistent, and the treatment for most ills largely consisted of bleeding the patient of what little strength he had left; one passenger reported that he had been bled a dozen times before reaching Goa, but somehow he managed to survive both his illness and the treatment. Hordes of rats roamed the decks at night unchecked. In the stifling heat of the tropics, food quickly turned putrid and the water became so foul that "men are forced to stop their noses when they drink," as one experienced traveler noted. Another was

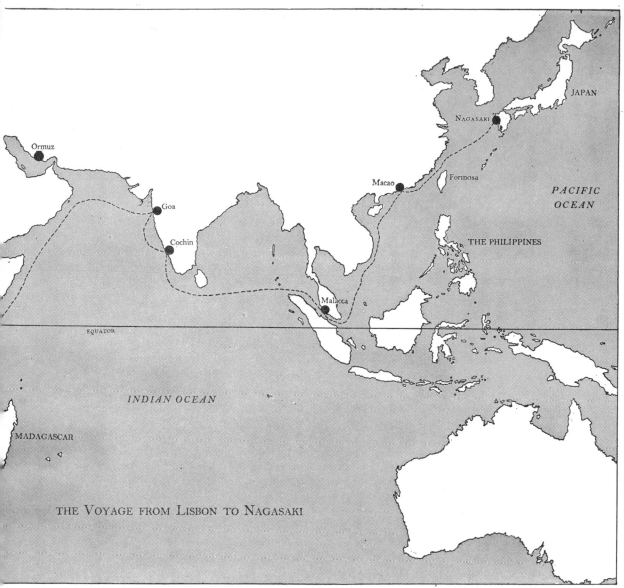

THE VOYAGE FROM LISBON TO NAGASAKI

probably not exaggerating when he briefly observed, "The ships are mighty foul and stink withal." The fine Royal Hospital at Goa proved its indispensable worth when the Lisbon ship put into port, for sometimes as many as three hundred patients were admitted and cared for until they had recovered from the effects of the voyage. The larger carracks might sail from Lisbon to the cheers of the crowds and the salute of guns with a thousand or more passengers and crew, but disease and mishaps could reduce this number to half or even less by the time Golden Goa was sighted.

All things considered, sea travel to the Indies in the sixteenth and seventeenth centuries could by no means be termed a luxury voyage. Yet, on the other hand, it should not be forgotten that there were also prosperous and uneventful voyages, free from storms, disease and other untoward incidents. But although the *Nanban* screens, painted by Japanese artists in the early seventeenth century, invariably depict the Portuguese *nao* entering Nagasaki harbor all shipshape and Bristol fashion, to borrow a phrase from another nautical tradition, in reality many of these carracks must have arrived in a battered and ragged state at the end of their lengthy voyage. Although the passage from Macao to Nagasaki was relatively short in duration, sailing conditions in the China Sea were extremely dangerous during the typhoon season, and various ships were lost on this last leg of the journey. In 1573, for example, a richly laden carrack was suddenly caught by a storm within sight of the Japanese coast, heeled over within minutes and only one man survived the disaster.

As regards the final events that led up to the arrival of the Europeans in Japan, the story may be briefly told. In 1517 a Portuguese embassy set out from Malacca and reached Canton in an attempt to establish official commercial relations with China. While the ambassador

Tomé Pires waited to travel to Peking, a contingent under Jorge Mascarenhas sailed off to explore the Ryukyus, the chain of islands to the south of Japan. This expedition, however, failed to reach its objective and put in at Fukien instead. Pires also failed to obtain an audience at the imperial court and returned in May, 1521, to Canton, where on account of the complaints of the former ruler of Malacca and the arrogant behavior of the Portuguese captain Simão de Andrade, the ambassador and his retinue were imprisoned and spent the rest of their lives in a Chinese gaol.

Pires, incidentally, had heard about Japan from the Chinese traders and sailors whom he had met in the course of his travels, and thus he mentions the island of *Jampon* in his celebrated *Suma Oriental*, composed mainly at Malacca between 1512 and 1515. This appears to have been the first time a European writer used the name, as opposed to the medieval term Cipangu found in Marco Polo's account. The actual name "Japan" is not a Japanese word, but was probably derived from the Malayan *Japun*, or *Japang*, which in turn originated from the Chinese *Jihpenkuo* (pronounced *Nihon-* or *Nippon-koku* in Japanese), the "Land of the Sun Origin." The first European cartographer to use the name was Giacome Gastaldi, who published a map in 1550 showing an island labeled *Giapam*.

Undeterred by the fate of Pires' embassy, the Portuguese continued to ply along the east coast of China in junks, anchoring at remote islands and coves, and conducting a forbidden but profitable trade with the local inhabitants. It was during one of these commercial voyages that the Europeans first reached Japan. A junk carrying three Portuguese was bound for the Chinese port of Ningpo when it was blown to the northeast by a typhoon and eventually fetched up on the coast of Tanegashima, an island to the south of Kyushu. Their names were Antonio Peixoto, Francisco Zeimoto and Antonio da Mota, and it appears likely that they landed in September, 1543. According to Japanese records there was a crew of a hundred men on board and one of them acted as interpreter by scratching ideographs, common to both China and Japan, in the sand on the beach. Despite the language barrier the Portuguese received a hospitable welcome and in due course sailed back to Ningpo. The news of their discovery set off a scramble there among Portuguese merchants, who hurriedly embarked for Japan to take advantage of the lucrative market. Such was their haste that they sailed, in the memorable phrase of Fernão Mendes Pinto, "against the wind, against the monsoon, against the tide and against reason," and they accordingly paid the penalty for their nautical rashness.

Some Portuguese traders reached Bungo in Kyushu about 1544, and were there saved from the cupidity of the local daimyo by the intercession of his young son, Ōtomo Yoshishige, who ever after remained a staunch friend of the Europeans. Mendes Pinto also arrived about this time and has left a lively account of the introduction of the European arquebus into the country; for many years after these firearms were called *tanegashima teppō* in Japanese after the name of the island where they were first imported. A year or so later Jorge Alvares visited Japan and stayed for a short while at the port of Yamagawa on the southern tip of Kyushu. When Alvares met Saint Francis Xavier at Malacca towards the end of 1547, he introduced him to Yajirō, a Japanese who had left his country on a Portuguese ship. At Xavier's request Alvares wrote an admirable four-thousand-word description of Japan, the earliest firsthand report composed by a European. Although admitting that he had not traveled more than three leagues inland, Alvares provided a remarkably detailed account of the Japanese, their dress, food, crops, weather, social customs, Buddhism and Shintō.

Together with his missionary companions and Yajirō, who had since been baptized as Paul of Holy Faith, Xavier sailed from Goa in April, 1549, transferred to a junk at Malacca in June, and landed at Kagoshima on August 15, 1549. From that date onwards the varying fortunes of the Europeans in Japan are fairly well documented. Japan's century of contact with the West had begun.

1. A Portuguese merchant ship in Nagasaki harbor, as depicted by a Japanese artist of the Kanō school in the late sixteenth or early seventeenth century. Detail from a pair of six-panel *Nanban* screens; Suntory Art Museum, Tokyo.

S·P·FRACISCVSXAVERIVSSOCIETISV

26

3. Portrait of Toyotomi Hideyoshi (1536–98) (detail). Kōdai-ji, Kyoto.

◀ 2. Saint Francis Xavier. Portrait by an unknown Japanese artist, after 1623; color on paper; 61 × 49 cm.; Kobe Municipal Museum of Nanban Art. The Latin inscription erroneously reads *Societatisu*, instead of *Societatis Jesu*. The Japanese characters are extremely difficult to decipher, but they appear to spell out Xavier's name phonetically. The two characters below the "A" of FRĀCISCUS read "The Fisherman," which has given rise to the theory that the portrait may be the work of the Christian artist Pedro Kanō, a member of the famous Kanō school of painting.

4. The *Nanban-ji* ("The Temple of the Southern Barbarians"), the Japanese name for the Jesuit church built in Kyoto in 1576. This painting for a fan is the work of Kanō Motohide and is one of a series of illustrations depicting famous sights of Kyoto. 19.7 × 50.6 cm.; Kobe Municipal Museum of Nanban Art.

5. Autograph Letter of Takayama Ukon (1553–1615), mounted as a *kakemono*. Kirishitan Bunko, Sophia University, Tokyo. This letter of the Christian daimyo is an invitation to a tea gathering, and is dated the third day of the fifth month; the year is unknown. Renowned for his skill in the tea ceremony, Takayama was a disciple of the famous tea master Sen no Rikyū (1520–91).

大佛殿

日巖院

耳塚

6. Europeans in Kyoto. Detail from a *rakuchū rakugai* ("In and Around Kyoto") screen; Nanban Bunka-kan, Osaka. European merchants are seen walking in front of the Hōkō-ji, which contains a large *daibutsu* statue. The Hōkoku Shrine, built in honor of Hideyoshi in 1599, is not shown. In the foreground stands the mound labeled *mimi-zuka*, which Richard Cocks noted during his visit on November 2, 1616. "Before the east gate of the temple of Dibotes stands a rownd hill of an endifferant biggnes, on the top whereof standeth a ston pillar . . . ; which hill, as I was tould, was made of the eares and noses of the Coreans which were slayne when Ticus Samme [Hideyoshi] did conquer that cuntrey som 24 or 25 years past."

7. European merchants trading at Nagasaki. Detail of part of a contemporary painting mounted as a *kakemono*; Kobe Municipal Museum of Nanban Art. ▶

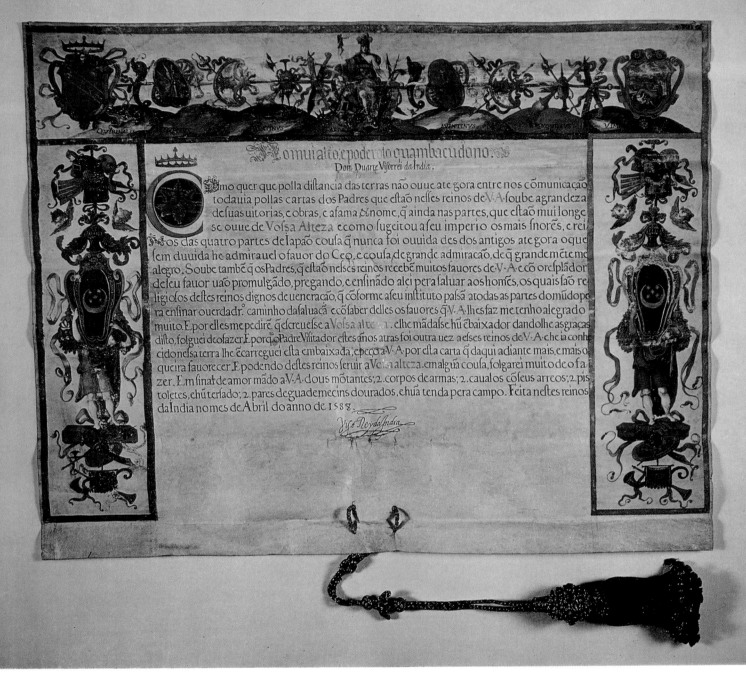

8. Formal letter of greetings, dated April, 1588, from Dom Duarte de Meneses, Portuguese Viceroy of India, to Toyotomi Hideyoshi. The letter was presented to the Japanese ruler by Alessandro Valignano, S.J., at Kyoto on March 3, 1591. 60.6×76.4 cm.; Myōhō-in, Kyoto.

THE EUROPEANS IN JAPAN, 1543—1640

THE EUROPEANS IN JAPAN, 1543—1640

The Work of Xavier, 1549–51

IT BEGAN with a chance meeting at Malacca in the year 1547. Writing on January 28, 1548, Francisco Xavier reported, "While I was in the city of Malacca, some Portuguese merchants of much credit told me the great news of some very large islands that have just been discovered; they are called the islands of Japan. . . . A Japanese named Angero [Yajirō] came with these Portuguese merchants."[1]

The discovery, if it may be called such, was made in 1543, when three Portuguese, Antonio da Mota, Francisco Zeimoto and Antonio Peixoto, reached the island of Tanegashima in a junk. They were kindly received by the local lord, Tanegashima Tokitaka, a vassal of the daimyo of Satsuma. The Japanese chronicle *Teppō-ki*, the "History of the Arquebus," composed between 1598 and 1640, describes the profound impression caused among the islanders by the foreigners and above all by their firearms. The story of the metalsmith, Kiyosada, who gave his daughter, the fair Wakasa, to the Portuguese captain in order to learn the secret of the manufacture of arquebuses, adds a romantic note to the introduction of these lethal weapons. Homesick for her native land, the girl wrote a poem that so impressed her Portuguese husband that he returned with her to Tanegashima.

The news of the discovery and its promising commercial possibilities drew a number of Portuguese ships to the coasts of Japan in the following year, and there the Portuguese came up against Chinese traders, who until then had enjoyed a virtual monopoly in foreign commerce with Japan. After calling in at Kagoshima one of the Portuguese ships continued around the eastern coast of Kyushu and eventually reached the port of Funai, the capital of Bungo Province. Prompted by his counselors, the daimyo planned to kill the foreigners and seize their cargo, but his eldest son, Ōtomo Yoshishige, later known by his Buddhist name Sōrin, successfully interceded on their behalf and during his long lifetime always remained a steadfast ally of the Portuguese. The captain of the ship was Jorge de Faria, and among his companions there was a young merchant named Fernão Mendes Pinto, who subsequently gained universal fame, not so much because he performed any heroic deeds himself, but because, in his

Diego Pacheco, S.J.

---

[1] F. Xavier, *Epistolae Xaverii*, G. Schurhammer, S.J., and J. Wicki, S.J., eds., (Rome: 1944), I, p. 390.

celebrated *Peregrinaçam*, he tended to attribute to himself the feats of his compatriots in all the oriental seas. Contrary to his claim, Pinto was not one of the original European discoverers of Japan, but he certainly knew how to publicize the event.

One of the ships that visited Japan in 1544 took on board a samurai of Kagoshima called Yajirō and carried him to Malacca so that he could consult with Xavier. As the two men did not in fact meet until 1547, Yajirō lived for three years with the Portuguese and was thus able to converse freely with the missionary. From Malacca, Yajirō and two Japanese companions traveled to Goa, where they were instructed in the Christian faith by a man who had also experienced the influence of Xavier, Cosme de Torres, the chaplain of the fleet of Lope de Villalobos. On May 20, 1548, the three Japanese received baptism from the bishop of Goa, Fray João de Albuquerque, and Yajirō was thenceforth known as Paul of Holy Faith. With improvisation characteristic of the work of Xavier, events followed rapidly until the missionary and his group of companions found themselves on the beach of Kagoshima on August 15, 1549.

On the eve of leaving Malacca to sail to Japan, Xavier had written laconically, "Our party is made up of three Portuguese and three Japanese, who are very good persons and good Christians."[1] Nevertheless, none of the three Europeans who landed at Kagoshima that day was in fact Portuguese. They were Francisco Xavier, aged forty-four, born in the austere mountainous region of Navarre; Cosme de Torres, thirty-nine, from Valencia; and Juan Fernandez, twenty-three, from Cordoba. But Xavier was well aware that, regardless of the nationality of the Europeans involved, the mission itself belonged to the Portuguese *padroado*[2] —a fact that has to be kept in mind if the later political and religious problems of the Japanese mission are to be properly understood.

A few weeks after their arrival at Kagoshima, the men of Tenjiku (India), as the strangers were called, were received by the daimyo Shimazu Takahisa and asked permission to teach their religion. The audience was held in most favorable circumstances, for Shimazu believed that the presence of Xavier would attract Portuguese merchants and their lucrative trade to his territory, and so he readily granted the request. Thus Xavier began his work in Japan. He became friendly with the local Buddhist monks and instructed the relatives and friends of Paul, baptizing in all about a hundred persons. Progress then came to an abrupt halt when the monks began to see in him a dangerous rival and brought pressure to bear on the daimyo. Shimazu realized that Xavier was not going to be a commercial asset after all and withdrew his favor, although he did not allow the missionary to leave his domains. Some months of apparent inaction followed, but in reality the time was well spent as the missionaries carefully studied the situation and prepared for their future work. The letters written by Xavier at this time not only show his efforts to understand the people and their psychology but also indicate that, despite growing hostility, the Japanese had already won his heart.

In September, 1550, the small missionary group finally managed to depart from Kagoshima, leaving behind there Paul of Holy Faith, who had given himself so unstintingly to the work of Xavier. His place was taken by a recently baptized Japanese of eighteen years of age, called Bernard, who became a faithful companion of Xavier in his journeys through Japan. He later accompanied the missionary to Goa, and from there he traveled on to Lisbon and Rome, thus becoming the first Japanese to reach Europe. He entered the Society of Jesus and died at Coimbra in Portugal in 1557 as he was preparing to return to his native country. The second stage of Xavier's work in Japan took place in Hirado, and there he met with a similar reception. The daimyo Matsuura Takanobu received him with every sign of friendship, which was doubtless inspired by the presence of a Portuguese merchant ship anchored in the port. But Xavier

---

[1] Xavier, *Epistolae Xaverii*, II, p. 111.
[2] Portugal and Spain had agreed to limit their activities to different areas in Asia. Thus Macao was part of the Portuguese *padroado*, while the Philippines belonged to the Spanish zone of influence. Japan was generally considered to fall within the Portuguese area, but the matter was disputed.

did not commit himself here; moreover, he now had a trustworthy interpreter in Juan Fernandez, who by this time was able to express himself in Japanese. Accompanied by Fernandez and Bernard, he pressed on to his goal, the great city of Kyoto, the capital where the *dairi*, or "emperor," resided. Before leaving Hirado, he baptized the Kimura family, which had provided him with hospitality during his stay at the port; from this family would later come many Christians and martyrs, among whom was Sebastian Kimura, the first Japanese priest.

A necessary stop was made on the way at Yamaguchi, the prosperous capital of Ōuchi Yoshitaka's domain and an important cultural center. Xavier stayed there during the months of October and November and managed to meet the daimyo, but his work met with obstinate resistance. The journey from Yamaguchi to Kyoto was made in the depths of winter and followed the overland route as far as Iwakuni, whence the remaining part was made by boat to Sakai, the flourishing port of central Japan. This epic journey, made through deep snow and seas infested by pirates, would later serve as an inspiration to many of his successors. But the difficulties and sufferings experienced en route were insignificant when compared to Xavier's disappointment on his arrival at the capital. The city had been devastated in the fighting between the troops of Miyoshi Chōkei and Hosokawa Harumoto, as both men strove to control the powerless shogun Ashikaga Yoshiteru. Xavier was unable to obtain an imperial audience, but in any case an interview would not have served any purpose, for the emperor Go-Nara was a mere figurehead without any political power.

At the beginning of January he started his journey back to Kyushu with the knowledge, gained from hard experience, that if his work was to be successful, the favor not of the imperial court but of the individual daimyo would be required. He also knew that one of the most influential daimyo was Ōuchi Yoshitaka, whom he had already met, and so he began forming a new plan of action as he traveled by boat to Hirado. In the spring he returned to Yamaguchi, but this time he went in his capacity as papal legate, suitably robed in accordance with his diplomatic rank and carrying with him exotic gifts. He obtained permission to preach and established himself in a temple called Daidō-ji, which the daimyo provided for him. Although initial progress was slow, the time came when he was too busy to instruct the numerous catechumens and debate with the Buddhist monks. The number of Christians quickly reached five hundred, and most of them belonged to the samurai class. But without any doubt the neophyte who was to contribute most to the Japanese church was a half-blind minstrel, a native of Hirado, who decided to hang up his *biwa* (a four-stringed Japanese lute) and follow Xavier. In the history of the Japanese mission he is known as Brother Lourenço.

In September, 1551, the ship of Duarte da Gama reached the port of Funai, bringing news and letters from India. In order to meet the Portuguese and try to convert Ōtomo Yoshishige, who had succeeded his father as daimyo the previous year, Xavier left Yamaguchi and set out for Bungo. He left behind Cosme de Torres and Juan Fernandez to continue his work, and they were not destined to meet again. In the event, Xavier did not manage to convert Ōtomo, but he made such a deep impression on the young noble that missionaries would always be free to work in Bungo. The letters from India urged Xavier to return, and he reluctantly decided to leave Japan. His experience of the unsettled conditions in the country was to be completed at the end of September, just before he sailed, when he received news that a sudden rebellion had destroyed the city of Yamaguchi and with it, the church there. It was as well, perhaps, that he did not know that his friend Ōtomo Yoshishige had actively helped to bring about the revolt.

Xavier began the Japanese mission and laid the foundations of a work that was to continue for a century. It is interesting to note that for many years missionary work did not extend beyond the places where he himself had left his impact; moreover, the Christian communities founded by him persevered with an astonishing vitality, despite great trials. Although using different methods, his immediate successor was able to continue his work successfully and maintain the high standards set by the founder of the mission.

The Contribution of Cosme de Torres, 1551–70

Although inevitably overshadowed by Xavier the saint and Valignano the administrator in the history of the Europeans in Japan, Cosme de Torres played a vital role in forming the Japanese mission during his twenty years of supervision. Stout in figure and genial by nature, he possessed an inexhaustible energy beneath his simple appearance. Following the example of Xavier, he did not rely on preconceived and rigid plans but was constantly on the move, setting up his headquarters wherever circumstances permitted. His work was unobtrusive but efficient; he was a pioneer in adaptation and knew how to implant this spirit in his colleagues.

After the setback at Yamaguchi, Torres once more began his work in the city. In the five years that elapsed before another rebellion in 1556 gave political power to Mōri Motonari, the number of Christians there increased to about two thousand. Using Yamaguchi as his base of operations, Torres also ministered to the small Christian communities in Hirado and Bungo, and with the help of the first two bonzes to be converted he again tried, but without success, to work in Kyoto. The fresh crisis at Yamaguchi in 1556 obliged the missionaries to move on, and they accordingly gathered in Bungo, where the daimyo was friendly but the inhabitants, especially the upper classes, were distinctly hostile. Torres left Yamaguchi with his health broken, but he continued to direct the missionary work with unabated vigor.

Among the Jesuits in Bungo a new and important recruit was the merchant and doctor, Luis de Almeida, whom Torres had admitted into the Order in Japan. Belonging to a family of "New Christians," or converted Jews, Almeida had graduated at Lisbon, and as the business associate of Duarte da Gama he had already visited Japan several times. He decided in 1556 to donate his considerable fortune to the Japanese mission and dedicate the rest of his life to the apostolate. His money was invested in Macao commerce, providing the necessary capital for the mission, and thus began the controversial participation of the Jesuits in the silk trade. Almeida founded a hospital for the destitute in Funai, an institution that is a landmark in the history of Japanese medicine, for he introduced European surgery and taught the science to his helpers; in addition, he imported Chinese medicines and worked with Japanese doctors. He was also responsible for the financing of the hospital and received generous contributions for this purpose from the Portuguese merchants. From the missionary point of view, however, the work of the hospital tended to retard the progress of conversion among the Bungo samurai, who apparently did not appreciate the missionaries' concern for the outcasts of society.

Three years later, further political disturbances in Kyushu once more forced the Jesuits to concentrate in Bungo. Torres refused to be discouraged; his experience of the political instability of Japan had already taught him the difficult art of adapting his work to circumstances. He sent the Jesuit Gaspar Vilela and Brother Lourenço to make a third attempt to establish a base in Kyoto; the two men finally managed to settle in the capital in November, 1559, and even obtained an audience with the shogun, Yoshiteru. But their opponents were influential and numerous, and with the secret support of Matsunaga Hisahide they obliged Vilela to retire to Sakai. The missionary remained there building up a Christian community until September, 1562, when he was once more able to return to the capital.

The same year, 1562, was decisive for the expansion of missionary work in Kyushu. On the instructions of Torres, Almeida left the direction of the Funai hospital to others and began an itinerant apostolate first in the region of Hirado, then in Bungo, and finally in Kagoshima. It was at this last place that he received an important summons, for the affairs of the mission had once more become linked to the trading ship from Macao, and Almeida accordingly made his way to Yokoseura. Situated in a lovely bay and facing what is now Sasebo, the small town belonged to the territory of Ōmura Sumitada. As a daimyo Sumitada was not important; his domains were small and lacked wealth, and his military resources were inferior to those of neighboring daimyo. His position even within his domains was insecure, for he himself belonged by birth to the house of Arima and had been adopted by the previous daimyo of Ōmura. But the twenty-nine-year-old Sumitada was a man of foresight and enterprise. He had heard a great deal about the Portuguese who traded at Hirado, the port belonging to his political rival Matsuura, and now with astute timing he invited both the foreign merchants and missionaries to his territories. The invitation, moreover, was unusual in that it was accompanied by a concrete proposal; he offered the port of Yokoseura to the missionaries and promised to exempt the Portuguese traders from taxes for ten years. As far as Sumitada was concerned, the plan had definite advantages; for if all went well, not only would he win for himself wealth and fame but he would also deliver a hard blow against his enemy and rival.

At the beginning of July, 1562, the ship of Pedro Barreto entered the port of Yokoseura, and in the middle of the same month Almeida arrived with full powers to negotiate with Sumitada. The agreement was concluded within a few days, and in the following month Torres and Fernandez arrived with various Japanese helpers. From that time onwards, the development of Yokoseura was rapid. The missionaries stationed there were able to begin work in Ōmura and also minister to the Christians of Hirado and other neighboring regions. In the spring of 1563, Almeida extended missionary work to the lands of Arima. Finally, in June of that same year, Ōmura Sumitada received baptism with some twenty of his nobles in the small church of Yokoseura after receiving intensive instruction. He was the first Christian daimyo.

Various theories have been advanced to explain why he became a Christian, but historians who suggest merely commercial motives to encourage Portuguese trade commit a grave injustice as well as an obvious historical error. For they ignore all the contemporary evidence and confuse two different events: the concession of the port and the baptism of the daimyo. The handing over of the port to the missionaries was made explicitly for financial reasons. It was a clever political move, and it shows that although Sumitada was well aware of the relation between missionaries and merchants, he nevertheless knew at the same time how to distinguish between the two parties. His baptism was a religious event resulting from personal conviction attested by missionaries who knew him well, and this is proved by his faithful perseverance in the difficult years that followed. It was not necessary for him to become a Christian in order to continue the trade that he had already secured; in fact, in view of the precarious political situation within his territory, his conversion was liable to weaken his authority and jeopardize the profits of the foreign trade. Sumitada clearly realized this possibility and for this reason delayed his decision for some time.

From the missionary point of view, the work at Yokoseura was highly successful and raised many hopes for the future. But the aggressive attitude of Sumitada towards Buddhism and the scheming of Gotō Taka-aki, the illegitimate son of the previous daimyo, brought these hopes to an end. On August 17, 1563, a rebellion broke out in Ōmura and at the end of November, just as the Portuguese ships were about to leave for Macao, groups of armed men set fire to Yokoseura. Once again the missionaries were obliged to take refuge either in the islands of Hirado or in the territory of Bungo. Neither the port nor the church of Yokoseura was rebuilt. The small town thereupon passed from history, but not before it had made its contribution in both the political and religious fields. Yokoseura was the prototype of another experiment that was to acquire far greater fame, for the history of Nagasaki begins in Yokoseura.

As a result of the dispersion of the missionaries after the razing of Yokoseura, the next few years were spent in the reorganization of the Christian communities in Hirado and the establishment of the church in Arima. At the same time that progress was halted in Yokoseura, work in the Gokinai region around Kyoto began to advance. Three officers were deputed by Matsunaga Hisahide to conduct a judicial examination of Vilela and Brother Lourenço. The verdict was apparently decided beforehand, but the eloquence of Lourenço unexpectedly won the day, and the three officials, one of whom was known as Takayama Hida-no-kami, were converted to Christianity. Some weeks later, the family of Takayama received baptism in the castle of Sawa, and among the new Christians was an eleven-year-old boy who received the name of Justo. This was Takayama Ukon, who later figured so largely in the history of the Japanese mission. From that time onwards, Vilela and Lourenço, ably assisted from 1565 by Luis Frois, were able to expand their work with greater security. In the castles of central Japan conversions among the samurai class became more numerous, and not a few of those receiving baptism were military officers or lords of small territories.

In the political field, the moment was opportune for rapid advancement, and among those striving to inherit the power of the decadent Ashikaga, the young daimyo of Owari, Oda Nobunaga, began to make progress in a remarkable way. Before Nobunaga obtained absolute control, however, Matsunaga Hisahide managed to expel the missionaries once more from Kyoto by obtaining an imperial decree against them. But the Christian community in central Japan had taken deep root and mission work continued to expand. In Kyushu the apostolate was conducted mainly by traveling missionary groups under the direction of Torres, and their aim was to achieve the evangelization of entire areas and thus obtain some stability. In Kyoto and the surrounding districts, however, the preaching was conducted principally among the samurai families and was carried out by a series of talented missionaries. In the early years Vilela, and then Frois, both ably assisted by Brother Lourenço, made an outstanding contribution; their work was later continued by Organtino Gnecchi, Gregorio Cespedes, Pedro Morejon, and a select group of Japanese Jesuit Brothers.

Vilela was a practical and determined man, possessing a toughness that enabled him to surmount the severest hardship. Frois, on the other hand, was more intellectual and had a keener perception of the values of Japanese culture, as his letters and *História* amply demonstrate. His ironic sense of humor earned him more than one rebuke from superiors but undoubtedly helped him to overcome the considerable difficulty of living alone for five years in central Japan. Vilela had won the favor of the Ashikaga shogun; Frois, in his turn, obtained the friendship of Oda Nobunaga, and by this means was allowed to return to Kyoto. His memorable meeting with Nobunaga at his castle at Gifu, described by Frois with such a wealth of detail, began a new era for the Gokinai mission. It is not without interest that this meeting was arranged by a military officer who was then known as Tokichirō. When Toyotomi Hideyoshi became absolute lord of Japan and prided himself on being the first to realize the danger of allowing foreign priests in Japan, he omitted to mention this early service to the missionaries.

In Kyushu the missionary work also prospered and steadily advanced like a series of waves radiating from various centers: Kuchinotsu in Arima; the Hirado Islands, where Juan Fernandez died in 1567; the Gotō Islands; Shiki, to the north of Amakusa; Fukuda, the new port of the Portuguese in Ōmura. In 1567 Luis de Almeida began missionary work in a small unknown village called Nagasaki.

Torres was finally able to establish a base of operations in the capital of Ōmura in 1568, and thus, after five years of preparation, missionary work began there. With the close collaboration of Ōmura Sumitada, he drew up the plans for the new port of Nagasaki, although he did not live to see them put into effect. In the spring of 1570 he was taken seriously ill and retired to All Saints Church, built by Vilela at Nagasaki in the previous year. There, in July, he received news of the arrival of his successor, Francisco Cabral, at the port of Shiki. Torres and the rest of the missionaries, with the exception of Frois at Kyoto, gathered at Shiki at the summons of Cabral to discuss future plans and policy; when the meeting ended in August, Cabral, accompanied by Almeida, began a tour of the whole mission.

The aged and sick Torres, however, remained in Shiki and died there on October 2, 1570. In the same year Vilela returned to India, and in one of his letters he described the state of the Japanese mission at the time of his departure. There were some forty Christian communities established between Kyoto and Kagoshima, and some of them, such as Hirado, possessed numerous churches; the number of baptized Japanese had already reached thirty thousand.

Cathay

Quinfay

INDIA superior

Archipelagus 7448 insularũ

Zipangri

Chamaho

Panuco Inf. Tortucarũ

Terra flor

Iucatana

Inf. ſdonum

Nou

Catigara

Inf. infortunatæ

9. Detail from an early sixteenth-century map of Asia, showing the island of Zipangri, or Zipangu (Marco Polo's name for Japan), to the southeast of China. From Sebastian Munster, *Cosmographiae Universalis Lib. VI*, Basel, 1559. Museum of the Twenty-Six Martyrs, Nagasaki.

10. Map of East Asia, at the beginning of the period of European contact with Japan. Japan is shown midway between China and America. From Abraham Ortelius, *Theatrum Orbis Terrarum*, Antwerp, 1574.

11. Map of Japan, at the end of the period of European contact. Although some of the geographical features are exaggerated, the map is nevertheless reasonably accurate. From Antonio Cardim, S.J., *Fasciculus e Iapponicis Floribus*, Rome, 1646.

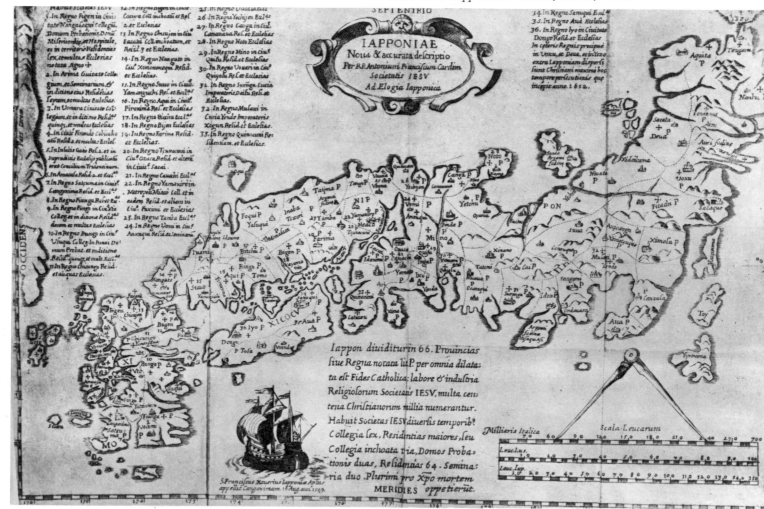

12. European merchant at Naga-saki. Detail from a pair of six-panel *Nanban* screens. Nanban Bunka-kan, Osaka.

13. A Japanese "with his Cotan [sword] by his side, and Dagger or Cuttbelly," a sketch in the manu-script of the Englishman Peter Mundy, made at Macao in 1637. Bodleian Library, Oxford: Rawlin-son MSS., A. 315, f.149.

P. Iulianus Nacaura Iappon, Societ · IESV olim Romam legatus ad Summū Pontificem pedib⁹ sulpēsus, & in fouea cingulo tenus depressus · quarta die moritur Nagasachi 21 · Octob 1633 · in odiū Fidei

P. Hieronymi de Angelis Siculus, Societ · IESV viuus concrematus in odium Fidei Yendi, 4 · Decemb · 1623 ·

14. The martyrdom of the Japanese Jesuit Julian Nakaura at Nagasaki in 1633. Nakaura was one of the four young Kyushu nobles who visited Portugal, Spain and Italy from 1584 to 1586. From Antonio Cardim, S.J., *Fasciculus e Iapponicis Floribus*, Rome, 1646.

15. The martyrdom of the Sicilian Jesuit Girolamo de Angelis at Edo (Tokyo) on December 4, 1623. Angelis reached Japan in 1602 and was the first European to visit the island of Ezo (Hokkaido). From Antonio Cardim, S.J., *Fasciculus e Iapponicis Floribus*, Rome, 1646.

16. A missionary priest celebrating Mass in the Japanese-style chapel of the Jesuit residence at Nagasaki. Detail from a pair of six-panel *Nanban* screens, signed by Kanō Naizen (1570–1616). Kobe Municipal Museum of Nanban Art.

Martinho Hara   Michael Chijiwa   Mancio Itō

17–19. Portraits of three of the Kyushu nobles, drawn by Urbano Monte during their visit to Milan in July, 1585. From Beniamino Gutierrez, *La Prima Ambascieria Giapponese in Italia*, Milan, 1938.

20. A mural painting in the Vatican Library showing the grand procession escorting the Kyushu delegates to an audience with Pope Gregory XIII at St. Peter's, Rome. From Nagayama Tokihide, *Collection of Historical Materials Connected with the Roman Catholic Religion in Japan*, Nagasaki, 1926.

21. A group of missionaries awaiting the arrival of the procession of
Portuguese merchants at Nagasaki. The figures dressed in black are
Jesuit priests and students, while in front of the curtained doorway
stand an elderly *dōjuku*, or "lay catechist," and two friars. Detail from
a pair of six-panel *Nanban* screens signed by Kanō Naizen (1570–1616).
Kobe Municipal Museum of Nanban Art.

The Macao Ship and the Port of Nagasaki

The commercial possibilities arising from the accidental discovery of Japan encouraged the Portuguese traders in the Far East to set up a permanent base of operations. The merchants began taking advantage of the safe haven offered by the bay named after the goddess Ama on the south coast of China, and there at Amacao, or Macao, they set up a small base in about 1555. Two years later formal permission was obtained from the Chinese authorities, and the new settlement could be considered firmly established. From that time on, the City of the Name of God, to give Macao its full title, rapidly developed. In 1563 two Jesuits, Francisco Perez and Manuel Teixeira, arrived there with the intention of proceeding to Canton. When this plan proved impossible, they decided to establish a residence in Macao next to the hermitage of Santo Antonio. The Jesuits remained in this place until 1582, when they moved to the site that would be later occupied by the great Church of the Mother of God and the College of St. Paul. Three years after their arrival the bishop Melchior Carneiro reached Macao and duly started there the Misericordia fraternity and other works of charity, which played a large role in the life of Macao and later indirectly influenced Christian life in Japan.

As far as commerce was concerned, the Portuguese arrived in the Far East at an extremely opportune time, and secure in their new base at Macao, they were in an excellent position to exploit the situation to the full. On account of the devastation wreaked by the *wakō*, or Japanese pirates, relations between China and Japan were far from cordial, and trade was officially prohibited between the two countries. Thus the recently arrived "Southern Barbarians," or *Nanbanjin* as the Europeans were unflatteringly dubbed by the Japanese, with their large ships capable of holding a great deal of cargo were able to act as commercial intermediaries. They transported to Japan the silk and gold of China, and then returned to Macao carrying Japanese silver obtained from the Sado and Iwami mines. The demand for European firearms, which had attracted much attention when the Portuguese first reached Japan, soon subsided.

The discovery of Japan led to the foundation of Macao, and trade from this port in turn required another commercial base on the Japanese coast. It is interesting to follow the Portuguese ships as they searched the coast of Kyushu for such a port, which had to be conveniently situated and politically stable. Kagoshima, the first port used by the Portuguese ships, apparently did not meet these conditions, for the Portuguese showed little inclination to make use of its facilities, although their ships sometimes wintered in the vicinity. In the year after the discovery of Japan, the ship of Jorge de Faria entered the port of Funai and for some time this city, belonging to a friendly daimyo, appeared to satisfy their needs. But Funai did not provide adequate shelter in time of storms, and it was also situated on the east coast of Kyushu, thus obliging ships to make a long detour around the island. So the Portuguese began to frequent the port of Hirado and for a while this became their principal base. As well as possessing great scenic beauty, Hirado offered attractive facilities, for the port was well protected against typhoons and was close to the commercial city of Hakata. But although the daimyo Matsuura was anxious to promote foreign trade, he showed himself hostile towards the Portuguese and Christianity, and in 1561 the Captain-Major[1] Fernão de Sousa and sixteen of his company met their deaths in a quayside brawl at Hirado.

The next port to be tried was Yokoseura, which, although somewhat remote from the commercial routes, nevertheless offered good conditions. Various concessions were made by Ōmura Sumitada, but the Portuguese ships used this port only in 1562 and 1563. In the following year Pedro de Almeida was obliged to use Hirado once more, but this was the last visit of the Portuguese to this port. In about 1565, Sumitada designated another port in his domains at the foot of the small castle of Fukuda. But from the beginning, the use of this port was regarded as only provisional; overland communications were poor, the town was in-

---

[1] The traditional title of the captain of the Portuguese ship that sailed every year to Nagasaki.

conveniently situated and there was no defense against winds from the south. Moreover, the daimyo Matsuura, irritated by the loss of Portuguese trade, decided to take his revenge by joining forces with some Sakai merchants and attacking the ship of João Pereira anchored at Fukuda. With the help of the small galleon of Diogo de Meneses, Pereira managed to repulse the attack, but the unfortunate incident told against Fukuda. For some time the small port of Kuchinotsu appeared a suitable haven, but the arrival of the ship of Tristão Vaz da Veiga in 1567 encouraged Sumitada to look for an even more suitable anchorage. This was to be Nagasaki, the official port of the Macao ship from 1570 onwards.

Pl. 32
The bay of Nagasaki is a superb natural port; various islands guard its entrance and two chains of hills protect its deep and safe water. Some small villages were situated around the bay, at the top of which, some distance from the open sea, stood the castle and village of Nagasaki at the foot of some low hills. Its *tono* ("lord"), a retainer of Ōmura, was Nagasaki Jinzaemon, who was married to a natural daughter of the daimyo. Jinzaemon was probably one of the nobles who had received baptism at Yokoseura, for he was already a Christian when Almeida first visited Nagasaki in 1567.

It is not possible to put a definite date to the beginning of the negotiations between Cosme de Torres and Ōmura Sumitada concerning Nagasaki, but the matter was probably discussed when the daimyo visited Kuchinotsu in 1567. This meeting took place some time between the arrival of Tristão Vaz da Veiga in June and the beginning of missionary work in Nagasaki in the last months of the same year. In 1568 Torres stopped at Nagasaki on his way from Fukuda and posted Vilela there in December, leaving Fukuda without a missionary. From then onwards the importance of Nagasaki steadily increased. A church was built next to the residence of Jinzaemon, and it was there that Torres retired in the spring of 1570 and that the first meeting between Cabral and Sumitada took place in the autumn. At about this time the Jesuit Melchior de Figueiredo began sounding the bay to prepare for the opening of the port.

The Jesuit historian Luis de Guzman specifically names Torres in these negotiations concerning the future of Nagasaki; other contemporary writers do not mention him directly but attribute to an unnamed missionary the plan of turning Nagasaki into the port for the Macao ship. According to these authorities, Sumitada agreed to allow an uncultivated promontory to be used as a refuge for Christians expelled from other regions and as a port for foreign traders, and he instructed Jinzaemon to carry out the project. Exiled Christians and merchants connected with the Macao trade began to settle there, and within a matter of months Nagasaki had become a small town with its residents living in six wards, which they named after their native cities. At the end of the cape, next to the site reserved for the dock, Figueiredo built a small church. The ship of Tristão Vaz da Veiga entered the bay at the beginning of 1571, and the history of the port of Nagasaki had begun.

The details of the agreement between Torres and Sumitada are not known, but one fact remains quite clear—there was not the least concession of lands or rights to the Portuguese, and the foreign traders had to pay charges for port and trading facilities. But Nagasaki offered great advantages and in the following decade the Macao ship stopped there every year, with the exception of 1573, when Antonio de Vilhena was shipwrecked off the Amakusa Islands, and 1579, when Alessandro Valignano, the Jesuit Visitor, directed the ship of Lionel de Brito to Kuchinotsu. By that time the city of Nagasaki already possessed some four hundred houses and depended in large measure on the trade with Macao. "If the ships were to stop coming here for two or three years," wrote Valignano, "Nagasaki would be ruined."

Despite this somewhat uncertain future, Nagasaki had already acquired great importance not only for Ōmura Sumitada and the Japanese mission but also for other neighboring daimyo, who coveted the wealth that entered through the port. The most dangerous of these neighbors was the ruler of Saga, Ryūzōji Takanobu, who planned to take over the whole of the Hizen region. The fear that Ryūzōji might appropriate for himself the port of Nagasaki and that

Portuguese trade might return to Kuchinotsu prompted Ōmura to take a further important step. He offered Valignano the port of Nagasaki as a means to finance the mission of Ōmura. Although there are few contemporary documents concerning the actual founding of Nagasaki, there is a good deal of evidence in the letters of Valignano concerning its concession. It is strange, therefore, that not a few modern historians have erroneously interpreted the action of Sumitada. The agreement did not involve the concession of Japanese territory to foreign powers, nor was it wrung from a reluctant daimyo by the insistence of Valignano. All the contemporary evidence agrees that the plan originated with Sumitada, who insisted that the Visitor "should accept this port for the Church," adding that he "would regard it as good fortune if he accepted it."

Before committing himself Valignano discussed the matter with nearly all the missionaries in Kyushu. As a result of these consultations, a document was drawn up on June 9, 1580, whereby Ōmura Sumitada and his son Yoshiaki conceded to the Society of Jesus not only the port of Nagasaki but also the neighboring village of Mogi, which was necessary for free access to the port from the region of Arima. Valignano accepted the donation on condition that the missionaries were free to leave Nagasaki whenever they wished, and the agreement with this proviso was later approved by the Jesuit General, Claudio Aquaviva, to whom Valignano fully explained the transaction in a letter dated August 15, 1580. This letter, still preserved in the Jesuit archives in Rome,[1] is perhaps the most important document relating to this matter and provides ample evidence to refute any suggestion that Nagasaki became a Portuguese colony. Nagasaki was neither a colony nor the possession of Portugal or of any other foreign nation, and as far as Valignano was concerned, Ōmura Sumitada continued to be "lord of the land." With the help of Valignano's legal training, the daimyo drew up the code of law by which the city would be governed and the necessary jurisdiction would be given to the Japanese official chosen by the Jesuits to administer the city. With the exception of the anchorage fees, which the Jesuits received as rent, all other taxes and dues were paid directly to the daimyo. The money paid to the missionaries was divided into three parts: one for the maintenance of the port, another for the Nagasaki church, and the third for the Jesuit residence at Ōmura. Thus all the money remained within Sumitada's territory. In addition, the daimyo had in Nagasaki a place of sanctuary in time of danger; this was not an insignificant consideration, for Sumitada had already experienced the need for such a refuge.

The political foresight of Sumitada and the legal acumen of Valignano combined to realize the plan. Nagasaki was an innovation in various respects, and one of its most interesting features was its legislation. The text of its laws has not been preserved, but the general lines can be deduced from Valignano's letters. There was a clear distinction between civil and criminal cases and between ecclesiastical and secular jurisdiction, and the severity of traditional Japanese penalties was considerably mitigated. The Superior of the Jesuits in Japan chose the *yakunin*, or "city governor," whose term of office lasted a year, although he could be deposed for sufficient reasons. This official was obliged to govern the city in conformity with the laws drawn up by Sumitada, and Valignano warned the mission Superior not to interfere in the administration of justice. The *yakunin* was assisted in his office by the *otona*, or "heads of wards," according to the definition of the term in the Portuguese-Japanese dictionary, *Vocabulario da Lingoa de Iapam*, composed and printed at Nagasaki some years later. This first influence of Roman law on Japanese legislation did not always result in the smooth running of the city, for the men who frequented the port were accustomed to the summary justice of Japan and therefore did not always feel the same respect towards the more benevolent code of Nagasaki. In general, the population of the city was made up not of samurai but of merchants and laborers. It was a homogeneous community, united above all by the common Christian faith; all the leading citizens were members of the Misericordia fraternity, set up

[1] Jesuit Archives, Rome: Jap Sin 81, ff. 277—279.

according to the rules of a similar organization founded at Macao in 1569 by Bishop Carneiro.

Nagasaki never actually belonged to the Portuguese, but the city was certainly the scene of close contact between East and West. Europeans and Japanese lived together and enjoyed the same rights and liberty. Foreigners could freely move about the territory and quite a number of Portuguese, and later Spaniards, settled in the city and married Japanese. The full history of the city in the first half-century of its existence is still to be written, but it contains great interest from the point of view of law and sociology. It also explains some of the difficulty later experienced by the first governors appointed by the Tokugawa regime to subjugate the Christian population.

The Period of Cabral, 1570–80

According to Valignano, the death of Cosme de Torres in 1570 ended the first period of the Christian mission in Japan. The ten years during which his successor, Francisco Cabral, held office formed a period of complex transition. They were years of undoubted progress; various daimyo in Kyushu were converted, the number of Christians increased rapidly, and Nagasaki continued to develop and fulfill the hopes that had been placed in the experiment at its foundation. The number of missionaries also rose as new recruits arrived in the country; the mission became independent of Goa and was affiliated to the new diocese of Macao. On the national level, political power at last began to stabilize under the strong rule of Oda Nobunaga. In Europe, the death of Dom Sebastian of Portugal led to the temporary union of that country with Spain, while in Rome Gregory XIII, a great friend of the Jesuits, was elected pope.

In Kyushu missionary work continued along the lines laid down by Torres and made good progress in the regions of Ōmura, Arima, Amakusa, and Bungo. After much hardship and danger the entire territory of Ōmura was converted, and according to the reports of 1576 there were some fifty thousand Christians living in that region. When compared with the small bands of missionaries, consisting of two or three priests and a few Brothers and catechists, this large number may give rise to some doubt about the genuine nature of these conversions. But the initial conversion is only the first step and the subsequent religious formation was achieved by a careful organization that ensured that the periodic visits of the missionaries were combined with the continuous work of resident catechists.

As a result of the labors of Luis de Almeida, the daimyo of Arima and Amakusa were baptized in 1576. But Arima Yoshinao died soon afterwards, and his successor, Harunobu, swayed by those who saw in his predecessor's death a sign of divine punishment, persecuted the Christians and caused a number of them to abandon their new faith. In Bungo the political situation became increasingly unstable; the daimyo continued favoring the missionaries, but many of his leading vassals were openly hostile. But an unexpected event in 1575 changed the situation when Chika'ie, the second son of the daimyo, received baptism, thus bringing his father, Ōtomo Sōrin, nearer to making a similar personal decision. This finally happened three years later, and after arranging his complicated matrimonial affairs, Ōtomo was baptized by Cabral in his castle at Usuki on August 28, 1578. In veneration of his old friend Xavier he chose the name of Francisco, which he later proudly incorporated in Latin letters in his seal. He had traveled a long road since meeting Xavier twenty-eight years previously, and he had overcome numerous obstacles on the way, including difficulties that sprang from his private life and those caused by the faulty Japanese of some of the missionaries.

A few days after his baptism the army of Bungo marched off to reconquer the territory of Hyūga, which had been seized by Shimazu from the Itō family, close relations of the Ōtomo. Although he had already placed the government of his domains into the hands of his eldest son, the inefficient Yoshimune, the old warrior accompanied the expedition, for now he dearly

THE
SOUTHERN
BARBARIANS

wished to realize one of his dreams. His plan was to establish a Christian society in Hyūga, and he spared no effort in obtaining information about the legislation of Christian states; to this end he took with him Cabral and Almeida as advisers. But his plan was rudely cut short when the forces of Bungo were utterly routed at the battle of Mimikawa, and it was with the greatest difficulty that Sōrin managed to retire to his castle at Usuki. Although the cause of the disaster was due to the carelessness of Yoshimune and his staff, the rumor that the tutelary deities of Bungo were displeased by Sōrin's baptism once more began to circulate. In those difficult moments the spirit of Ōtomo Sōrin was put to a severe test, but although he was in real danger of losing all he possessed, his faith remained unshaken.

In central Japan events were developing in a very different way. With his military genius, strong will, and harsh voice, Oda Nobunaga continued to overcome all the obstacles in his way. The terrible punishment that he inflicted on the militant monks of Mount Hiei served as a grim warning to his adversaries, and by deposing the shogun Yoshiake in 1573 he clearly signaled the end of the long Ashikaga dynasty. He continued to fight against Araki Mura-shige, and in these wars some of the principal Christian samurai were killed or exiled. Taka-yama Ukon and the Christian community of Gokinai were placed in grave danger when Nobu-naga encamped around the castle of Takatsuki, but the situation was saved by Ukon's action of boldly delivering himself unarmed into the hands of Nobunaga. The ruler recognized his noble character and pardoned his father, Takayama Dario, for his sake, and returned his fief of Takatsuki.

On the eve of the arrival of Alessandro Valignano in 1579, the number of Christians reached almost a hundred thousand, that is to say, an increase of seventy thousand in nine years. Six daimyo had received baptism; the missionaries numbered forty-three and among them were eight who had recently arrived as the advance party of the Visitor's expedition. But neither the statistics nor the reports of that period show the increasing malaise that existed among the missionaries as a result of Cabral's policy. The superior was a man of undoubted talent, an indefatigable worker, and well prepared for the work of the direct apostolate. But the mentality and outlook of this former soldier had been formed by his experience in India and prevented him from understanding the Japanese people. As a result, the pessimistic tendency of his character cast a shadow over the work and future of the whole mission.

Cabral was opposed to the formation of an indigenous clergy, believing that the Japanese were not ready to receive the priesthood. He systematically withdrew his men from the study of the language and declared that it was impossible for Europeans to learn Japanese; his views on this subject should be taken into account when some modern writers use his statements to prove that neither Frois nor any other missionary of that time could express himself well in Japanese. Moreover, Cabral dealt with the Japanese members of the Order as if they were second-class Jesuits and thus gave rise to considerable bitterness and divisions. Finally, he made no attempt to adapt himself to Japanese customs, nor did he ever come even remotely near to appreciating the cultural values of Japan.

This is certainly a formidable indictment of Cabral's policy, but it should not be forgotten that the principal source of information about his work in Japan is found in the letters of Valignano, and Valignano himself considered Cabral the man most suited to lead the Japanese mission if he could correct these defects. The sane humanism and spirit of adaptation that so distinguished Torres and his colleagues Almeida and Fernandez were noticeably lacking in Cabral. But despite his pessimism he never took the extreme position of some modern critics, who would detect in Japan a fundamental incapacity to receive Christianity. Compared with such writers, Cabral was indeed an optimist.

The First Visit of Valignano, 1579–82

Pl. 48

On board the great ship of Lionel de Brito that entered the harbor of Kuchinotsu on July 24, 1579, was Alessandro Valignano, the Visitor of the Jesuit missions in India and Japan. At that time he was a man of forty-one years of age and had spent the previous five years in India. A boisterous youth, in which he had experienced both trial and prison, a doctorate in law at the university of Padua and later studies in Rome, his appointment as Visitor at the early age of thirty-three years, and his strong personality all combined to make him a man of whom much could be expected, but from whom serious errors could be feared. It is certainly true that here and there in the work of Valignano defects inherent in his character and attitude can be discerned, for he had excessive self-confidence, a certain authoritarian manner, and a lack of moderation in his criticism of others. But these defects are insignificant when compared with his work and achievements, and he was clearly the ideal man to deal with the crisis in the Japanese mission. For at that time vision and firm administration were badly needed, and the letters of the men who worked with him or under his direction clearly show that Valignano possessed, perhaps to excess, both these qualities.

His first impression on arriving in Japan was a feeling of disillusion. In Arima the sad results of the premature death of the daimyo Yoshinao were still being felt, while Ōtomo Sōrin possessed only a shadow of his former power. Ryūzōji Takanobu, the greatest enemy of Christianity in Kyushu, was at the gates of Shimabara with his army and at the same time was threatening Ōmura. The situation was very different from what he had expected, and the Visitor blamed his mistaken impressions on the reports of the missionaries who had tended to describe the situation in Japan in the rosiest light possible. In this Valignano was not being completely fair, for it is sufficient to read these letters carefully to note in them hints of all the problems of the mission, except perhaps the basic problem of the incompatibility of Cabral.

But, as Valignano himself would later point out when explaining his point of view to the Jesuit General, it was extremely difficult to understand "the things of Japan" from Rome or Goa. With more experience he would later learn to distinguish the authentic values hidden below the agitated surface of Japanese society; but at that time he had only just arrived and his feeling of disappointment was strong. This disappointment colored his judgement, and his first descriptions of Kyushu and of some of the people there are worthy of the pen of Cabral. But there is something in these early pessimistic accounts that smacks of rhetoric and seems to indicate that he was not entirely convinced of everything he wrote. This is shown by the fact that from the very beginning of his stay in Japan he began working as if his real opinion did not correspond completely to what he wrote, for he still followed a preconceived plan based largely on the reports that he criticized so strongly.

But hardly had the Visitor disembarked at Kuchinotsu when Arima Harunobu, who until a short time previously had been persecuting Christians, came to welcome him and asked for baptism and also Portuguese help in the war against Ryūzōji. At that moment Valignano must have learnt something that was to be so often repeated in his later experience: the instability of the political situation in Japan was liable to upset in a moment the most carefully made plans. He must have also experienced the difficulty of drawing the line between religion and politics, between the urgency of preaching the gospel and the price of Chinese silk.

When he continued his journey to Bungo a year later, however, nearly all of the most pressing problems had been solved. The negotiations concerning the concession of Nagasaki had been successfully concluded, and a truce between Arima and Ryūzōji had restored peace to Hizen for the time being. The conversion of Harunobu was a difficult task and proved both the firmness of the Visitor and the goodwill of the daimyo. At the end of February or the beginning of March, 1580, Harunobu received baptism from the hands of Valignano and was thenceforth known as Don Protasio in the European letters. With the territory restored to peace and the

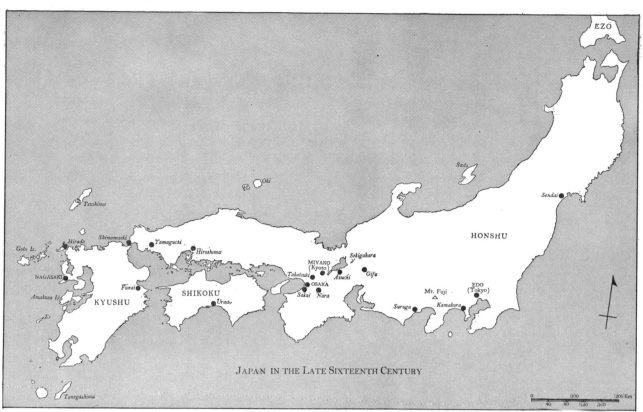

JAPAN IN THE LATE SIXTEENTH CENTURY

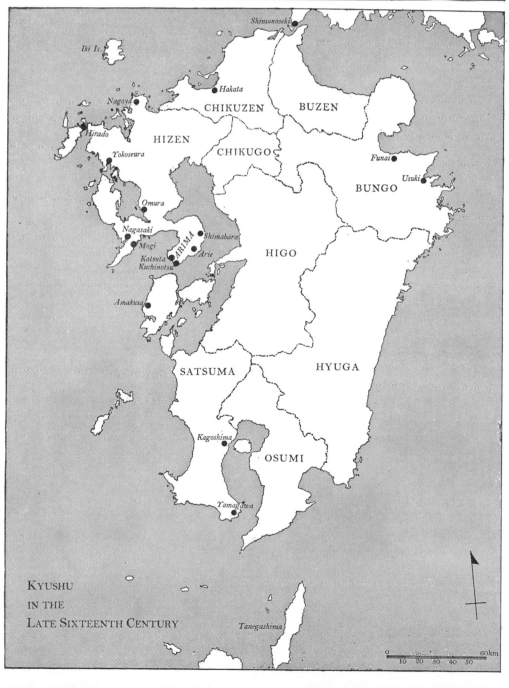

KYUSHU

IN THE

LATE SIXTEENTH CENTURY

ruler baptized, Valignano was able to devote himself fully to implementing some of his long-term plans. The plan most dear to him was to establish three seminaries, one at Arima, another in Kyoto, and a third one, which in the event was never begun, in Bungo, for these schools would guarantee the continuation and future of the Japanese church. Hinoe-jō, or Arima Castle, is today merely a hill with cultivated terraces, but it may be considered the starting point of Valignano's policy of renovation, for Kita-Arima, the small village at the foot of the castle, marks the site of the first Christian seminary in Japan.

Between June and August of 1580 he summarized his ideas in a series of memoranda in which may be found all the fundamental ideas of the report he made at the end of the visitation. He dealt with a wide variety of topics, ranging from the division of the mission into the three regions of Shimo, Bungo and Kyoto, to the fundamental question of the formation of a Japanese clergy. Many of his decisions were based on a simple premise. As the Christian community in Japan was completely new, it would have to develop along the lines of the primitive church and thus there should be no premature promulgation of ecclesiastical law for which the Japanese Christians were not ready. When Valignano put all these ideas on paper and began translating them into reality, the *consultas*, or "councils of missionaries," of Bungo, Azuchi, and Nagasaki had yet to be held. He had still not met Ōtomo Sōrin, nor had he been introduced to the sophisticated society of central Japan. The fundamental lines of his policy were laid down during the first year of his visitation, while he resided by the placid waters of Ariake and Nagasaki bays.

Pl. 25

Leaving Nagasaki and Arima, Valignano arrived in Bungo on September 14, 1580, and on March 8, 1581, he was once more on his way to Kyoto. His stay in Bungo was therefore brief but rich in results. Of all the people whom the Visitor met in Japan, Ōtomo Sōrin was undoubtedly the man who exerted the deepest influence on him. Valignano visited other daimyo to present his compliments or ask favors, but in Ōtomo he met an intellect that made him feel more than once like a pupil. In no other encounter can the meeting between East and West, with their differences and mutual comprehension, be better represented. The principal topic of their conversations was the problem of missionary adaptation to Japanese life and mentality, and Ōtomo held strong views on the matter. For the daimyo, as well as for Takayama Ukon, conversion to Christianity should not involve a loss in cultural inheritance but ought in fact to produce a spiritual enrichment. Ōtomo emphatically expressed his mind to the Visitor and urged that the Japanese church should follow this course. The impression that his words caused is evident in the writings of Valignano, and it is noteworthy that the council of missionaries in Bungo unanimously approved the article referring to the need for adaptation.

Ignoring, for the time being, the systematic opposition of Cabral, Valignano continued to press ahead with his plans and established two Jesuit houses of formation in Bungo—a novitiate in Usuki, at the foot of Ōtomo's castle, and a college in Funai. In both these houses Japanese and European candidates would begin their studies for the priesthood. Before resuming his journey the Visitor found time to revise the current catechism that had been composed by Cabral; this revision was one more step in the history of this work, which began with the rough notes of Xavier, translated by Yajirō, to be succeeded in due course by the book of questions and answers of Vilela, the catechism of Melchior Nuñez and the text translated and revised by Torres.

On the journey towards Sakai through the picturesque Inland Sea, Valignano was able to experience at first hand the danger of pirates mentioned so laconically in the letters of Xavier; in fact, the Visitor only managed to escape the peril thanks to the sturdy rowers provided by Ōtomo and the opportune intervention of Diego Hibiya Ryokei as the party reached Sakai. But, on leaving Sakai, Valignano began what can only be called a triumphal progress. Christian lords in the castles guarding the road to Kyoto entertained him royally and competed among themselves in their hospitality. The reception was somewhat different from Xavier's experience some thirty years previously, and the change was due, of course, not so much to Valignano himself but to the men who had gone before him. The visitation of the Gokinai region had a double climax. The first was strictly religious and took place at Takatsuki, the fief of Takayama Ukon; the second, which would remind Valignano of the splendor of his Renaissance Italy, was in Kyoto. Takatsuki was already a fully developed Christian community, and Valignano celebrated Holy Week and Easter Sunday with a crowd of some twenty thousand people, Christians and pagans, who had flocked there from neighboring regions. On Easter Sunday, March 26, he continued with his party to Kyoto, where the preparations for his audience with Oda Nobunaga were well advanced.

Valignano was then forty-three years old and Nobunaga was forty-seven years. Both were in the prime of their lives and at a crucial point in their work. Nobunaga, the undisputed lord of central Japan, had just built the city and castle of Azuchi on the banks of Lake Biwa as a symbol of his power and looked forward to the future with justified confidence. For his part, Valignano saw his plan of making Japan into a center of mission work for the whole of the Far East already taking shape. The success that had crowned his early efforts and the overwhelming reception at Takatsuki and Kyoto increased his optimism. Both men were alike in many respects, for both had greatness of vision, strength of will, foresight, and the tendency to impose their views on others; but as regards their view of life, however, the two men differed radically.

The embassy of the Visitor afforded Nobunaga a splendid occasion to show off his power and glory, not only to the foreigners but also to the whole population of the capital and the nobles of the court. Valignano's solemn reception represented the official recognition that Xavier had vainly sought in Kyoto so many years previously. Splendid gifts were exchanged on both sides, and the reception culminated in a grand festival celebrated in the capital on April 1, when Nobunaga exhibited his equestrian skill in front of the guest of honor, the emperor Ōgimachi, and an enormous crowd of spectators.

Valignano took the opportunity to try to implement some of the decisions taken in meetings with missionaries and Christian lords; Azuchi was, moreover, an ideal place for establishing new bonds of friendship with the neighboring daimyo. As a result of the work of Organtino, conversions among influential people had already started in Gokinai. The conversion of the elderly daimyo Kyōgoku Takayoshi and his wife deserves special mention, because Maria Kyōgoku was the sister of Asai Nagamasa and was therefore closely related to the family of Nobunaga. Organtino had also made much progress with the foundation of the Azuchi seminary by the time Valignano arrived. The building had been constructed on a magnificent site provided by Nobunaga, and the first pupils, mostly sons of samurai and vassals of Takayama Ukon, were already in residence. In this first group of pupils was a sixteen-year-old boy, Paul Miki, the son of Miki Handayu, an officer in the service of Nobunaga. Paul knew Valignano and Nobunaga personally and probably also one of the ruler's officers, Hashiba Chikuzen, later to be known as Toyotomi Hideyoshi. The paths of their lives were later to cross in an unforeseen way.

Pl. 58

The Jesuit Visitor remained at Azuchi until the second half of August, as Nobunaga wanted him to witness the Bon Festival in honor of the dead. When he was finally able to begin the return journey to Kyushu, Valignano carried in his luggage Nobunaga's final gift—a magnificent *byōbu*, or "screen," on which was depicted the city of Azuchi and which would later be sent to Rome as a gift to Gregory XIII.

At the end of 1581, Valignano was once more back at Nagasaki, and in a meeting there with all the missionaries he was able to sum up the results of the three eventful years of his visitation. The meeting also ratified the acceptance of Nagasaki, and several of the participants, such as Figuereido, Vaz, and Almeida, had taken an active part in the foundation of the port ten years previously. Vaz and Almeida had only just returned from Macao, where they had been sent by Valignano to receive ordination to the priesthood in recognition of their outstanding services to the mission.

It was at this time that the Visitor was considering a plan in which he placed much hope, for it involved nothing less than an embassy to the pope from the Christian daimyo of Kyushu. The project had been in his mind for some time, but the final decision was not made until shortly before his departure from Japan, and it was then necessary to work quickly to complete the arrangements for the expedition in time. He had first thought of Jeronimo Itō, a nephew of Ōtomo Sōrin, as the representative of Bungo, but, as the boy was then in the seminary at Azuchi and time was short, his cousin, Mancio Itō, was chosen in his place. The representative of the daimyo of Arima and Ōmura was to be Michael Chijiwa, a relative of both rulers. To complete the party, Julian Nakaura, the son of the lord of Nakaura Castle in the peninsula of Nishi-Sonogi, and Martinho Hara, son of one of the leading vassals of Ōmura, were chosen as companions to the two ambassadors; two other Japanese, Constantino Dourado and Brother Jorge Loyola, accompanied the legates as attendants. Valignano's plan was very concrete in its intentions and far simpler than what in fact resulted. The expedition had the dual purpose of creating a favorable atmosphere in the courts of Madrid and Rome, where Valignano wanted to obtain important favors for the Japanese mission, and of informing the Japanese of the splendor and power of Europe through the reports of the young men on their return. His instructions concerning the dress and lodging of the Japanese boys clearly show that he did not intend them to go to Europe as princes. But their reception surpassed all expectations, and the overwhelming success of the mission gave rise to jealous rumors that cast doubt on the noble rank of the young men. Modern biographical data, however, clearly refutes the charge that the young ambassadors were boys of common birth without any connection with the daimyo whom they represented.

The origin of the embassy offers more interest to the historian. The speed with which the preparations for the mission were made has given rise to some speculation that Valignano arranged the whole affair without reference to the daimyo concerned. Admittedly, the Visitor himself stated that the original idea was his, but originating a plan is one thing and perpetrating a deliberate fraud is another, and when the party returned six years later with the reply and gifts of the pope, the reception accorded to the young men by Arima Harunobu, Ōmura Yoshiaki, and Ōtomo Yoshimune clearly showed that the daimyo considered them as their representatives. In the case of Ōtomo, the recognition was all the more significant as Hideyoshi had by that time proscribed Christianity and Yoshimune, son of Sōrin, had renounced his faith.

Although the organization of the embassy must have fully occupied Valignano's attention before he embarked from Japan, he still had to face a more urgent problem, on which would depend in large measure the continued success of his visitation, for it was obvious that a new mission superior was required. The state of the mission was then far different from the situation which Valignano had found on his arrival three years previously and thanks to his opportune intervention many problems had been solved. He had strengthened the bonds of friendship with the Christian daimyo and other important personages, including Oda Nobunaga himself. The religious life of the different Christian communities was thriving, and the seminaries and houses of formation had been duly established. New missionaries were preparing for their work by studying Japanese, and the norms that the Visitor had laid down concerning the urgent need for adaptation had been generally accepted. But the problem remained as to whom he could entrust the continuation of his work.

In 1581, Cabral was relieved of the responsibility of office, and returned to India in indifferent health, while Gaspar Coelho was chosen to succeed him. Valignano himself was not entirely happy about his choice but admitted that there was no better candidate available; if the Visitor felt obliged to limit the field to the Portuguese members of the mission, his choice was certainly considerably restricted. Moreover, in the situation at that time, he could hardly have foreseen the dire results that the innocent blunders of Coelho would eventually cause.

But at the same time it may be wondered whether his choice of Coelho, whom he praised as docile, was not influenced by the fear that a man of stronger personality and deeper knowledge of Japanese affairs might interfere with the plan that he had so carefully made for the mission.

Accompanied by the young ambassadors, Valignano sailed from Nagasaki in the ship of Ignacio de Lima on February 20, 1582. He left behind him every indication of a bright and successful future for the mission. But when discussing the concession of Nagasaki in a letter to Rome in 1580, the Visitor had remarked, "Japan is a country of many changes and without any stability." His experience during the three years of the visitation had afforded him considerable opportunity to verify the truth of this observation; but on departing from Nagasaki with the satisfaction of a job well done, he could not have foreseen how quickly and deeply the vicissitudes of Japanese political life were going to affect his work.

Only four months after Valignano had left, Oda Nobunaga died on June 21, 1582, in the flames of Honnō-ji in Kyoto, where he was caught off his guard by the treachery of Akechi Mitsuhide. With Nobunaga disappeared the city of Azuchi, which symbolized his power and dreams, and the seminary was burned to the ground; the students managed to escape in time and were taken by Organtino to Takatsuki. Akechi met a violent death soon afterwards, and from the resulting political confusion emerged the new figure of Nobunaga's former lieutenant, Hashiba Chikuzen, later known in Japanese history as Toyotomi Hideyoshi.

The Enigma of Toyotomi Hideyoshi, 1582–98

The historical period dominated by Toyotomi Hideyoshi poses various questions, many of which, especially those concerning the motives for his actions, still remain without adequate answer. The problem does not concern merely secondary matters insufficiently documented in historical sources, for a satisfactory explanation of such important national events as the invasion of Korea and the execution of the *kanpaku*, his nephew Hidetsugu, is still lacking, not to mention issues linked more closely to his private life, such as the condemnation of the great tea master, Sen no Rikyū. For Hideyoshi invariably kept to himself the ultimate reasons for his decisions. Thus it is not only the deeds but also the personality of Hideyoshi that make this period especially intriguing. His complex character was full of contrasts, and, in order to understand the events in which he intervened, a psychological study of the man is just as necessary as research into historical sources.

Hideyoshi was born in 1536 at Nakamura, a small village in the region of Owari. His name, Kinoshita Tokichirō, was changed several times as he advanced up the social scale. He was known as Hashiba Chikuzen when he won the favor of Oda Nobunaga and as Toyotomi Hideyoshi when he finally obtained supreme power; in Japanese historical accounts he is generally referred to as *taikō*, or "retired regent," a title that he assumed in 1592. Hideyoshi was sensitive about his humble origins and liked to pass himself off as a member of the illustrious Fujiwara clan. With his initiative and remarkable talent for taking full advantage of circumstances he was able to rise from being the son of a lowly samurai to become the absolute lord of Japan, and this remarkable advance, unprecedented in Japanese history, did not fail to have an effect on his character.

At the age of twenty-two he entered the service of Oda Nobunaga and was already his leading general when the ruler met his violent death in 1582. The treachery of Akechi Mitsuhide prepared the way ahead for Hideyoshi at an opportune moment, for at that time he had nearly all of Nobunaga's army under his command and was therefore able to appear on the scene as the righteous avenger of his lord. The fratricidal strife between Nobunaga's sons presented him with yet another opportunity of which he was not slow to take advantage, and

Pl. 3

*THE
EUROPEANS
IN JAPAN*

he managed to dispose of the ruler's legitimate successors either by force or by cunning. This role of usurper also left its mark on his complicated character and increased his natural suspicions and fears.

In the three years following the death of Nobunaga, Hideyoshi confirmed his dominance of the home provinces in central Japan. He then proceeded methodically to bring the rest of the country under his control by his military campaigns in Shikoku in 1585, Kyushu in 1587, and Kanto in 1590; at the successful conclusion of the last campaign he was the absolute lord of Japan. Hideyoshi was well aware of his undisputed position and was not spared the corruption of power. He raised fantastic buildings and organized lavish festivals, eclipsing the memory of his predecessor; but this deleterious tendency is best seen in his international policy, which culminated in his greatest error, the disastrous invasion of Korea.

In addition to his military and political career, Hideyoshi's private family life has also to be taken into account. The two figures of his sister and, above all, his mother, for whom he bore a passionate love, appear throughout his life. Women, in fact, played an important role in his life, especially after his rise to supreme power. His legitimate wife did not provide him with the male heir for whom he so ardently longed, and of all his concubines only the famous Yodogimi, a niece of Nobunaga, presented him with sons. The first was Tsurumatsu, whose death in 1591 at the age of two plunged the ruler into deep grief, while the second was Hideyori, born in 1593 when the ruler was already fifty-seven years of age. His birth gave rise to a popular rumor, reported not without complacency by the ironic pen of Frois, that cast doubt on the child's paternity.

In his desire to keep supreme power within his family, Hideyoshi had recourse to the adoption of his nephew Hidetsugu, who was duly awarded the title of *kanpaku*, or "regent," in 1592. But Hidetsugu had the misfortune of being found unworthy of the office precisely when the birth of Hideyori assured the dictator of direct succession. The tragic conclusion of the affairs is one of the most obscure episodes in the life of Hideyoshi and resulted in the execution of Hidetsugu, as well as his entire family and retinue, in 1595. From that time until his death three years later Hideyoshi gave signs of increasing senility and mental unbalance.

His home policy brought a halt to the incessant civil wars and provided a period of much needed political stability. Agrarian reforms and the redistribution of fiefs not only increased his revenues but enabled him to control more effectively the centers of possible opposition. His famous "Sword Hunt" disarmed the peasants and tied them even more closely to the soil. The militant Buddhist monks, already severely chastened by Nobunaga, also experienced the heavy hand of his rule and lost their aggressive power once and for all.

At this juncture Hideyoshi came up against a relatively small group of people who did not fit into any traditional political category; these were, firstly, the missionaries and their converts, and secondly the foreign merchants, who supported them. In his younger days Hideyoshi may have regarded them with a curiosity not unmixed with some sympathy, for these men were pioneers trying to advance into traditional Japanese society much as he himself was doing; later he saw them enjoy the favor of Nobunaga at Azuchi, and their influence among many of the samurai did not escape his sharp attention. At that time he did not have political responsibility, and was, moreover, fully occupied in military operations; but after he succeeded Nobunaga and became ruler of Japan, Toyotomi Hideyoshi would also have to take up a position regarding the Christian movement. It was now no longer a matter of dealing with that singular pair, Luis Frois and Brother Lourenço, whom he had introduced to Nobunaga. The church in central Japan was thriving and baptisms among the noble classes continued to increase. Two outstanding figures of the time, the daimyo Gamō Ujisato, married to a daughter of Nobunaga, and Kuroda Yoshitaka, Hideyoshi's close friend and comrade-in-arms, received baptism in 1584, while the conversion of the commander of his cavalry, Makimura Toshisada, obviously did not go unnoticed.

But, at the beginning, Hideyoshi did not appear to pay a great deal of attention to the movement, for he was still busily consolidating his power, and the aggressive Buddhist monks of the Shingon sect appeared a far more pressing problem. In 1585 he destroyed the monastery of Negoro in the Kii Peninsula and thus concluded the work, begun by Nobunaga, of subjugating the Buddhist church. In the same year he finished building his new castle at Osaka, and following the example of his predecessor he offered a site to the Jesuit missionaries, who transferred thither their seminary from Takatsuki. To a certain extent the move was fortunate, for only a short time afterwards Takayama Ukon was promoted to the fief of Akashi and left Takatsuki. Economically Takayama gained by the exchange, but in view of subsequent events it may be questioned whether the move was a reward for his merits or rather the first step towards isolating this fervent Christian soldier from Kyoto and Osaka.

In many ways the year 1586 is most important in the history of the relations between Hideyoshi and the Europeans. In Kyoto and Osaka the conversions among the samurai reached a scale that may well have appeared alarming to the ruler. In Kyushu the forces of Shimazu Yoshihisa, daimyo of Satsuma, threatened Bungo and occupied Nagasaki, thus providing Hideyoshi with the long-desired opportunity to intervene in those distant provinces. It was precisely at this critical juncture that the Jesuit Superior, Gaspar Coelho, went to Osaka to present his compliments to the ruler.

To all appearances the visit was a complete success. Hideyoshi showed himself at his most affable as he personally guided his Portuguese guest and his companions around the great castle and showed them his treasure. He doubtless enjoyed provoking the admiration of the foreigners, to whom only a few moments previously he had confided his plans to conquer Korea and China. But at the same time his keen intelligence was no doubt dwelling on some of the promises that the ingenuous Coelho had let slip during the course of the conversation. Overwhelmed by Hideyoshi's confidences, the Jesuit had offered to intervene on the ruler's behalf and ask the Portuguese to help him in his campaign against China; but what was worse, he had promised to secure the collaboration of the Christian daimyo in the forthcoming Kyushu campaign. If anything could arouse the suspicions of Hideyoshi, it was the alliance between missionary and daimyo.

Takayama and other Christians were understandably alarmed when they heard of these promises, but Coelho could not be persuaded that he had acted rashly for he genuinely believed that he had thereby won the favor of Hideyoshi. Some months later during the Kyushu campaign he again visited the ruler at his camp in Yatsuhiro and received an even more cordial reception, which left poor Coelho eagerly looking forward to a third visit. A third visit he was certainly to have, but it would be his last.

By the time Hideyoshi entered Kyushu, the vanguard of his army, commanded by the Christian daimyo Kuroda Yoshitaka, had already forced the Satsuma troops to retire. Hideyoshi conducted the campaign until its successful conclusion and then stopped at Hakata to redistribute the territories. The two contestants, Ōtomo and Shimazu, both suffered a drastic reduction in their possessions, while among the new powerful figures appearing in Kyushu were the Christian lords—Konishi Yukinaga in Uto, Kuroda Yoshitaka in Nakatsu, and Mori Hidekane in Kurume. As a counterbalance, the fief of Kuwamoto was awarded to Katō Kiyomasa, the enemy of Konishi and a fervent disciple of the Buddhist Nichiren sect. In the summer of 1587 Ōmura Sumitada and Ōtomo Sōrin both died, but their sons inherited their estates, and Ōtomo Yoshimune finally received baptism at the urging of Kuroda.

Coelho traveled to Hakata in order to congratulate Hideyoshi on his successful campaign and in another of his genial errors he arrived in a well-equipped *fusta*, or "foist." Hideyoshi inspected the ship and was not sparing in his admiration. Moreover, he asked Coelho to convey to the Portuguese captain Domingos Monteiro his desire to see the great Portuguese *nao*, or "carrack," anchored at that moment at Hirado. Up to that time relations between Hideyoshi and the Portuguese merchants had been distant and superficial, but the expedition into Kyushu had made the ruler realize the advantages to be gained from foreign trade. But his first step towards establishing closer relations ended in disappointment when Monteiro came in person to explain that he was reluctant to bring his heavy ship round to Hakata as he was unfamiliar with the port. Hideyoshi appeared satisfied with his explanation and with his accustomed generosity dismissed Monteiro with a handsome gift. It was July 24.

Twenty-four hours had not passed before Takayama had been stripped of his possessions and the missionaries ordered to leave Japan. The reason for Hideyoshi's volte-face is still a mystery and will probably never be known. Possibly the change was not quite so sudden as it appeared and was part of a carefully considered plan that the ruler had been waiting to put into operation at a suitable moment. Between the festival atmosphere of July 24 and the announcement of the sentences, Hideyoshi did nothing more than meet with some of his intimate followers and send two messages. One was to Takayama telling him to choose between apostasy and exile, and the other was to Coelho listing various accusations against the missionaries.

Takayama replied without hesitation that he was not prepared to renounce his religion, and he thereupon retired into seclusion in the domains of his friend Konishi Yukinaga. Historians have always been interested in the reasons that prompted Hideyoshi to change his attitude towards Christianity, but they generally mention only in passing this episode concerning Takayama. However, both events are closely related, and the concrete case of Takayama throws considerable light on the whole affair and leads to a better understanding of Hideyoshi's reasoning.

Of all the influential Christians who surrounded Hideyoshi, Takayama was the only one to receive the ultimatum. Two years later Hideyoshi allowed him to return into his presence once more, although he did not restore him to the rank of daimyo, and even invited him to join his close circle of friends in the tea ceremony. In the interval Takayama's religious fervor had not diminished nor had he stopped proselytizing, but at the same time he had not shown any hostility towards Hideyoshi. The ruler himself did not bear any particular animosity towards Takayama, but he saw in him a possible rallying point for those disaffected with his regime. Christianity now appeared to him as an insidious organization, and he believed that he at last understood its power and the threat that it offered to his security. In his eyes all the indications —the vain promises of Coelho, the zeal of Takayama, the advance of Christianity in Kyushu, the expansion of Portuguese trade, the hints of his anti-Christian physician, the monk Seiyakuin—pointed to the same alarming conclusion.

All the other suggested reasons, ranging from the refusal of Christian girls in Arima to join his household to the heady effects of the Portuguese wine that he freely imbibed that night, may well have played a part in the final decision, but the missionaries recognized that these were only secondary factors. Pedro Gomez, Coelho's successor, put forward his own explanation of the events when he wrote, "The same king [Hideyoshi] saw from his experience that all who received the law of God remained united among themselves as if they were brothers."[1] Years later another missionary, Francisco Pasio, recorded some confidences that Maeda Gen'i, the governor of Kyoto, had made to him, in which he attributed to Hideyoshi a statement made on hearing of the apostolate of the Franciscan friars: "They must not do this; if they continue to do so, I will find out who are the preachers and who are the converted, and I will punish them because I do not want this religion; for it is a religion of love and union and therefore detrimental to this kingdom."[2] Finally the Jesuit João Rodrigues noted in his work *Bispos da Igreja do Japão* that Hideyoshi told Bishop Martins in 1596 that the expulsion of the missionaries was due not to his personal displeasure with them, "but he

---

[1] Real Academia de Historia, Madrid: Cortes 576, n. 70, f. 5.
[2] Archivo de Indias, Seville: s.V, leg. 18, f. 168.

had done it because of certain Christian lords with whom he was not satisfied, thus giving to understand Justo Ukon Dono [Takayama], whose rare talents, prudence and military prowess he fully recognized; and seeing the union among Christians in Japan, he feared that he might take over the government."[1]

The message that shook Coelho out of his dreams, both real and metaphorical, in the early hours of July 25, 1587, should be studied in the light of these explanations. Hideyoshi asked four questions, which in fact were equivalent to four accusations against the missionaries. Why did they employ force to make conversions? Why did they destroy Buddhist and Shintō temples? Why did they kill and eat useful animals such as horses and cattle? Why did the Portuguese merchants deal in slaves? The last charge was not strictly directed against the missionaries but against the Portuguese merchants and their Japanese accomplices; in his reply Coelho pointed this out and asked Hideyoshi to intervene and stop the abuse. In the same way the Jesuit rejected the other accusations, blaming the destruction of temples on the excessive zeal of converts and emphatically denying the charge of eating horsemeat. The only fault that he was prepared to admit was the practice of eating beef and he promised strict amendment on this point.

Hideyoshi did not prolong the debate but at daybreak sent copies of the expulsion decree to Coelho and Captain Monteiro. Prescinding from the other accusations, he emphasized in the edict the destruction of temples and the incompatibility of Christianity with the traditional religions of Japan. The missionaries were given twenty days to leave the country, although it was obviously impossible for the Jesuits working in central Japan to comply with the order at such short notice. At the same time Hideyoshi extended a friendly hand to the Portuguese merchants provided they did not interfere with the national religions of Buddhism and Shintō.

Pl. 26

The missionaries did not leave Japan. Coelho asked for an extension of time, explaining that the Portuguese ship did not have enough room to carry all the missionaries from Japan. Hideyoshi granted the respite, but at the same time he ordered the Jesuits to assemble at Hirado to await transport and issued a series of decrees designed to destroy the church in Japan. But most of these orders remained on paper; Hideyoshi returned to Osaka and the missionaries quietly began to reorganize their work. Nobody supported Coelho's wild attempts to seek military aid against Hideyoshi, and both missionaries and Christian daimyo wisely chose the path of prudence. Coelho died in 1590, and under the direction of his successor, Pedro Gomez, the mission continued to expand not only in Kyushu but also among the samurai class in Osaka and Kyoto. The seminary and college were reestablished away in Arima and Amakusa, while Nagasaki, which Hideyoshi had placed under his immediate jurisdiction, reverted for the time being to the territory of Ōmura and continued to remain the center of the Japanese church.

Why did Hideyoshi not insist on the enforcement of his orders? The question intrigued his contemporaries and even today still presents a mystery. Basing their interpretation on Luis Frois, some authors believe that the expulsion decree was the result of a night of orgy, during which Seiyakuin managed to inflame the dictator's suspicions; once he had calmed down, he could not withdraw his orders, but at the same time he did not feel inclined to enforce the decree. Other authors prefer the view of Valignano, who believed that Hideyoshi had been planning the decree for some time and that his show of friendship towards Coelho was merely a cloak to mask his real intentions while he awaited an opportune moment. According to this theory, the reason why the decree was not put into effect was to be found in Hideyoshi's fear of losing the Portuguese trade, which with the annexation of Nagasaki to the central government promised to be a lucrative source of revenue.

But it may well be that both these interpretations, although containing perhaps part of the truth, are far too simple. In order, for example, to maintain foreign trade, it would have been

THE EUROPEANS IN JAPAN

---

[1] Real Academia de Historia, Madrid: Jesuitas, leg. 21, f. 320.

sufficient to leave only a small number of Jesuits at Nagasaki, as in fact Hideyoshi officially recognized on the occasion of Valignano's embassy in 1591. It is also necessary to bear in mind the general course of events after the edict and the imperfect information that the ruler received regarding the activities of the missionaries. For it is impossible to admit without qualification that Hideyoshi was perfectly informed of everything that happened in Japan. Like every feared dictator, he had begun to be isolated as those around him carefully vetted, to their own advantage, the information that reached his ears; an impartial reading of the events leading up to the martyrdom of the twenty-six Christians in 1597 clearly demonstrates this state of affairs. Moreover, the edict was not a popular cause and the men interested in accusing the missionaries and their faithful were not numerous, especially in the Christian regions of Kyushu.

A study of Hideyoshi's character is particularly helpful at this point. Except in his last years, he never showed himself eager to annihilate an enemy; he liked to be generous and he seemed to possess a natural instinct to conserve the species. He aimed at only reducing others to his power; when the enemy bowed his head in submission, he was inclined to withhold his arm. In the case of Christianity he probably experienced some surprise at not encountering the slightest resistance. The missionaries ostensibly conformed to his will; the Portuguese carried on with their trade; Takayama silently retired from the political scene; and the other Christian nobles continued in their allegiance. When faced with an adversary who withdrew in this fashion, Hideyoshi preferred to wait before delivering further blows. He had the patience of a man who was sure of his power.

Pl. 20

In July, 1590, Valignano returned to Japan for his second visitation and disembarked at Nagasaki with the young ambassadors. Their tour of the courts of Lisbon, Madrid, Rome and Florence had been a triumphal success, and their reception in Europe had far surpassed the hopes and desires of the Visitor. He could hardly have failed to be satisfied with the result of the expedition, for all the objectives had been achieved, from obtaining a papal bull confirming Japan as the exclusive mission of the Jesuits to introducing the first press of movable type into the country. As a tangible product of this press, which was to play such an important role in the apostolate, he brought with him a description of the historic journey to Europe already edited and printed.

Pl. 8

But the success of the mission to Europe would have been completely in vain if Hideyoshi could not be induced to withdraw his anti-Christian edict. Valignano therefore arrived prepared to meet the ruler in his capacity as ambassador of the Viceroy of India; carrying magnificent gifts and accompanied by the young Kyushu ambassadors, he reached Kyoto in the spring of 1591. After some hesitation Hideyoshi received him with great solemnity in the luxurious setting of his recently constructed Juraku-tei palace. Gifts were duly exchanged, and after diplomatic protocol had been satisfied the young legates performed on their European musical instruments, much to the pleasure of a most cordial Hideyoshi, who called for several encores. Although there was no formal repeal of the expulsion decree, the audience itself was tantamount to its withdrawal, for according to the recognized custom of the time readmission into the presence of a lord was an official sign of reconciliation. A wave of optimism swept through the Christian community, but the Visitor prudently warned against any premature display of rejoicing.

Valignano's visit to court coincided with another of the crucial times in Hideyoshi's career and was one of a series of embassies and pseudo-embassies that figured so prominently during the last years of the ruler's life. Now that the Kanto campaign had been successfully concluded and national unity had at last been achieved, his attention was drawn to the neighboring countries of China, Korea and the Philippines; it was time to begin translating into reality the dreams that he had described to Coelho four years previously. In order to dedicate himself more fully to international affairs, he arranged for the office of *kanpaku*, or "regent," to be

22. Posthumous portrait of Tokugawa Ieyasu (1542–1616) (detail). Rinnō-ji, Nikko.

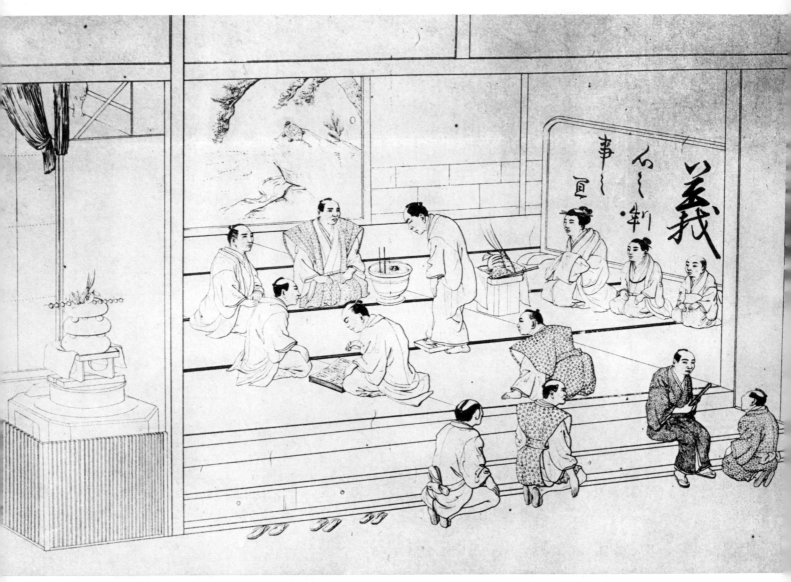

23. The *e-fumi* ceremony, in which citizens were obliged to trample on a plaque of Christ or Our Lady to prove that they were not Christians. From Naga-yama Tokihide, *Collection of Historical Materials Connected with the Roman Catholic Religion in Japan*, Nagasaki, 1926.

24. Our Lady of the Rosary *fumi-e*, set in a wooden board. 10.8 × 7.6 cm.; Tokyo National Museum.

25. Portrait of Ōtomo Yoshishige (1530–1587), daimyo of Bungo in Kyushu. Ōtomo was baptized and received the Christian name Francisco in 1578, but in this posthumous portrait he is featured wearing Buddhist robes. Zuihō-in, Daitoku-ji, Kyoto.

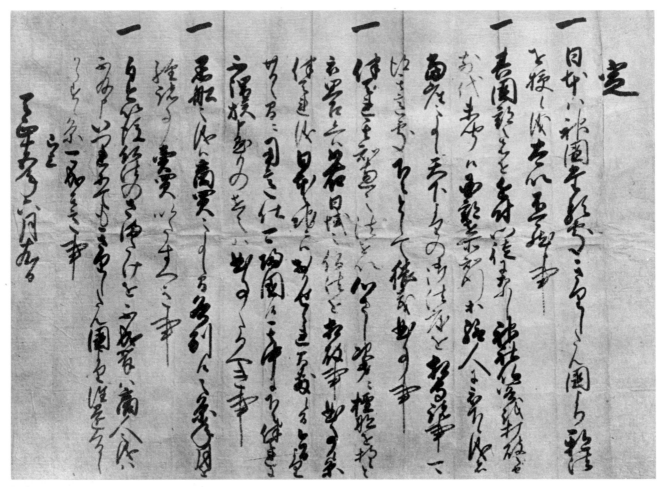

26. A contemporary copy of Hideyoshi's decree—one of the fifteen
made—issued in July, 1587, expelling
all missionaries from Japan. Matsuura
Shiryo Museum, Hirado.

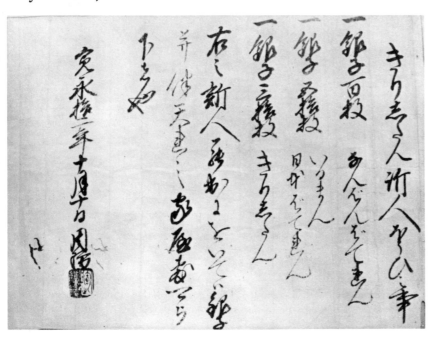

27. Notice, dated 1635, offering various rewards for information leading to
the arrest of missionaries and Christians. Kirishitan Bunko, Sophia University, Tokyo.

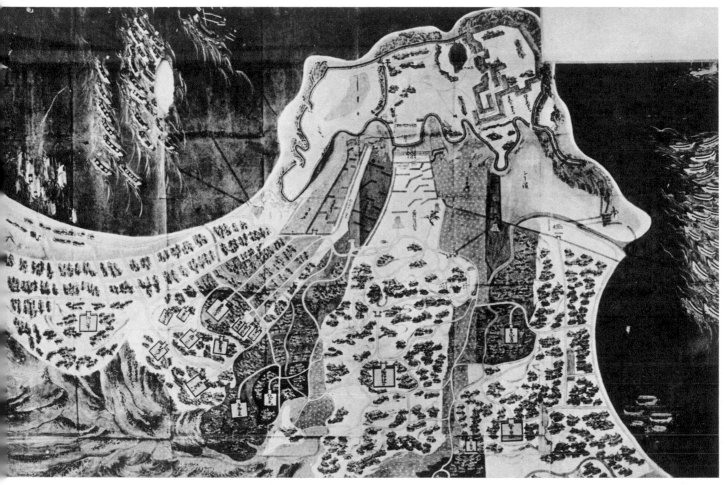

28. A seventeenth-century map of Shimabara penin- (top right-hand corner) and the besieging shogunal
sula, showing the relative positions of Hara Castle troops during the Shimabara Rebellion, 1637–38.

29. The release of Yamada Emonsaku after the capture of Hara Castle by Tokugawa troops in April, 1638. From the block-print book *Shimabara-ki.*

30. The assault on Tomioka Castle, Amakusa, by peasants in January, 1638. After this attack the rebels crossed over to Shimabara, joined the insurgents on the mainland and occupied Hara Castle. From the seventeenth-century block-print book *Shimabara-ki.*

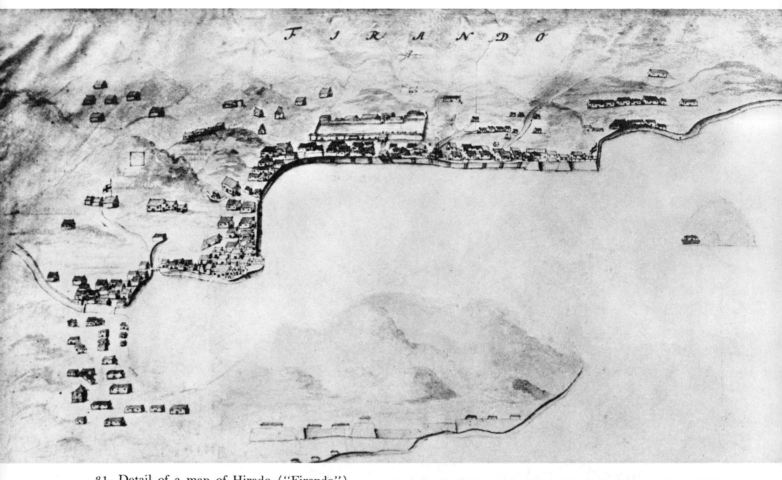

31. Detail of a map of Hirado ("Firando"), drawn in 1621. The building on the far left, flying the flag of St. George, is the English House, while the building on the far right, flying a tricolor flag, is the Dutch headquarters. The mansion of the ruling Matsuura family is in the center. From François Caron and Joost Schouten, *A True Description of the Mighty Kingdoms of Japan and Siam*, edited by C. R. Boxer, London, 1935.

32. A copy, made in 1898, of a seventeenth-century Japanese map of the city and port of Nagasaki. The artificial islet of Dejima, linked to the shore by a bridge, can be seen clearly. Prefectural Library, Nagasaki.

33. An eighteenth-century representation of the 1597 martyrdoms at Nagasaki. João Rodrigues is shown as one of the two European priests standing in the center of the picture, while Bishop Pedro Martins can be seen in the lower right-hand corner, viewing the scene from his house. From Fray Juan Francisco de San Antonio, *Chrónicas de la Apostólica Provincia de San Gregorio*, vol. III, Manila, 1744.

34. The bronze life-size statues of some of the 1597 Christian martyrs in the workshop of the sculptor Funakoshi Yasutake, prior to their erection in 1962 on the actual site of the execution at Nagasaki.

awarded to his nephew Hidetsugu at the beginning of 1592, while he assumed the title of *taikō*, or "retired regent." His relations with the Philippines date from 1591 and began on a discordant note. His message was delivered to the Philippines by the adventurer Harada Kiyemon and demanded an oath of submission from the startled governor, Gomez Perez Dasmariñas. The governor answered this ultimatum with his own embassy, which was led by the Dominican friar Juan Cobo. The embassy landed at Satsuma in 1593 and was received by Hideyoshi in the castle at Nagoya in Hizen, the military headquarters from which he directed the Korean campaign. There are many obscure points concerning Cobo's mission, and some of them will probably never be clarified, for the friar was shipwrecked and drowned on his voyage back to Manila. But one certain, albeit indirect, result of the embassy was the increase in tension between the Spanish and Portuguese merchants in Japan and Hideyoshi's order to pull down the principal church in Nagasaki.

As a result of Cobo's death, Harada decided to act on his own initiative; he returned to the governor of the Philippines and this time asked for some Franciscan friars to be sent to Japan. He may well have had a hand in compiling the letters that the Franciscans in Manila received purportedly from various Christians in Japan, for the contents of these messages clearly show that they were not genuine. Harada's negotiations were successful, and in 1593 a new legation reached Nagasaki and proceeded to Nagoya. Fray Pedro Bautista was a genuine ambassador, as may be seen in his credential letters still preserved in the archives of Pastrana in Guadalajara, Spain; he was accompanied by three other Franciscans, one of whom, Gonzalo Garcia, had formerly been a catechist of the Jesuits in Japan and acted as interpreter.

After their diplomatic mission had been completed, the Franciscans asked for permission to stay in Japan, but Hideyoshi refused the request in accordance with the 1587 expulsion decree. The friars then asked if they might visit Kyoto and see the magnificent buildings that had been raised there. Half-flattered and half-relieved to find a reason to comply with their request, Hideyoshi agreed and appointed an official to look after the party. When Bautista later complained of the restrictions and onerous attention to which his party was subjected, Hideyoshi took a further step and granted the friars the site of a former Buddhist temple in the capital. The Franciscans thereupon built a church and monastery, and also founded a small leper hospital in which they accommodated some of the local people. Attracted by their way of life, some Christians built their houses around the monastery and thus formed a small community. But the friars' public apostolate in the capital alarmed the Jesuits, who saw in their *modus operandi* an open challenge to Hideyoshi's decree. Objectively, the friars were certainly flouting the prohibition, but convinced that they had won not only the permission but also the favor of Hideyoshi, they did not interpret their work in this way. Bautista clearly shows this in a statement in one of his letters, which has often been overlooked. "While this king [Hideyoshi] lives, we can enjoy much security for he is like a father to us; he has given food to us as to the poor and also permission to build a monastery and church."[1]

Meanwhile the Japanese church continued to expand rapidly, and during the five years that followed the expulsion edict some fifty thousand people, mostly in Kyushu, received baptism. A select group of Jesuits worked in Kyoto and Osaka under the experienced direction of Organtino and their influence among the daimyo families steadily increased. Gracia Hosokawa, daughter of Akechi Mitsuhide and wife of Hosokawa Tadaoki, and the daimyo Kinoshita Katsutoshi, nephew of Hideyoshi's wife, were baptized despite the edict. Their example was followed by other influential people, such as Sō Yoshitomo, daimyo of Tsushima, Hosokawa Okimoto, brother of Tadaoki, and Tsutsui Sadatsugu, daimyo of Iga. Finally in 1595 and 1596 there was such a strong movement towards Christianity that Frois was led to exclaim, "Never up to now have so many nobles been baptized in the regions of Kyoto." Among these neophytes could be numbered the grandsons and heirs of Nobunaga, the sons of

[1] L. Perez, O.F.M., *Cartas y Relaciones del Japón* (Madrid: 1916-23), I, p. 76.

Maeda Gen'i, governor of Kyoto, Kyōgoku Takatomo, lord of Tanabe, who was also related to Nobunaga, and various close relatives of Ukita Hide'ie, daimyo of Okayama. These converts are specifically mentioned because they had two characteristics in common—all were young and all were closely connected to Hideyoshi either by political or family ties. It was an interesting development and in some ways recalled the similar movement towards Christianity inspired by Vilela and Brother Lourenço about 1563. But there was one important difference; the people who were now receiving baptism were well aware that they were directly opposing the will of the ruler. It may be asked whether these notable conversions passed unnoticed by Hideyoshi. Succeeding events show that in part they were overlooked, but at the same time this movement undoubtedly had some bearing on the second stage of the persecution, the martyrdom of the twenty-six Christians at Nagasaki.

The events that followed have been studied and described at great length, but the fundamental facts may be briefly stated. On October 19, 1596, the Spanish galleon, *San Felipe*, foundered at the entrance to the port of Urado in Shikoku while making the voyage from Manila to Acapulco in Mexico. The daimyo of Urado, Chōsokabe Motochika, seized the rich cargo on the orders of Hideyoshi; the Spaniards protested in vain against the confiscation through their ambassador, Fray Pedro Bautista, in Kyoto. These events coincided with the visit that Pedro Martins, the first bishop to reach Japan, paid on Hideyoshi. The atmosphere was tense, and orders were issued to compile a list of Christians living in the capital; the differences between Jesuits and Franciscans, Portuguese and Spaniards, deepened. On December 7, Martins embarked at Sakai to return to Nagasaki, and on the following day Hideyoshi finally ordered the detention of the Franciscans and their flock. Days of hope and uncertainty followed, during which time the captain of the galleon, Mathias de Landecho, together with various members of his company, arrived at Osaka. On December 31, sentence of death was pronounced on the prisoners and they were all transferred to Kyoto; three days later, after each had suffered the mutilation of an ear, they were paraded around the streets of the capital. They were then taken to Osaka and Sakai, and finally departed for Nagasaki on January 9.

Pls. 33, 34

The prisoners spent almost a month traveling in the bitter winter cold, and their heroic march ended on February 5, 1597, on the small hill called Nishi-zaka at the entrance of Nagasaki, where fastened to crosses they courageously died from the thrusts of lances. In all there were twenty-six martyrs—four Spaniards, one Mexican, one Indo-Portuguese and twenty Japanese, including three boys. Their splendid testimony stands out clearly in contrast to the background of intrigue and controversy.

It is extraordinarily difficult, if not impossible, to learn who was responsible, directly or otherwise, for the tragedy and to understand the reasons that caused Hideyoshi to take this extreme step. Many people had a role to play in the affair and as usual Hideyoshi kept his real reasons to himself. It is certain from the edict dated January 8, 1597, that the reasons for the executions were ultimately religious, but there were many other relevant factors at play before Hideyoshi made the final decision. The two events of the confiscation of the cargo of the *San Felipe* and the martyrdoms at Nagasaki are closely related. Hideyoshi and the martyrs appear as the protagonists in the drama, but different personalities—the Spanish sailors and the Portuguese merchants, Jesuits and Franciscans, the bonze Seiyakuin, friendly officials and hostile daimyo—all played out the lesser roles. All the elements and personalities in the early history of the Europeans in Japan seemed to converge in this episode. Hideyoshi found himself weighed down under a series of setbacks and misfortunes, which included the death of his nephew Hidetsugu, a great earthquake that had devastated his recently constructed palaces at Fushimi, the Korean war with its enormous cost and corresponding loss in prestige, the absurd Chinese embassy in 1596 that caused him to order a fresh invasion of the mainland, and finally his markedly declining health.

The episode also underlined differences in outlook. To the Spaniards the seizure of a ship belonging to a friendly power was incredible, and they regarded as monstrous the condemnation, without trial, of foreigners who, although they may have erred, still possessed the title of ambassadors. On the other hand, Hideyoshi was unaware of the rules of international conduct; the confiscation of a wrecked ship was a right commonly recognized in the Far East, and the summary execution of a man judged as dangerous to the security of the state was the prerogative of any lord. In his reply to the letter of protest from the governor of the Philippines, Hideyoshi appeared quite confident of his position; it apparently did not occur to him that before executing an ambassador it would have been fitting to have informed the friendly country concerned.

Hideyoshi's desire to lay his hands on the booty is clearly pointed out in Bautista's letters, but the charge has been indignantly denied by some of the ruler's modern admirers. But in order to understand the events of that time, it is necessary to study the real man as he is seen in the light of contemporary evidence and not merely a figure idealized as a hero.

Hideyoshi was generous, sometimes to the point of being lavish; but at the same time he coveted wealth and hoarded great quantities of treasure. He could give away a precious sword, knowing that its full value would not be appreciated by the recipient; but he was also capable of seizing prized tea utensils from the collection of the Sakai merchant Lucas Sosatsu, whom he unjustly condemned to death. It is also obvious that he could not have regarded the crew of the *San Felipe* as pirates or dangerous intruders, for he allowed them to remain at liberty without the least hindrance or punishment and offered no objection to their returning to the Philippines. In addition, the Franciscan missionaries had been advised by the Jesuits and some Japanese to work more unobtrusively, but they had not received the least official warning from the authorities, and the site on which they had built their church had been given to them by Hideyoshi himself. As in the case of Coelho ten years earlier, Hideyoshi's condemnation came as a complete surprise; the two events, in fact, were remarkably similar in many respects, but their consequences were tragically different. Between the two episodes much blood had flowed, and Hideyoshi had changed.

The Nagasaki martyrdoms appeared to presage an intensification of the persecution, but in the event little else followed. For Hideyoshi had reached the end of his career and was now engrossed by the one fixed idea of ensuring that his five-year-old son Hideyori should inherit the wealth and power accumulated during his sixteen years of rule. To this end he devised a scheme whereby his work would be continued after his death by a board of regents comprising Tokugawa Ieyasu, Maeda Toshiie, Mōri Terumoto, Ukita Hide'ie and Uesugi Kagekatsu.

At the side of the dying ruler was also to be seen the unexpected figure of João Rodrigues, for between the old dictator and the young missionary there was undoubtedly a bond of mutual friendship. Rodrigues, who had stood by the crosses and comforted the Nagasaki martyrs only the previous year, was concerned for the eternal salvation of his illustrious friend and tried to move him to repentance; Hideyoshi, for his part, gave no sign of this desired conversion but at the same time did not rebuff the priest. There was something very human in the conversation between the two men, and the fact that Rodrigues could thus speak to the dying ruler with impunity introduces an attractive note of affection in this last meeting between Toyotomi Hideyoshi and the men from the West.

From Sekigahara to Osaka, 1600–1615

Sekigahara is a key name in Japanese history, for the course that the country would follow for two and a half centuries was decided in a matter of a few hours on October 21, 1600, when Tokugawa Ieyasu decisively defeated his rivals and became absolute ruler of Japan. Although the battle was brief, its preparations can be said to have begun two years earlier at the moment of Hideyoshi's death. In a move that perhaps demonstrated his friendship but did not at all accord with his suspicious nature, the dying ruler entrusted the future of his son to the man who had most interest in supplanting him, Tokugawa Ieyasu. Hideyoshi's death thus brought about a change in the political scene that naturally affected the government's relations with the European powers and the Christian mission. Philip II died at the same time as Hideyoshi, and the decline of the Spanish Empire began to set in. In Japan itself the persecution was not renewed, and the movement of conversions continued.

Valignano arrived for his third visit in 1598, and was accompanied by the new bishop of Japan, the Jesuit Luis Cerqueira. While the bishop visited the domains of Konishi Yukinaga, the Visitor reorganized his forces; the experience of previous years had not diminished Valignano's energy but it had qualified his optimism. Jeronimo de Castro, one of the friars expelled from the country in 1597, slipped back into Japan in disguise. Positions were being taken for the next stage of events.

One of the great figures of the Japanese church, Konishi Yukinaga, the former admiral of Hideyoshi, fell from power as a result of Sekigahara and was executed; his territories passed to his enemy, Katō Kiyomasa. Gracia Hosokawa also died, but in this case her death benefited the Christian cause, for it won the friendship of her husband Tadaoki. Ieyasu redistributed the fiefs, and many territories changed hands; the reshuffle of power forced the missionaries to begin their work again in a number of places.

Pl. 22

When Jeronimo de Castro was apprehended and led before Tokugawa Ieyasu, the friar was agreeably surprised to find an ally and protector in the ruler. Ieyasu had been preparing for this moment, for he had been closely observing events and knew exactly what he wanted. His attitude towards international relations was both practical and visionary, and it contrasted strongly with the impulsive and arrogant policy of Hideyoshi. He wished to establish commercial relations with foreign countries without tieing himself to any particular nation and, as far as possible, to build up a Japanese mercantile fleet. If his plan to use Fray Jeronimo to establish new relations with Manila were successful, he would obviously be in a stronger position in his dealings with the Portuguese merchants and missionaries. His policy towards the latter was tolerant and without any sign of hostility, but it could hardly be called friendly.

At this juncture a new figure appeared on the Japanese scene. Will Adams, the English pilot of the Dutch ship *Liefde*, was a small figure with a long shadow, for his arrival in 1600 marked the beginning of the intervention of the English and Dutch, the bitter rivals of Spain and Portugal. The arrival of the disabled *Liefde* at Bungo had been accidental but opportune, for it coincided with the start of the Dutch commercial empire in the East Indies. Adams could also build ocean-going ships; this skill, in addition to his nationality, made him a very useful person in the plans of Ieyasu, who took him into his service and refused to allow him to leave Japan. From that time onwards the Englishman worked actively in his speciality of shipbuilding and at the same time helped to arouse Ieyasu's suspicions of the missionaries.

Partly because of the ruler's balanced character these suspicions were slow to form, and for the time being the future of the Christian community looked serene and promising. As a symbol of the new era just beginning, Bishop Cerqueira raised to the priesthood two Japanese ordinands, Luis Niyabara and Sebastian Kimura, the latter being the grandson of the samurai who had befriended Xavier in Hirado. Ieyasu continued to use the services of João Rodrigues, repeatedly receiving him in audience, and thus for some years the Jesuit linguist acted as a counterbalance to Adams. In Nagasaki the Portuguese still enjoyed their commercial monopoly as the promise of substantial trade with Manila had not been fulfilled, much to the disappointment of Ieyasu.

In 1603 Valignano left Japan for the last time. His third and longest visit had been fruitful, but its good effects were qualified to a great extent by his tenaciously held policy of maintaining the Jesuit monopoly of the Japanese mission. Undisturbed by the brief of Gregory XIII and the prohibition of Bishop Cerqueira, Franciscan, Dominican and Augustinian friars continued to arrive from Manila. Taking advantage of the door opened by Jeronimo de Castro, the Franciscans concentrated their efforts in the Edo region, while the other friars worked in different parts of Kyushu. The attitude of Cerqueira towards the newcomers was basically the same as Valignano's view, although for different reasons, and the bishop unfortunately lacked sufficient vision to resolve the anomalous situation. As a result the tension between the religious orders, although not between all their members, continued to the end.

It has already been noted that the attitude of Ieyasu towards the missionaries could be called tolerant but not friendly. The fact that no daimyo, with the exception of Kyōgoku Taka-tomo, received baptism after Sekigahara may be taken as an indication of his policy, although the upheaval in Japanese society at the time has also to be borne in mind. In addition, from the very beginning Ieyasu brought pressure to bear on the daimyo of Ōmura and Arima to renounce their faith and did not in the least oppose the local anti-Christian persecution waged by Katō Kiyomasa from 1602. Nevertheless, there were no great changes until 1609. The number of Christians continued to increase, although more slowly than before, at the rate of five thousand every year. In 1606 Cerqueira was received in audience by Ieyasu and in the following year the Jesuit Superior, Francisco Pasio, met both the ruler and his son, the shogun Hidetada. With the exception of two or three years when the Dutch blockade managed to prevent the annual voyage from Macao, Portuguese trade continued to flourish. Commerce with Manila took a course that did not displease Ieyasu; the Spaniards had not been able to establish trade in a regular fashion, but Japanese ships sailed between Nagasaki and Manila with increasing frequency. This latest development was irritating to the Portuguese in Macao, but it did not deter their compatriots in Nagasaki from often serving as pilots in these ships.

The year 1606 presented disquieting auguries. Valignano died in Macao, and a problem that had been brewing for two years at Nagasaki ended in the apostasy of Ōmura Yoshiaki. The city that had grown up outside the municipal limits of Nagasaki was a source of profitable revenue for Ōmura but caused considerable administrative difficulties to the Nagasaki governors appointed by the central government. One of these officials, Ogasawara Ichian, informed Ieyasu of the situation in some detail, and the ruler decided to annex the surrounding territory in exchange for other lands of much less value. Angry at the exchange and believing that it had been effected by the maneuvers of Rodrigues, Ōmura expelled the missionaries from his domains in 1605 and renounced his faith a year later.

With the Christian stronghold of Ōmura thus reduced and secure in his control of Nagasaki, Ieyasu now prepared for the next step of weakening the territory of Arima. The instrument chosen for this purpose was Hasegawa Sahioye, the brother of the ruler's favorite, Onatsu. Few men contributed as much as this governor of Nagasaki to prepare the ground for the expulsion of the missionaries and the general prohibition of Christianity. And as if trying to fit in with the plans of Ieyasu, various ships of the countries struggling for political and commercial influence in Japan arrived in 1609. The governor of the Philippines, Rodrigo de Vivero, was shipwrecked off the coast of Kazusa and was duly granted two audiences by Ieyasu. Two Dutch ships, which had been patrolling the straits of Formosa to ambush Portuguese shipping, sailed into Hirado. With the help of Will Adams, the Dutch commander Abraham Van der Broeck appeared at court and presented a letter of friendship from the Prince of Orange. The ships eventually left carrying Ieyasu's reply, and Jacques Specx remained at Hirado at the head of the new Dutch factory, or trading post.

In the same year of 1609 the Portuguese *Madre de Deus*, commanded by the Captain-Major Andres Pessoa, sailed into Nagasaki with its valuable cargo of merchandise and silk. A few months later a Japanese junk, under the command of the Chinese captain Kyubei, also put in. Kyubei had been sent by Arima Harunobu to the kingdom of Champa (Annam) to obtain a cargo of the precious incense called *kyara* and carried Ieyasu's certificate authorizing the voyage. On the return journey the junk had wintered at Macao, where a disturbance had broken out and the Japanese were severely punished by Pessoa. The Portuguese captain lost no time in presenting his version of the incident to Hasegawa, who persuaded him not to disturb Ieyasu by mentioning the matter at court. But when the Nagasaki governor heard the complaints of the Japanese crew of the junk, he decided to take the matter into his own hands.

The final result was Ieyasu's order to seize the *Madre de Deus*, and Arima Harunobu, to whom fell the duty of taking revenge on behalf of his offended subjects, directed the attack. After hard and protracted fighting, Pessoa himself fired the powder magazine to prevent the ship and its cargo from falling into the hands of the assailants, and the *Madre de Deus* sank to the bottom at the entrance of the port, near the island of Kaminoshima.

The loss of the ship affected many people, including the Portuguese and Chinese traders of Macao, the population of Nagasaki, and also the Jesuit missionaries who saw with dismay their revenue for two years disappearing with the ship. But the repercussions of the explosion that rocked the city of Nagasaki were even more widespread. The position of the Dutch was considerably strengthened; in addition, Ieyasu hardened his attitude towards the Portuguese, as may be seen by the measured tone of his reply to the ambassador from Macao, Nuño de Sotomayor.

The final decision to seize the ship has sometimes been attributed to the offer of Rodrigo de Vivero to divert Japanese trade to Manila. But the charge is unfounded because the negotiations of Vivero had as their sole aim the establishment of direct relations with Mexico, a commercial route that had no connection with the silk trade. Nevertheless, it is clear that even after the sinking of the ship, Ieyasu was still anxious to maintain friendly relations with the Portuguese.

Yet another result of the affair was felt in the territory of Arima. Its daimyo Harunobu was the hero of the day for the part he had played in the attack on the *Madre de Deus*, and in recognition of his services Ieyasu gave him a magnificent sword. But this prize was soon followed by another of doubtful value when the ruler presented his granddaughter Kunihime as wife for Harunobu's eldest son. The only drawback to this largesse was that Arima Naozumi, baptized as Miguel, was already married to a Christian girl belonging to the Hibiya family. Arima could see no way of escaping the dilemma and, repudiating his legitimate wife, Naozumi, accepted Kunihime in her stead. The young ruler thus placed himself in an irregular position regarding his religion and, at the same time, in a servile position vis-à-vis Ieyasu; his father, Harunobu, connived with the move and thus weakened his position as a Christian daimyo.

But before taking this step Harunobu had made a gesture that has perhaps not always been fully appreciated. By attacking and sinking Pessoa's ship he had hurt both the feelings and finances of the Portuguese missionaries. But the daimyo did not want to sever his relations with the church, and in the following year he helped the hard-hit missionaries in his realms with generous alms. The same attitude was taken by the leading officers who had taken part in the attack. Jorge Yuki Yaheiji, one of the oldest and most fervent Christians in Japan, was exiled for the faith two years later, while Adrian Takahashi and Leon Taketomi were martyred in front of Arima Castle in 1613. Their attitude recalls Valignano's remark in his *Apologia*, where, defending the patriotism of Konishi Yukinaga, the Visitor observed that the noble's faith did not involve servility towards either dictators or missionaries. "If he were to learn in some way that the Fathers wanted to hand over the country to the Spaniards, he would be the first to raise his sword against them."[1]

The Christians of Arima continued to give courageous testimony of their faith for many years, but the end was near for their daimyo. The combined efforts of Hasegawa and Kunihime, together with the ambiguous position of Naozumi and his father, brought about the fall of the daimyo and the consequent setback for the Christian cause in Japan. Wishing to recover

---

[1] Ajuda Library, Lisbon: *Jesuitas na Asia*, 49-IV-58, f. 80.

some castles, Harunobu asked the help of Okamoto Daihachi, a Christian in the service of Ieyasu's confidential adviser, Honda Masazumi. Okamoto readily accepted the commission and accompanying gifts, but apart from making deceitful promises he took no action. Exasperated by the lack of results, Harunobu decided to present his case to Ieyasu, only to be denounced by his son, Naozumi, who had been waiting for a suitable opportunity to depose him. Ieyasu condemned Okamoto to death and exiled Harunobu to the region of Kai, whither followed soon afterwards an order to commit suicide. Refusing to compromise his Christian conscience, Harunobu declined to obey, and in the last days before his execution he demonstrated the profound faith that had always distinguished him. But this tragic family history erased from the heart of Ieyasu the last feelings of sympathy that he had perhaps retained towards the Christian community. Naozumi apostatized under pressure from Hasegawa and began to persecute his Christian subjects but achieved little success; the martyrdoms at Arie in 1612 and at Arima in the following year were indications of the troubled times to come. But the Christians did not weaken and at his own request Naozumi was transferred to the region of Hyūga.

From that time onwards the policy of Ieyasu was clearly anti-Christian. João Rodrigues fell into disgrace and was obliged to retire to Macao in 1610, thus leaving the field free to Adams. As if to compensate for the favor that Honda Masazumi and the governor of Kyoto, Itakura Katsushige, had shown to the missionaries, the Zen monk Suden and the neo-Confucian scholar Hayashi Razan were appointed advisers at court and helped to formulate Ieyasu's policy against Christianity. A series of decrees was issued in Kyoto, reviving the old anti-Christian edicts and dismissing, in some cases punishing, the Christians in Ieyasu's service. In Edo the propagation of Christianity was forbidden, and when Fray Luis Sotelo violated these decrees by building a small chapel for lepers at Asakusa, some Christians were put to death. Sotelo's life was also placed in jeopardy, but he fortunately had a powerful friend and protector in Date Masamune, daimyo of Sendai. Date was also interested in trade with Mexico, and securing the liberty of Sotelo he sent the friar and his ambassador, Hasekura Tsunenaga, to Spain and Rome by way of Mexico.

Sotelo and Hasekura left Sendai on their way to Europe as Captain John Saris, carrying a letter from James I of England, reached Hirado in the *Clove*. Ieyasu granted him an audience and conceded to the English the same trading privileges as he had granted the Dutch. Leaving Richard Cocks as the manager of the English factory in Hirado, Saris left Japan at the end of 1613 and returned to England with Ieyasu's official reply. In the event, English trade did not flourish, but the presence in Japan of new enemies of the Portuguese strengthened Ieyasu's position. Only the last occasion was missing and this was duly supplied by Hasegawa misrepresenting an insignificant event. A Christian was sentenced to death for illegally minting silver and some of the faithful had knelt to pray for the condemned man at his execution. Hasegawa thereupon accused them of worshiping a criminal and went on to interpret in the same sense the great manifestations of faith that had accompanied the martyrdoms at Arima. On January 27, 1614, Ieyasu promulgated a long edict, drawn up by Hayashi and Suden, proscribing Christianity throughout the land and expelling all the missionaries. Shortly afterwards Takayama Ukon received a fresh invitation to apostatize, accompanied this time with the threat of exile abroad. As a reply to the ultimatum, Takayama set out for Nagasaki with his whole family.

Nagasaki itself was in a confused state. Bishop Cerqueira had recently died, and the clergy had elected the Jesuit Superior, Valentim Carvalho, as the vicar of the diocese. Carvalho was not exactly a conciliating character and his intransigent attitude in the following months led the Franciscan Superior, Diego de Chinchon, to adopt an equivocal position. Chinchon persuaded the Japanese clergy that Carvalho's election had been invalid, whereupon the clerics revoked their previous choice and elected the Dominican Francisco de Morales as the new

Pl. 44

vicar. Confident of the righteousness of his case, Carvalho adopted a strong line and threatened his adversaries with censures. Thus arose the so-called Nagasaki schism, which divided both missionaries and laity into two opposing parties. The validity of Carvalho's election was recognized in due course by the archbishops of Manila and Goa, and the unhappy affair slipped unmourned into history. Such an episode would be distressing at the best of times, but in the circumstances it was bitterly ironic.

In a demonstration of fervor the Nagasaki Christians organized penitential processions through the streets of the city. Exaggerated reports reaching Ieyasu gave the impression of a city in open revolt and served to increase further the hostility of the authorities. The missionaries gradually assembled at Nagasaki, where they were joined by Takayama Ukon and his family. The Jesuit Diego de Mesquita made a final attempt to plead with Ieyasu but was denied audience, and he died in a hut on Nagasaki beach shortly before the departure of the ships. During the last few days before their exile, all the missionaries were interned in the nearby villages of Fukuda and Kibachi to prevent them slipping away. Finally, on November 7 and 8, 1614, the *Nossa Senhora da Vida* and a junk sailed for Macao with some seventy Jesuits and a good number of their Japanese helpers on board; at the same time another junk left for Manila carrying about forty missionaries and the families of the exiled Japanese. But thirty-seven missionaries and almost a hundred catechists had succeeded in escaping the vigilance of the authorities, and continued to work in disguise among the three hundred thousand Christians throughout the country.

The fact that so many were able to remain behind while others slipped back from exile in the following years indicates connivance on the part of not a few local officials and, above all, the support of the people. Moreover, Ieyasu was then occupied by a more pressing problem, for the moment of direct confrontation with Toyotomi Hideyori had arrived. The armed struggle took place in two stages, known as the winter and summer campaigns, and finally Pl. 36 Osaka Castle, the Toyotomi stronghold, fell to the Tokugawa troops on June 4, 1615 and the house founded by Hideyoshi came to an end. Ieyasu had completed the violation of the solemn oath that he had made to Hideyoshi eighteen years previously.

The fall of Osaka had its repercussions in the prohibition of Christianity. As the power of the Tokugawa family was finally consolidated, any hopes for a change in the political situation finally disappeared. The presence of seven priests and numerous Christian samurai, with their crosses and standards, among the Osaka defenders did not pass unnoticed and served to inflame the anti-Christian sentiments of Ieyasu and his son, the shogun Hidetada. Only one of the unofficial chaplains, the Japanese priest Francisco Murayama, son of the Nagasaki official Murayama Toan, died in the actual fighting; the rest escaped with their lives, not as a result of Ieyasu's benevolence but thanks to the Christians and sympathizers who fought in the victorious army.

Only four months later the figure most representative of the Japanese church, Justo Taka-yama Ukon, died in Manila. The citizens of that city accorded him a magnificent reception on his arrival and the governor offered him a pension; but although finding himself in great poverty, Takayama declined the offer. The reason for his refusal was worthy of him, for a samurai who received an allowance was under obligation to offer his services in return and by that time Takayama was not in a position to do this. He was a man who did not sell himself. He had lived with the three men who had dominated the Japanese scene for the past fifty years, Oda Nobunaga, Toyotomi Hideyoshi and Tokugawa Ieyasu. All three had tried at one time or other to win him over by persuasion, flattery or threats, but none of them was able to record the victory.

35. The ruins of Azuchi Castle, built by Oda Nobunaga on the banks of Lake Biwa in 1576 and destroyed only six years later after the ruler's assassination. Luis Frois, S.J., visited the magnificent castle in 1581 and commented that "as regards architecture, strength, wealth and grandeur, it may well be compared to the greatest buildings of Europe."

36. The siege of Osaka Castle in the summer of 1615. Detail from a screen in Osaka Castle. After failing to take the castle by assault in the winter of 1614–15, Tokugawa Ieyasu made another attempt in the following summer and utterly routed the troops of Toyotomi Hideyori, the son of the former ruler, Hideyoshi. From then onwards the Tokugawa regime, which lasted until 1868, met with no further military resistance.

37. Hideyoshi viewing the blossoms at Yoshino. Detail from a pair of screens by Kanō Mitsunobu (1561–1608); Hosomi Collection, Osaka. On April 17, 1594, Hideyoshi went to view cherry blossoms at Yoshino, some forty miles south of Kyoto. He is seen here in this screen (which was discovered as recently as 1962) being carried in a palanquin into the Kimbu Shrine, with a man dressed in European clothing standing nearby as an interested spectator. Yoshino still attracts large crowds every spring, and the blossom at the top of the hill is traditionally at its finest on April 17 and 18.

38. A view of Kyoto in the early seventeenth century, showing Nijō Castle. Detail from a pair of *rakuchū rakugai* ("In and Around Kyoto") six-panel screens; Shōkō-ji, Toyama.

39. The Thousand-Armed Statue of Kannon. Sanjūsangen-dō, Kyoto. Richard Cocks visited the temple on November 2, 1616, and wrote about this statue, "And out of the side of it proceed many armes with hands, and in each hand on thing or other, as speares, sword, dagges, spades, arrowes, knyves, frutes, fyshes, fowles, beastes, corne, and many other matters and formes; and out of the head procead many littell heades."

40. The thousand statues of Kannon, described by Cocks as "standing on foote upon steps, on behind an others back, all apart on from an other, with glories over their heads, armes out of their sids, and littell heades out of the great." Sanjūsangen-dō, Kyoto.

41. The path leading to the Kanchū-an tea house, Nezu Art Museum, Tokyo. In his description of the Japanese tea house, João Rodrigues, S.J., observed, "The stones with which they pave the path make up one of the main expenses. . . . Although rough and unworked, they look as if they have appeared there quite naturally, and they have a certain grace, beauty and simplicity about them."

42. *Maple Tree*. Detail from a painting on wall panels in Chishaku-in, Kyoto, about 1593; attributed to Hasegawa Tōhaku (1542–1610). João Rodrigues often visited Kyoto during this period when some of the best mural decorations were being produced, and he wrote, "The walls are lined with paintings executed on many layers of paper. . . . The four seasons of the year may be represented, each one depicted by whatever blooms in that season. . . . Everything is done to imitate nature, so that you seem to be looking at the very things themselves. In the houses of the great lords and nobles these paintings and the doors of the rooms have a background richly painted in gold, and on this gold they depict the scenes in various suitable colors."

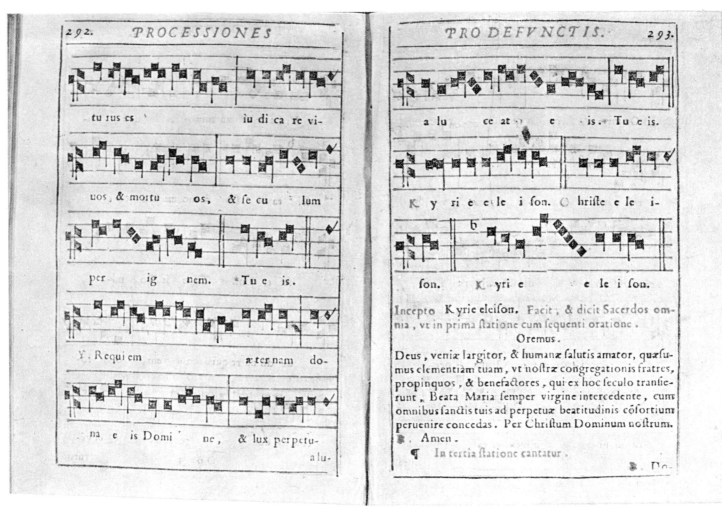

43. Two pages from Luis de Cerqueira, S. J., *Manuale ad Sacramenta Ecclesiae Ministranda*, a manual of liturgical services for the use of missionaries, published at Nagasaki in 1605. This was the only book printed in two colors by the Jesuit press in Japan. Kirishitan Bunko, Sophia University, Tokyo.

The Final Phase, 1615–40

Tokugawa Ieyasu survived his Osaka victory by only one year. According to the Jesuit annual letter of 1618, he spent his last days resting at his Suruga court and enjoying his favorite pastime of hunting. The account that this letter gives of him depicts a man conscious of having fulfilled his ambition and confident that his work would continue. The contrast between his tranquil state of mind and the anxiety and fears of the dying Hideyoshi is striking.

Perhaps because he could foresee the path that events would follow after his death, Ieyasu did not appear in a hurry to enforce his edicts against Christianity. While Japanese society settled down again after the Osaka upheaval, the hidden missionaries enjoyed a period of deceptive calm that made them hope for an improvement in the situation such as had occurred after the death of Hideyoshi. But when the change eventually came, it was decidedly for the worse. Ieyasu's successors possessed neither his vision nor his breadth of mind. They devoted their efforts to strengthening the authority of their family within Japan and they employed various methods for this purpose. They weakened the power of the nobility by strategic distribution and frequent transfers of fiefs belonging to the daimyo tied to the house of Tokugawa (*fudai daimyo*) and by placing debilitating economic burdens on the others (*tozama daimyo*); in this way they aimed at crushing all opposition, even of the intellectual order, to the *bakufu*, or shogunal government. In addition a policy of progressively isolating the country from all foreign contacts was adopted. Although this isolationist policy also tended to limit the power of the *tozama daimyo*, the measure was primarily an anti-Christian move.

The first step was taken in 1616, the year of Ieyasu's death, when the shogun Hidetada issued a decree limiting foreign trade to the ports of Nagasaki and Hirado. Shimazu Tadatsune at Kagoshima in the south of Japan wanted to develop trade with Manila, while Date Masamune at Sendai in the north awaited the return of his ambassador Hasekura Tsunenaga; both daimyo saw their expansionist policy cut short and the means of acquiring new wealth frustrated. The decree also had the effect of associating even more closely the two designated ports with the two rival blocks; Nagasaki was the center of Portuguese and Spanish trade, and Hirado was the English and Dutch base. For some time this situation afforded a clear advantage to the first group and an indirect support to the hidden missionaries.

It is, perhaps, tempting to present the history of the Europeans under the shogun Hidetada and Iemitsu, the successors of Ieyasu, as a series of anti-Christian decrees steadily increasing severity and a growing list of martyrs. But such a simplification runs the risk of making the account incomprehensible because it fails to take into consideration two important factors— the colony of foreign merchants and the Japanese people themselves. The Portuguese were tenacious in maintaining a trade that was vital for the very existence of Macao, and in their efforts to retain this commercial link they indirectly supported the anti-Christian measures; but at the same time they were incorrigible in smuggling missionaries into the country and lending them all possible help. This connection with the missionaries finally ruined the Portuguese trade. The Dutch and the English, on the other hand, were more disposed to collaborate with the *bakufu* in order to drive their rivals out of Japan, and the more determined group, the Dutch traders, were thus able to remain in the country permanently.

Despite this Portuguese aid, the work of the missionaries could not have continued but for the support of the Christian laity and the benevolence of not a few daimyo who neglected as far as possible to enforce the persecution edicts. The sympathy of the people was shown in a special way in Nagasaki. Although ruled by a *bugyō*, or governor appointed by the central government, the day-to-day administration of the city depended to a large extent on the *daikan*, or vice-governors, and the *otona*, or ward officials. The situation was greatly eased by a change of governor in 1615, when the anti-Christian Hasegawa Sahioye was succeeded by his nephew Hasegawa Gonroku. The new governor differed greatly from his uncle, and although his name is inevitably associated with many martyrdoms he in fact avoided bloodshed as much as possible and invariably acted with courtesy and sympathy during the Christian trials.

For many years the position of *daikan* had been held by Antonio Murayama, an interesting and somewhat enigmatic character who figured prominently in the early history of Nagasaki. As a young merchant he employed his considerable talent to amass a large fortune and in time he became one of the wealthiest citizens of Nagasaki. His ready wit and astuteness won for him the favor of Hideyoshi, who, unable to pronounce his Christian name correctly, called him Toan. He took an active part in the divisions between missionaries and passed from the side of the Jesuits to that of the Dominicans, whom he helped to establish at Nagasaki in 1609. For some years he lived separated from his wife, and his conduct caused considerable scandal in the city; but the persecution in 1614 brought about a radical reform in his way of life, and he publically confessed his repentance in the penitential processions of that year.

The change in Murayama coincided with another in the opposite sense in another Nagasaki citizen, Juan Suetsugu Heizo, who had long been his rival. Suetsugu secretly abjured his faith and accused Murayama of misappropriating funds and protecting hunted missionaries. The case dragged on intermittently for two years, but finally Murayama and his family were condemned to death, and Suetsugu took his place in the administration of the city. The fall of Murayama freed the hands of the *bugyō*, and from 1619 onwards the hunt for missionaries and their helpers began in Nagasaki. One of the first martyrs was Murayama's son Andres, who was convicted of sheltering a Dominican priest in his house.

But even before this execution there had been another in Ōmura, which was especially noteworthy as the first case in which foreign priests were put to death since the 1597 martyrdoms. As a result of working secretly and making use of catechists, letters and nocturnal visits, the missionaries were bound to lose contact with certain sectors of the Christian population with a consequent loss of fervor in these communities. Recognition of this fact, together with the allegation that the missionaries exhorted others to martyrdom but avoided it themselves, moved three friars from Manila, a Franciscan, a Dominican and an Augustinian, to embark on a tour of public preaching through Ōmura. The Christians of some villages immediately responded to the call, but when the news reached the ears of Ōmura Sumiyori, grandson of Sumitada, the daimyo was forced to intervene. The three friars were imprisoned and, together with a Jesuit captured elsewhere, were subsequently decapitated.

The enterprise of the friars, it is true, animated the Christians and banished any suspicions concerning the integrity of the missionaries, but at the same time it obliged Sumiyori to become a persecutor and intensified the search for missionaries in Nagasaki. Their action gave rise to new polemic about the correct policy to adopt in time of persecution. The controversy remained for the most part on the theoretical level, for the majority of missionaries continued to work secretly, realizing that public preaching played straight into the hands of the persecutors. An interesting contemporary document, written in a diffuse style and weighed down with quotations, sets forth the Jesuit position, based on the principle that the greatest good of the Christian community would be achieved by the secret apostolate that neither provoked the authorities nor abandoned the faithful, and this norm in fact became the regular basis of apostolic work. In general the missionaries could be divided into two classes; itinerant missionaries moving from one place to another, secretly visiting different communities; and others working unobtrusively within a city, such as Nagasaki, or in one particular region, such as Shimabara, ministering to one or several Christian centers.

After the blows of 1617 and 1619 there followed an interval of relative calm. The progress of missionary work continued and a considerable number of baptisms was recorded. In another effort to halt this advance the *bakufu* then promulgated a new law, threatening to punish not only the owner of a house in which a missionary was discovered but also his neighbors. Some priests arrested in the region of Hizen were taken to the harsh prison of Suzuta to await the decision of the shogun, and it was generally believed that they would be exiled from the country. But at this juncture there occurred an apparently insignificant event that was to cause widespread repercussions and that brought together in a remarkable way all the parties concerned in the political and commercial struggle. On July 22, 1620, the English frigate *Elizabeth* belonging to the Fleet of Defense intercepted off the coast of Formosa a Japanese junk plying between Manila and Nagasaki with the certificate, or *goshuin*, of the shogun. Two Spaniards were found hiding among the cargo of deer skins and they were immediately suspected of being disguised missionaries. They were taken to Hirado and shut up in the prison of the Dutch factory, where they were severely tortured to force them to reveal their identity. If it could be proved that the pair were missionaries, the junk and its cargo would be awarded to the Dutch and English; on the other hand, if no such admission were forthcoming, the foreign merchants were liable to incur the displeasure, if not the punishment, of the shogun.

The prisoners steadfastly refused to confess and finally a complicated trial took place in the residence of the daimyo of Hirado. The picture could not have been more complete, for every kind of interest was involved. The governor of Nagasaki, Hasegawa Gonroku, and the daimyo of Hirado, Matsuura Takanobu, presided over the proceedings, while Richard Cocks and Jacques Specx represented the English and Dutch interests. Spanish merchants, such as Alvaro Muñoz, and a Portuguese contingent, led by Luis Martins de Figueiredo, attended from Nagasaki. The apostate Suetsugu Heizo and the renegade priest Thomas Araki were also present, together with the Japanese crew of the junk and its captain Joaquin Diaz Hirayama, a Japanese domiciled in Manila. From the prison of Suzuta were brought the Jesuit Carlo Spinola, the Dominican Francisco de Morales and the Franciscan Pedro de Avila.

Various interesting facts became evident during the course of the trial, and none was so marked as the isolation in which the accusers found themselves. A large part of the population of Hirado was Christian and favorably disposed towards the two prisoners and, above all, towards the Japanese crew of the junk. In addition, the junk and its cargo belonged to Nagasaki and the citizens of that city had no desire to see it fall into the hands of the foreign merchants. As regards the officials, Matsuura was the son of a fervent Christian and had been baptized shortly after his birth. Although he officially appeared as an ally of the English and Dutch, his sympathies lay with the prisoners, for whom he provided an abundant banquet at which was served Spanish wine, given to the daimyo, ironically enough, by Richard Cocks shortly before. For his part, Hasegawa knew one of the prisoners personally but declined to identify him, for he wanted to save the crew and avoid bloodshed. The governor showed such a friendly attitude to the prisoners that Cocks accused him in his diary of being a secret Christian.

The hearing finally ended when the two prisoners, the Spanish Augustinian Pedro de Zuñiga, son of a viceroy of Mexico, and the Flemish Dominican Luis Flores, admitted that they were priests and the case was referred to the shogun. A sequel to the trial complicated the situation even further when the Dominican friar Diego Collado, together with some Japanese helpers, tried to snatch Flores from prison; the attempt failed and documents were found on the unsuccessful rescuers that compromised various Portuguese in Nagasaki. The consequences of the trial and rescue attempt were severe. Hidetada condemned to death the two priests, Hirayama and his crew, as well as all the Christian prisoners confined in the goals of Suzuta and Nagasaki. In August and September, 1622, the executions were carried out on the small hill of Nishi-zaka at Nagasaki where the twenty-six martyrs had died in 1597. The so-called Great Martyrdom took place on September 10 when fifty-one martyrs, including Carlo Spinola, Sebastian Kimura and other outstanding missionaries, were put to death either by the sword or by fire.

Not satisfied by these harsh sentences, Hidetada further ordered the severance of relations with Manila and Mexico, and in addition the captain-major of Macao, Jeronimo Macedo, was interned in the prison of Ōmura. Macedo was accused of smuggling missionaries into the country, and his name was implicated in the abortive rescue of Flores. The punishment did not break his spirit and he continued helping missionaries, especially those occupying adjoining cells, until his death in 1632.

Pl. 15

In 1623 Iemitsu succeeded his father Hidetada in the office of shogun and from the very beginning his attitude towards Christianity was made perfectly clear. He treated the daimyo who had gone to Edo for his investiture to the spectacle of a mass martyrdom in December of that year when fifty Christians were burnt at the stake; among the victims was the Sicilian Jesuit, Girolamo de Angelis, who in the course of his work became the first European to visit the island of Ezo, or Hokkaido. But the general measures taken towards controlling the Christian population as a whole were more significant than the sporadic executions of martyrs. A further development in the policy of national isolation was the prohibition, under pain of death, of traveling overseas; the same penalty was laid down for Japanese residents living abroad who returned to their native country. Thus Iemitsu brought to an end the ambitious plans of his grandfather, Ieyasu, to establish a mercantile fleet. At the same time the Anglo-Dutch alliance of the Fleet of Defense came to an end, and in 1623 the English merchants left Hirado, leaving the Dutch, Portuguese and Chinese to dispute the foreign trade.

Pl. 14

The persecution measures began to be transformed into a highly organized system which steadily increased in efficiency. Torture became more refined and was aimed at producing apostates rather than martyrs; the cross and sword were replaced by the stake and freezing water. These methods were succeeded in turn by immersion in the sulphurous water of the Unzen springs and finally by the *ana-tsurushi*, or suspension head downwards in a pit. This torture, the most terrible of all the torments, became general about 1633 and succeeded in wringing out the apostasy of the Jesuit Christovão Ferreira; in the same year more than thirty missionaries died as martyrs in the pit or at the stake. Among these victims was Julian Naka-ura, one of the Kyushu legates who had traveled to Rome in 1582. All four youths had become Jesuits on their return to Japan; Michael Chijiwa left the Order and abandoned his faith a few years later, but the other three persevered and were ordained as priests. Mancio Itō died young, and Martinho Hara, the intellectual of the group, was exiled to Macao; only Nakaura was able to remain in Japan and worked mostly in the territory of Arima until his martyrdom.

THE
SOUTHERN
BARBARIANS
Pl. 23
Pl. 27

With the compulsory registration of all citizens at their local Buddhist temples and the setting up of neighborhood organizations bound by the inhuman law of collective responsibility, the Christian population might have appeared firmly under control. But in fact the disguised missionaries continued traveling throughout the country with the support of the people. Some, such as Juan Bautista Baeza, managed to remain twelve years in Nagasaki without falling into the hands of the authorities, while Giacome Giannone spent seventeen years working in the region of Shimabara. It is not known when Fray Diego de San Francisco died, but he exercised a long and heroic apostolate in the north of Japan for many years. These and many other cases would not have been possible without the loyal collaboration of the ordinary people, and it was for this reason that severe punishments were inflicted on those caught providing accommodation and help to the missionaries. The *bakufu* also instituted other measures, such as the *e-fumi*, or rite of trampling on a religious plaque or picture as a sign of rejection of Christianity; edicts placing a price on the heads of the missionaries and their helpers were published on notice boards, and a strict registration of domiciles was kept.

Pl. 32

In 1635 the authorities took another step and this was to be the final measure before the definitive decree of *sakoku*, or "national isolation." The government ordered the wealthiest merchants of Nagasaki to contribute to the construction of an artificial island, sited a few yards from the shore, to serve as a quay and a residence for the Portuguese. The island, known as Dejima, "the island that juts out," was shaped like an extended fan and was joined by a narrow bridge to the promontory where the Jesuit college had once stood. As there was a guard post at the entrance of the bridge, the Portuguese were in effect interned and remained completely cut off from the mainland, for only trusted people were allowed to cross over to the island during the day for commercial reasons.

With the Portuguese thus taken care of, Iemitsu issued another decree that bore his characteristic imprint and ordered all the children of mixed marriages to be deported from Japan. As a result, 287 children of Portuguese traders and Japanese wives were sent to Macao, while others were obliged to leave for Dutch possessions. The international relations that had begun at Tanegashima ended at Dejima, and once more a young Japanese girl, homesick for her country, lamented her fate. This time the heroine was called Oharu, and her letter, written on pieces of cloth, is still preserved in Hirado. Her monument is at Nagasaki in the Chinese temple of Shofuku-ji, near the site of her father's house. But for Oharu, exiled to Djakarta, there was to be no chance of returning.

Despite these stringent measures five missionaries managed to enter Japan in 1637, but they were unfamiliar with the country and were captured immediately. More important for the authorities was the belated arrest and execution of Kintsuba, the popular name of the Japanese Augustinian Thomas de San Agustin. For many years the work of this legendary figure had been a cause of deep concern for the Nagasaki bugyō, who little realized that the disguised friar was living in his own official residence. By this time only five missionaries remained at liberty in all Japan and most of them were working in the remote northern regions.

At the end of 1637, an insignificant event in Arima provoked the greatest tragedy of the entire persecution, the rebellion of the Shimabara peasants. Matsukura Shigemasa, a man of considerable integrity, had succeeded Arima Naozumi in the government of the territory, and although not a Christian he tolerated the presence of missionaries in his fief for several years; he was aware that nearly all the peasant population of the region was Christian and saw that the work of the missionaries was beneficial to maintaining peace. Five Jesuits were working in the peninsula of Shimabara in 1632, when during the absence of the daimyo one of his governors apprehended Pedro Paulo Navarro and informed the central government of his arrest. Matsukura was unable to prevaricate any further and was obliged to begin a persecution that steadily grew in ferocity.

He was succeeded by his son, Matsukura Shigeharu, who was despotic, cruel and also hard pressed for money; the construction of the large castle at Shimabara was a heavy burden on his modest revenues, and as if this were not enough, he was also obliged to contribute to the building of Edo Castle. The victims, of course, were his peasants. In addition to the services that they had to render free in the salt mines of the daimyo, they also saw their meager crops disappearing in the form of outlandish taxes—taxes on births and taxes on deaths, taxes on doors and taxes on windows. If a man could not pay or fled to avoid payment, his children were sold as slaves. Shigeharu obviously did not realize that he was playing with fire, for many of these peasants had served in the army of Konishi Yukinaga and had been some of the finest soldiers of Japan; they thus did not possess the inexhaustible patience of men who had been chained to the land all their lives. One day a farmer killed a tax collector who had misused his daughter, and the spark was quickly fanned into a blaze. The peasants armed themselves, and failing to take by assault Shimabara Castle they withdrew and took refuge in the abandoned Hara Castle; this had formerly belonged to the house of Arima and consisted of a series of small embankments, with the sea on three sides and protected by a ditch. There they were joined by groups of peasants from Amakusa, who had risen against the tyranny of Terazawa Katataka, son of a former governor of Nagasaki. It was the end of December, 1637.

It has been calculated that some twenty thousand men, together with seventeen thousand women and children, took refuge in the castle. As their leader there appeared a seventeen-year-old youth, Masuda Shirō, better known as Amakusa Shirō, the son of a former samurai in the service of Konishi Yukinaga; behind this legendary and idealized figure a group of experienced rōnin, or masterless soldiers, organized and directed the resistance. Not all of the rebels were

demned as common criminals and that this had happened in the case of some *korobi bateren*.

The unhappy end of the Rubino expedition stopped any further attempt to send missionaries into Japan, and the Christians had to be abandoned to their own devices. Only from time to time did rumors, impossible to verify, reach Macao and Manila through Chinese merchants from Nagasaki. The desire to know the fate of these Christians moved the authorities in Rome to allow an Italian priest, Giovanni Battista Sidotti, to defy the *sakoku* decree. He landed at Yakushima in 1708 and met a heroic death in the *kirishitan yashiki* some seven years later.

Given the lack of documents concerning these last years, the total number of martyrdoms cannot be calculated with any precision. It is impossible to agree with authors who suggest a figure almost equivalent to the number of Christians, but nor can the limiting of the martyrs to a few hundred be accepted. Excluding the victims of the Shimabara rebellion, in which the women and children can be considered as martyrs, the figure of three or four thousand is by no means exaggerated, and nobody knows the large number of Christians who died as a result of exile and hardship.

The Christians in Japan did not die out. Prepared for this contingency by the missionaries, groups of the faithful continued to exist underground and showed an astonishing fidelity. The Christians living in Urakami, on the outskirts of Nagasaki, in the villages of the western coast of Nishi-Sonogi, and in isolated groups on the remote islands of Gotō, Hirado and Amakusa, continued to hand down their religion from father to son and secretly administer the sacrament of baptism. A quick look at the map shows that Christianity persevered in those regions where mass conversions had formed a religious milieu, and it was there that the hidden missionaries had been able to prolong their apostolate and prepare the faithful to resist persecution. This cohesive atmosphere also preserved most of the groups from the greater internal danger of their religion gradually degenerating into a meaningless ritual, as actually happened in the case of those communities known today as the *hanare*, "the separated ones."

In 1865 the hidden Christians appeared once more in Nagasaki before the astonished gaze of the Japanese authorities and the Western world. There were still some twenty thousand of them and they had preserved their religion for more than two centuries, patiently awaiting the time when the men from the West would once more be allowed to return to Japan.

THE

SOUTHERN

BARBARIANS

JAPAN DESCRIBED:

THE REPORTS OF THE EUROPEANS

JAPAN DESCRIBED:

THE REPORTS OF THE EUROPEANS

Michael Cooper, S.J.

Tales of travel and exploration have long exerted a special fascination, and the accounts of the medieval travelers, such as Marco Polo and Friar Odoric, who boldly ventured into the distant and exotic lands of Asia, for centuries stirred the imagination of Europe. Their colorful stories of marvels and prodigies, suitably illustrated by quaint woodcuts, provided the educated European with the vicarious thrill of exploring uncharted oceans and lands beyond the bounds of Christendom, much as the science fiction enthusiast today shares the hazards of space travel from the comfort and security of his armchair.

Marco Polo's vague reference to the mysterious island of Cipangu aroused much interest and added impetus to exploration, for his brief report not only described the wonders of this fabulous country but also mentioned its immense wealth. Thus when Europeans finally reached Japan in the middle of the sixteenth century and identified the island kingdom with the legendary Cipangu, there was considerable demand for information about this most easterly nation. If the subsequent reports were a good deal more prosaic then Polo's hearsay description, the fact that they were genuine eyewitness descriptions compensated for any loss in exotic detail, just as the sober accounts of lunar exploration in recent years have surpassed in interest even the most imaginative fantasies of science fiction.

Apart from the contributions of a few Portuguese merchants, such as Jorge Alvares and Fernão Mendes Pinto, information about Japan during the first forty years of its contact with the West was provided almost exclusively by Jesuit missionaries. Ever since its foundation in 1540, the Society of Jesus has encouraged the exchange of letters to strengthen the bond of union among its members throughout the world. An early instruction issued in 1553 suggested that Jesuit missionaries should describe in their letters not only their work but also the region in which they lived—"the weather, the degrees of longitude, the dress, food, housing, numbers and customs of the inhabitants . . .; just as other accounts are written to satisfy curiosity, so let our men also write in the same way."[1] The Jesuits in Japan responded with a will and began sending back to Europe lengthy accounts, usu-

---

[1] Letter dated August 13, 1553; in *Monumenta Ignatiana, Epistolae,* V (Madrid: 1907), p. 330.

ally in Portuguese or Spanish. Some of these early examples leave much to be desired, for the formidable language barrier and the frequent civil wars precluded a thorough knowledge of the country and its people. Nevertheless, despite these obstacles, the reports of pioneers such as Gaspar Vilela and Luis Almeida provide remarkably detailed descriptions of various aspects of Japanese life.

When the letters finally reached Europe, they were often copied and circulated to Jesuit houses for public reading in the refectory. But interest in the newly discovered country was not confined to members of the Order, and it was not long before these accounts were included in the published collections of letters from Jesuit missions in different parts of the world. The Japanese reports soon became by far the most popular of the missionary accounts, and the first of a long series of collections devoted entirely to letters from Japan was published at Coimbra in 1565. The widely publicized embassy of the Kyushu nobles, who made the grand tour of the courts of Lisbon, Madrid, and Rome in 1584–86, served to quicken public interest even more, and a bulky volume, containing over two hundred letters covering the first forty years of the mission, was put out at Evora in 1598.[1] Some of the letters included in this volume are extremely long and run to the size of minor treatises; this is particularly true of the official Annual Letters, which from 1580 onwards give a full report on Jesuit work in Japan year by year.

As the mission gained a precarious stability, full-length accounts of the history and work of the church in Japan, together with a great deal of material about the country itself, were produced by Alessandro Valignano, Luis Frois, João Rodrigues and others, but none of these works was published until recent times. Some manuscript accounts still remain unedited to this day in various European archives. Such works were composed by men of experience and perception, and they present an engrossing picture of Japan as seen through the eyes of intelligent and sympathetic Europeans. Towards the end of the sixteenth century other religious orders began to work in Japan, but on the whole the letters of the Franciscan, Dominican and Augustinian friars concerned only the progress of the mission and the development of the persecution, and thus they do not greatly add to the picture of Japanese life. Various Spanish laymen, such as Bernardino de Avila Giron, Rodrigo de Vivero y Velasco and Sebastian Vizcaino, also recorded about this time their impressions and experiences, but their writings remained unpublished until recent years.

With the arrival of the English and Dutch merchants a new chapter in the European accounts of Japan begins, for the letters and reports of Will Adams, John Saris and Richard Cocks throw considerable light on areas not described by the missionaries. Their down-to-earth observations have a particular value as the Protestant traders wrote from a different religious and political viewpoint, for practically all the information about Japan until then had been supplied to Europe by Catholic Spaniards, Portuguese and Italians. The contribution of the employees of the Dutch East India Company reached its greatest importance after Japan retired into national isolation, for the Dutch were the only Europeans allowed to continue their trade. Although they were obliged to lead a restricted life at Dejima, a number of highly talented men, such as François Caron, Engelbert Kaempfer, Carl Peter Thunberg and Isaac Titsingh, managed to keep Europe at least partially informed about a country that, after a century of contact with the West, had again retired into the seclusion that once characterized the mysterious Cipangu.

The reports on Japan during this century have a special interest and value on several counts. In the first place they describe a particularly eventful period of Japanese history, when the struggle to gain absolute control of the nation produced a succession of outstanding men who dominated the political scene and had considerable contact with the foreign visitors. The European reports do not merely satisfy idle curiosity but also make a contribution to the

[1] *Cartas que os Padres e Irmãos da Companhia de Jesus Escreverão dos Reinos de Iapão e China*, Evora, 1598.

historical knowledge of those times, and several of these accounts have recently been carefully translated and edited in Japanese. Moreover, some of the better informed writings bring out the character of the leading political figures more clearly than do many of the Japanese historical sources, for contemporary chronicles were composed in such stiff formal language that the personality of the rulers often remains hidden behind a respectful screen of honorific narrative. One letter of Frois about his informal conversations at Gifu is more informative about Nobunaga the man than any number of official records.

But the European reports do more than merely provide historical information, valuable though this may be. They tell of the encounter between men of radically different religion and culture, outlook and tradition; they tell of problems of mutual misunderstanding and prejudice between East and West that still remain basically unresolved in the world today. They describe an encounter that affected not only Japan but also indirectly Europe as well. For just as the Chinese called their country the Middle Kingdom and regarded people living outside its frontiers as ill-bred barbarians, so also Europe, less explicitly perhaps, looked on the rest of the world as inferior. Papal bull and national treaty divided the unexplored Asian world into Iberian zones of influence without the least reference to the inhabitants of these regions. But the letters from Japan, and even more so from China, spoke of an advanced and sophisticated civilization that had developed independently of the West. The more discerning and objective observers even admitted that in some respects Japan was superior to European countries. The belated realization that the West did not possess a monopoly of culture, that civilization could no longer be simply equated with Christendom, was eventually to produce far-reaching effects in the development of European thought.

A comprehensive survey and an evaluation of all the European writings during this century of contact are clearly impossible within the present limits; any such attempt would inevitably degenerate into a tedious and inadequate catalogue of authors and titles. Instead, a brief study of three individual writers, two Portuguese and one Englishman, will provide a more personal and detailed impression of what the Europeans had to say about Japan. The first of the chosen trio reached Japan in 1563, the last to leave departed in 1623; they spent a combined total of seventy-seven years in the country and their residence spanned the middle period of the century under study. Together they are chosen to represent all the Europeans who came to Japan and committed to writing their impressions of the country.

JAPAN

DESCRIBED

LUIS FROIS *(1532-97)*, *the Faithful Scribe.*

I am Portuguese and was received into the Society of Jesus at Lisbon some thirty-five years ago. In the same year I left for India, where I studied for fifteen years and looked after the secretarial work of the Father Provincial of India. About twenty years ago I left India and came to Japan, and for the most part I am the man who has written the general letters to India and Europe concerning the work of the Society in this province.[1]

Thus wrote Luis Frois in 1582 about his life's work, and it is characteristic of the Portuguese Jesuit, who wrote over a hundred letters about Japan and the progress of the mission, that he should modestly dismiss his own contribution in three sentences. In addition to writing his own letters, Frois also edited a number of lengthy annual reports on Jesuit work in Japan by collating information received from missionaries stationed throughout the country. He furthermore spent years of patient enquiry and research compiling a detailed history of the Japanese mission.

Pl. 45
Although writing primarily about missionary work in Japan, Frois was by no means averse to including additional material concerning the country and its inhabitants. A translation of one of his letters written in 1565 may be found in *The History of Travayle*, which was published in London in 1577 and contains the earliest account of Japan to be printed in English. In this particular letter Frois gives a lively description of Buddhist temples, the monastic foundation at Kōya, funeral ceremonies, the strange *yamabushi* hermits, religious suicide, and the mysterious island of Ezo (modern Hokkaidō), where the Ainu natives are described in *The History of Travayle* as "savage men, clothed in beastes skynnes, rough bodyed with huge beardes, and monstruous muchaches, the which they hold up with little forkes as they drynke." Small wonder that the Jesuit letters made popular reading even in Reformation England. Small wonder, too, that the authorities in Rome considered some of Frois' early accounts somewhat too exuberant. "A great deal about the heathen sects and superstitions should be deleted from this letter," noted one Jesuit severely, "because such things do not edify, and they are very long and prolix; besides, the many marvels related make the other accounts less creditable."[2]

The effusive style of the young missionary was eventually replaced by a more mature approach, and in the place of letters containing a jumble of undigested impressions and information, Frois began sending back carefully constructed reports giving a comprehensive survey of events in Japan. He showed an unflagging zeal in dispatching the news to Europe, and historians have good reason to be grateful to him as his accounts deal with not only missionary progress but also contemporary political developments as well. Although conscious that he was the chronicler of the Jesuit mission and its work, Frois never hesitated to write about secular events, and towards the end of his career he produced separate treatises on such diverse topics as the progress of the Japanese military campaign in Korea, the reception of the Chinese embassy in 1596, and the downfall and death of Toyotomi Hidetsugu.

Frois was a writer who happily combined quantity with quality, and he obviously took great care in cultivating a literary style and in editing his material. Above all he strove to ensure accuracy, basing his reports on his personal experience whenever possible and then on the testimony of trustworthy witnesses. "Now I was not an eyewitness to this," he begins one account cautiously, "but this is what they say about it." He was also a most meticulous and exact writer; he often descends to minute details, but he is usually successful in not allowing them to swamp his work or get out of control. In his account of Valignano's audience with Hideyoshi in 1591, for example, he not only lists the ruler's gifts to the visitors but pauses to calculate their exact value.

---

[1] Letter written in Kuchinotsu on November 5, 1582; in Jesuit Archives, Rome: Jap Sin 9, f. 94.
[2] Jesuit Archives, Rome: Jap Sin 5, f. 205v.

Some lords then appeared carrying two large trays, on each of which were piled 100 silver bars, and another tray with four silk robes, called *kosode*. They offered these gifts to Father Valignano on behalf of Hideyoshi, and he duly expressed his gratitude with another bow and returned to his place. Then the two priests went forward one by one, and Hideyoshi gave each of them . . . a similar tray with 100 silver bars and two silk *kosode*. He then summoned one by one the four nobles and all the Portuguese and the pages, and he ordered each one to be given a small tray with five silver bars and one silk *kosode*. But he commanded that Brother João Rodrigues and Brother Ambrosio Fernandez . . . should each be given a tray with 30 silver bars and two silk *kosode*.

Now each silver bar is worth four taels and three mace, so the gift to Father Valignano was worth 860 taels, while the two priests received the same, that is, 430 taels each. The present to each of the two Brothers was worth 258 taels, while the rest received gifts worth 21½ taels each. This gives a total of 2,494 taels, and this does not include the 36 silk robes, which were worth an additional 100 taels.[1]

Frois was in an excellent position to report the news accurately to Europe. He was described in 1581 as the most fluent Japanese linguist among the missionaries, and in his responsible office of secretary to Valignano and other superiors he traveled widely and had access to confidential information. Above all, he had the journalistic knack of being present when newsworthy events were taking place. In 1565, for example, he was received in audience by the shogun Ashikaga Yoshiteru shortly before the ruler's violent death. Although not actually present at the battle of Mimikawa, he met the defeated Bungo forces straggling home and received firsthand reports of the disaster. He knew Oda Nobunaga particularly well and on various occasions spent hours talking with him. This is how he describes in 1569 the man who began the work of unifying Japan.

This king of Owari would be about thirty-seven years old, tall, thin, sparsely bearded, extremely warlike and much given to military exercises, inclined to works of justice and mercy, sensitive about his honor, reticent about his plans, an expert in military strategy, unwilling to receive advice from subordinates, highly esteemed and venerated by all, does not drink wine and seldom offers it to others, brusque in his manner, despises all the other Japanese kings and princes, and speaks to them over his shoulder as if they were lowly servants, obeyed by all as the absolute lord, has good understanding and judgement. He despises the Buddhist and Shintō deities and all other pagan superstitions. Nominally belonging to the Hokke sect, he openly denies the existence of the creator of the universe, the immortality of the soul and life after death. He is upright and prudent in all his affairs and intensely dislikes any delays and long speeches.[2]

Pl. 47

Japanese sources confirm this description, except perhaps the reference to justice and mercy, two qualities that were not very prominent in Nobunaga's career, but Frois was somewhat prone to seeing the good side of Japanese rulers who favored the Christian mission.

Some of the most memorable passages in Frois' writings occur when he describes the grandeur of the castles that he visited. "I wish I were a skilled architect or had the gift of describing places well," he notes wistfully after Nobunaga had shown him around Gifu Castle. But he then goes on to give an excellent account of the great building, despite declaring that "the exquisiteness, perfection and arrangement of the chambers are quite beyond my powers of description, for I simply do not possess the necessary vocabulary, as I have never seen their like before." Some years later Nobunaga conducted him around Azuchi Castle, which had been profusely decorated by the painter Kanō Eitoku and his disciples, and Frois sets down his impressions for the benefit of his readers in Europe.

JAPAN

DESCRIBED

[1] Ajuda Library, Lisbon: *Jesuitas na Asia*, 49-IV-57, ff. 152v–153.
[2] Letter written in Kyoto on June 1, 1569; in *Cartas* (1598), I, f. 257v.

On top of the hill in the middle of the city Nobunaga has built his palace and castle, which, as regards architecture, strength, wealth and grandeur, may well be compared with the greatest buildings of Europe. Its strong and well-constructed surrounding walls of stone are about sixty spans in height and even higher in many places. Within these walls there are many beautiful and exquisite houses, all of them decorated with gold and so neat and well fashioned that they seem to reach the acme of human elegance. In the middle there is a sort of tower, which they call *tenshu*, and indeed it has a far more lovely and splendid appearance than our towers; it consists of seven storeys, all of which, both inside and out, have been fashioned to a wonderful architectural design. The walls within are decorated with designs richly painted in gold and different colors, while the exterior of each of the storeys is painted in various colors. Some are painted white with their windows varnished black according to Japanese usage and they look extremely beautiful; others are red or blue, while the uppermost one is entirely gilded.

The *tenshu* and all the other houses are covered with bluish tiles, which are stronger and lovelier than any we use in Europe. The corners of the gables are rounded and gilded, while the roofs have fine spouts of a very noble and clever design. In a word, the whole edifice is beautiful, excellent and brilliant. As the castle is situated on high ground and is itself very tall, it looks as if it reaches to the clouds and can be seen from afar for many leagues.[1]

Pl. 35

Today all that remain of the glory of Azuchi are the overgrown, ruined walls on a remote hill by Lake Biwa, a warrior's dream and perhaps symbolic of the fate of the dictator. But a few castles still survive from that time; although not so splendid as Azuchi, they continue even today to produce in the foreign visitor a feeling much akin to Frois' wonder and admiration.

While staying at Kyoto, Nobunaga was caught off his guard by a treacherous attack organized by Akechi Mitsuhide on June 21, 1582, and Frois vividly reports the event in a fine piece of descriptive writing.

When Akechi's men reached the palace [actually the Honnō-ji temple] gates, they at once entered as nobody was there to resist them because there had been no suspicion of their treachery. Nobunaga had just washed his hands and face, and was drying himself with a towel when they found him and forthwith shot him in the back with an arrow. Pulling the arrow out, he came out carrying a *naginata*, a weapon with a long blade made after the fashion of a scythe. He fought for some time, but after receiving a shot in the arm he retreated into his chamber and shut the doors.

Some say that he cut his belly, while others believe that he set fire to the palace and perished in the flames. What we do know, however, is that of this man, who made everyone tremble not only at the sound of his voice but even at the mention of his name, there did not remain even a small hair that was not reduced to dust and ashes.[2]

Frois also came to know Nobunaga's successor, Toyotomi Hideyoshi, and met him on a number of occasions. He was in the party of missionaries shown around Osaka Castle by the ruler in 1586, and he served as interpreter in the cordial but crucial meetings between Hideyoshi and Gaspar Coelho prior to the publication of the expulsion edict in July, 1587. Hideyoshi's love of pomp and ceremony gave Frois a special opportunity of exercising his descriptive powers, and the Jesuit recounts at length the colorful pageantry of court processions. He carefully describes the magnificent procession of June, 1596, when the three-year-old Hideyori was formally presented to the emperor and received official court rank. He also recounts the procession of the Chinese ambassadors to Kyoto four months later and appears

---

[1] J. A. Abranches Pinto and Y. Okamoto, eds., *Segunda Parte da Historia de Japam* (Tokyo, 1938), pp. 245–246. [2] Letter written in Kuchinotsu on November 5, 1582; in *Cartas*, II (1598), f. 65.

44. One of the two suits of Japanese armor presented by Tokugawa Hidetada to Captain John Saris on September 19, 1613, at Edo (Tokyo) as a gift to James I. The Armoury, Tower of London.

ers may peruſe theſe foure volumes of Indiſhe matters written long agoe in Italian, and of late compendiouſly made latin, by *Petrus Maffeius* my olde acquaynted friend, entitulyng the ſame, *De rebus Iaponicis*. One whole letter out of the fyſt booke thereof, ſpecially entreatyng of that countrey, haue I done into Englyſhe word for word, in ſuche wyſe as foloweth.

Aloiſius Froes, to his companyons in Ieſus Chriſt, that remayne in China and Indie.

THe laſt yeere, deare brethren, I wrote vnto you from *Firando*, howe *Coſmus Turrianus* had appoynted me to traueyle to *Meaco*, to help *Gaſpar Vilela*, for that there the harueſt was great, the labourers fewe, and that I ſhould haue for my companyon in that iourney *Aloiſius Almeida*. It ſeemeth now my parte, hauing by the helpe of God ended ſo long a voyage, to ſigniſie vnto you by letter ſuche thinges ſpecially as I myght thinke you woulde moſt delyght to knowe. And becauſe at the begynnyng *Almeida*

45. An extract from Richard Willes, *History of Travayle*, London, 1577, giving the beginning of an English translation of a letter written by Luis Frois, S.J., at Kyoto in February, 1565. This was the first printed account of Japan in English.

46. Second page of an autograph letter of Saint Francis Xavier to John III of Portugal, written at Amboina on May 16, 1546. Museum of the Twenty-Six Martyrs, Nagasaki.

106

47. Oda Nobunaga (1534–82), a portrait by Kanō Motohide. 70.3 × 31.5 cm.; Chōkō-ji, Aichi Prefecture.

48. Portrait of Alessandro Valignano, S.J. (1539–1606), who made three visits to Japan and was received in audience by both Oda Nobunaga and Toyotomi Hideyoshi. From J. F. Schütte, S.J., *Valignanos Missionsgrundsätze für Japan*, vol. I, Rome, 1951.

Mr Wickham, yor letter dated in Ximonaxeque the 19th of August
came to my handes the 28th ditto. And as towchinge the cace of the
bottell & the crose staffe, they were put into the shipp with
the other thinges before receaued, the same day yor letter
came. & yow need not feare domageinge for no man
hath entred into the howse since that tyme.

And as towchinge yor other request, I wish yow had thought
of the matter before yor departure from hence, & then yow
might haue had my Astralobia alonge with yow. & no doubt
had yow done the lyke with a comon sort, or else when
yow wrot yor letter yow had made the Generall & Mr
Adames acquainted with the matter, I wold haue sent a
man expres alonge with them. otherwais the md wold not
by any meanes lett yow haue necessary an instrument. &
comon sort is not knowinge how to furnish them such
as it in this place. yf that shold haue byn lost.
And besydes this yow must consider, that yow, theise and
all the rest of vs are vnder the comand of a Generall
whoe no doubt wold be as forward as any man in such a
matter or any other that is for the benefett of the Honorable
Company. yet yow may think he might haue byn somewhat
to be offended both with yow Mr & my selfe yf we had
sent away these Instruments So secretly & haue sent
downe to both of vs, not mentioninge one word
hereof. Soe yow must pardon vs both, for that matter
for the falt is not owrs, nether do I see yor motion
is vnreasonable, yf it had byn handled as it ought to haue
byn donne. All our Company are well, only Mr provost
Mr Sirs, & very weake god comfort him. there hath
some had an extreme fluxes with hath donne much
hurt, both in this place & Langasaque. As yet no newes
of the warrs heir, & is not reported this yeare
thes com downe deepest indeede, yet we cannot
tell any thinge for the rest & refer me to my
letter to the Generall & rest from Ferando in Japan
15th September 1613.

Yor lovinge frend
Ric Cocks

49. Autograph letter, dated September 18, 1613, Hirado, from Richard Cocks to Richard Wickham, the English commercal agent in Kyoto. India Office Library, London.

Mr. Wickham, your letter, dated in Ximonaxeque,[1] the 19th of August,
came to my hands the 28th ditto. And as tuchinge your case ofe
bottells & Crose staffe, they were put into the house with
the other things before receaved the same day you dep[ar]ted f[ro]m
hence. & you need not feare romageinge for no man
hath entred into the rowme since that tyme.
And as tuchynge your other request I wish you had thought
of the matter before your dep[ar]ture from hence, & then you
might have carid my Astralobia alonge with you. & no doubt
have doone the lyke with a Semy Cercle,[2] or yf when
you wrot your letter you had made the Generall[3] & mr.
Adams Accoynted with the matter, I wold have sent a
man expres alonge with them. otherwais the m[aste]r will not
by any meanes p[ar]te with soe necessary an Instrument as the
Semy Cercle is, not knowinge how to furnish hym selfe
in this place yf that should have byn lost.
And besyds this you must consider that your selfe and
all the rest of us are under the command of a General
whoe no dowbt wold be as forward as any man in this
matter or any other that is for the benefyt of the honora.
Company.[4] yet you may think he might have just occation
to be offended both with the m[aste]r & my selfe yf we had
sent away these Instruments, he writing p[er] same con-
veance to both of us, not mentionynge one worde
thereof. Soe you must p[ar]don us both for that matter
for the falte is not ours. Nether do I say your motion
is unreasonable, yf it had byn handled as it ought to have
byn doone. All our Company are well, only mr pawlyng[5]
is sick, & very weake god comfort hym. Also we
have had an exstreme Tuffon which hath doone much
hurt both in this place & Langasaque.[6] As yet no news
of the macow ship & so not expected this yeare.[7]
Here com downe dyvers merchants, yet we cannot
sell any thinge. for the rest I refer me to my
lettr to the Generall & rest from ferando in Japan le
18th Septembr 1613.

Your lovinge frend
Ric Cocks

[1] Shimonoseki. The English merchants sailed into Hirado on June 11, 1613; on August 7, John Saris, Will Adams, Richard Wickham and others started on their journey to Ieyasu's court at Suruga, via Shimonoseki, leaving behind Richard Cocks to attend to business at Hirado.
[2] The semi-circle, or graphometer, was an instrument for measuring angles in surveying.
[3] John Saris.
[4] The East India Company.
[5] William Pawling, master mate of the *Clove*, died shortly afterwards at Hirado on September 27.
[6] A severe typhoon, "that I never saw the like in all my life" as Cocks noted elsewhere, hit Hirado and Nagasaki on September 7.
[7] The ship *Nossa Senhora da Vida* ran aground off Macao, and so there was no official Portuguese voyage to Japan in 1613.

51. The interior of a traditional Japanese tea house. "They do not make use of spacious rooms and richly decorated apartments for this gathering . . . instead, the desired effect is gained by a tiny cottage, thatched with straw and reeds. . . . Everything is left in its original state; there is no artistry nor genteelness apparent, but only natural elegance and age." João Rodrigues, S.J., writing about 1620. The Sa-an tea house, Gyokurin-in, Daitoku-ji, Kyoto.

◀ 50. *Autumn Moon over Lake Tung-t'ing*, by the Japanese artist Kenkō Shōkei (second half of fifteenth century); ink on paper; 36 × 23.8 cm.; Hakutsuru Museum, Hyōgo Prefecture, Japan. The first of the series entitled *The Eight Views of Hsiao-hsiang*. The rivers Hsiao and Hsiang meet in southern China and flow into Lake Tung-t'ing. "The first scene is a certain famous place with the clear autumn moon reflected in the water; they go out on autumn nights to gaze at the moon in a sad, nostalgic mood." —João Rodrigues.

52. The *Daibutsu* at Kamakura. Cast in 1252, the bronze statue is 42 feet high. Richard Cocks visited the monument in October, 1616, and described it as "a mighty idoll of brass . . . made siting cros legged (telor lyke) . . . it is a wonderfull thinge."

to have been particularly intrigued by the Chinese musical instruments, especially the gongs.

But the grandest ceremonial procession took place in May, 1588, when the seventeen-year-old emperor Go-Yōzei, accompanied by the former emperor Ōgimachi, honored Hideyoshi by visiting his Jūraku-tei palace in Kyoto. Frois' hearsay account of this glittering occasion is of special interest as the event is also recorded at length in contemporary Japanese chronicles. "On a propitious day chosen by soothsayers" the cavalcade set out for the imperial palace to escort the young emperor back to Jūraku-tei.

> First of all there went ahead on horseback seventy men robed in crimson damask, wearing small hats like crowns; their court robes were fashioned after the Chinese style with long and wide sleeves. The harnesses of their horses were made of crimson silk thread, while their saddles and stirrups were lacquered a shining black with fine gilt decoration. Each carried in his hand a kind of scepter as if he were one of our kings at arms, and each was attended by a score of servants robed in black, except for six dressed in white. The ranks of these men were captains of arms, superintendants of estates, justices of Sakai and of other such places.

> Following in due order in the second place were the *kuge*, or gentlemen who directly serve the emperor. They wore on their heads different insignia, which were hats covering the ears rather like the hats of the Chinese mandarins; they carried small bows, like Turkish ones, in their hands and a few arrows in their sashes. They also proceeded on horseback, accompanied by many people according to ancient ceremony.

> In the third place came the illustrious kings and titled lords of different kingdoms [of Japan]. They also numbered seventy and wore a very fine and rich type of robe called *kara-ori*. Each was accompanied by two or three hundred servants and had a shoe-boy dressed in white next to his horse.

Then followed seventeen carriages bearing important Buddhist monks related to the imperial family, and after them came fifteen carriages in which traveled the emperor's lady courtiers.

> In the sixth place there came two very large oxen, covered with scarlet satin drapes on which were embroidered the arms of Hideyoshi; the shoes of the oxen were made of crimson thread, as were also the reins by which they were led. In the seventh place came a triumphal carriage, its wheels lacquered black and shining like mirrors. It was drawn by a single large ox, richly decorated like the previous pair. Its hooves and horns were gilded, and it was garlanded with many silk flowers and roses. Inside the carriage was a richly decorated litter, with the proud tyrant Hideyoshi within just like an idol.[1]

Frois died at Nagasaki in 1597. Had he been spared a few more years it is surely not over-fanciful to imagine a black-robed foreigner standing on a nearby hill overlooking the plain of Sekigahara, busily taking notes on the progress of the battle as Ieyasu obtained the victory that established the Tokugawa family as rulers of Japan for the next two and a half centuries. But, appropriately, Frois' last work concerns the mission that he served so faithfully for thirty-five years, and he lucidly narrates the events leading up to the martyrdom of the twenty-six Christians at Nagasaki on February 5, 1597. With his customary diligence he completed the twenty-chapter account within five weeks of the executions; his own death was only four months away. In the introduction to the treatise, Frois observes:

> Above all, this work attempts to declare the pure and simple truth, for this is the principal ornament and foundation of all historical writing.[2]

It is a fitting epitaph to his work as chronicler of the Japanese mission.

---

[1] Ajuda Library, Lisbon: *Jesuitas na Asia*, 49-IV-57, ff. 33–34.
[2] Luis Frois, S.J., *Relación del Martirio de los 26 Cristianos* ed., R. Galdos, S. J., (Rome: 1935), p. 3.

RICHARD COCKS *(d. 1624)*, *the Harassed Merchant.*

To lay aside the elegant writings of Frois and begin reading the mundane notes of Richard Cocks is rather like turning from the classical *Taiheiki* to the earthy *Hizakurige*. Gone are the meticulous accounts of religion and politics, castle and court, and in their place is artlessly described the humdrum round of events in the life of an English merchant living in a foreign and largely incomprehensible country. Yet, although contrasted in style and content, the contributions of Frois and Cocks are in fact complementary. For while the Portuguese missionary provides a comprehensive survey of religious and political developments, the English merchant records in his diary the insignificant events in the life of the common people. In his writings Cocks often presents some of the less wholesome aspects, not to say the seamy side, of Japanese life, and by introducing this dimension completely lacking in the missionary letters, he makes it possible to form a more balanced picture of Japan in the early seventeenth century.

In some respects it can perhaps be argued that Cocks is the most interesting of all the Europeans who left on record their impressions of Japan during this period. As in the case of his fellow countryman Samuel Pepys, it never occurred to the merchant that his diary would ever be read by others, and he freely notes down his intimate thoughts and feelings. As a result of his engaging candor and uninhibited comments the personality of the writer clearly emerges, and it is impossible not to feel sympathy and affection for him in his many trials. This is in sharp contrast to the writings of the self-effacing Frois, who was always conscious that he was composing his reports for a wide audience and deliberately maintained an impersonal style.

Richard Cocks was possibly a native of Coventry, but little is known about his early life. When the English East India Company established a trading post in 1613 at Hirado, some forty miles northwest of Nagasaki, Cocks was appointed the factor, or manager. He made several visits to court at Edo and Kyoto, and was granted a brief and totally silent audience with Hidetada in September, 1616. But despite the outward display of cordiality on the part of court officials, Cocks found it increasingly difficult to obtain and renew satisfactory trading privileges for the English merchants.

Nor was life at Hirado much easier for him. His initial stock, to the value of £5,650, consisted mainly of cloth, wool and cotton goods, but the Japanese much preferred the fine Chinese silk imported by the Portuguese. Commercial expeditions to Siam and Cochin China proved costly failures. Money was advanced to the wily Li Tan, a Chinese merchant, to obtain trading rights in China, but nothing more substantial than vague and glowing promises was ever received. The English had also to contend with the rival Dutch merchants in Hirado, and Cocks was more than once exasperated ("The devell hawle some of them for their paines") by their policy of undercutting his prices by selling cheap. Although theoretically united in their common dislike of the "papistecall" Portuguese and Spaniards, the English and Dutch were constantly feuding and their mutual antagonism culminated in an armed attack on the English factory.

But Cocks' chief source of worry was his task of trying to maintain some semblance of order among the unruly crews of visiting English ships, and there are constant references in his diary to desertions, drunken brawls, thefts, floggings, mutiny, and even hangings. On one occasion he steps in at the last moment to stop a duel; on another he tries to get his drunken sailors out of the local stews. The arrival of the *Hozeander* in the autumn of 1615 brought more trouble for the harassed manager.

> September 7. Mr. Hunt, the master of the Hozeander, fell out with Roland Thomas, the purcer. Soe they went together by the eares. I condeme them both very much; but surely they were drunk, espetially the master, and I think he is crazed in his witts.[1]

---

[1] N. Murakami, ed., *The Diary of Richard Cocks* (Tokyo: 1899), I, p. 53.

But Mr. Hunt was not the only miscreant.

> January 19 [1616]. Mr. Dorington, the mr. mate of Hozeander, mad show as though he were lunatick, talking idly; but I thynk he counterfeteth. A strange kind of people they are all of them which came in this shipp.[1]

There were other untoward incidents before the *Hozeander* finally sailed from Hirado, and it is not surprising that Cocks notes dolefully:

> The very truth is, here doe I confess before God and the world, I never did see a more unruly company of people, and are far worse then they in the Clove, although they were bad enough.[2]

To add to his difficulties Cocks also experienced considerable trouble with his staff in the English factory, and the most trying member was undoubtedly Mr. Thomas Nealson.

> June 26 [1617]. Mr. Nealson, being drunk yistarnight (as he is seldom sober), fell a quarreling with Mr. Totton and used hym out of fation; and because I reproved hym for it, willing hym to goe into his chamber and sleepe, he fell out with me and cald me ould drunken asse, geveing me many thretnyng speeches not sufferable.[3]

The following day a repentant Mr. Nealson "wrot me that he was sory of that which passed yisternight, promesing amendment; which God grant." Sad to relate, Cocks' pious wish was not granted, and references to Mr. Nealson's tipsy revels continue to crop up regularly in the diary. Another member of the staff, Mr. Richard Wickham, could also prove uncooperative on occasion, and to encourage him to mend his ways Cocks thoughtfully lent him his copy of "St. Augustyn Citty of God." The alcoholic Nealson was presumably considered beyond hope of reform and received nothing more uplifting than "The Turkish History."

But Cocks does not limit his remarks to the squabbles and escapades of the Europeans but conscientiously notes down rumors and items of news that came his way. He received, for example, a firsthand report on the fall of Osaka Castle in 1615.

Pl. 36

> June 2. We had news today that Ogosho Samme [Ieyasu] hath taken the fortres of Osekey and overthrown the forses of Fidaia Samme [Hideyori]. Others say that most of the forses of Fidaia Samme issued out of the fortrese, and sallid out 3 leagues towards Miaco [Kyoto], but were encountred by the Emperours forses and put to the worse, many of them being slaughtered and the rest driven back into the fortresse, etc.
> June 7. After dyner came a Franciskan frire, called Padre Appolonario, whom I had seene 2 or 3 tymes in Firando [Hirado] heretofore. He was in the fortres of Osekey when it was taken, and yet had the good happ to escape. He tould me he brought nothing away with hym but the clothes on his back, the action was soe sudden; and that he marvelled that a force above 120,000 men (such as was that of Fidaia Samme) should be soe sowne overthrowne. He desired me for God's sake to geve hym somthing to eate, for that he had passed much misery in the space of 15 daies, since he departed out of the fortres of Osekey. So, after he had eaten, I gave hym 15 mas [mace] in plate; and soe he departed.
> June 20. . . . They say the taking of this fortres hath cost above 100,000 mens lives on the one parte and other, and that on the Prince Fidaia Sammes part no dead man of accompt is found with his head on, but all cut ofe, because they should not be knowne, to seek reveing aganst their frendes and parents after. Nether (as som say) can the body of Fidaia Samme be fownd; soe that many think he is secretly escaped. But I cannot beleev it. Only the people of these sothern parts speake as they wold have it, because they affeckt the yong man more then the ould.[4]

JAPAN

DESCRIBED

---

[1] *Ibid.*, I, p. 101.   [2] *Ibid.*, I, p. 94.   [3] *Ibid.*, I, p. 265.   [4] *Ibid.*, I, pp. 2–3, 5–6, 12.

In the following year Cocks reports the rumors concerning the failing health and death of the victor, Tokugawa Ieyasu, and shows how news, distorted or otherwise, about the mighty, aloof rulers of the country gradually filtered down to the common people through various sources. At first he is sceptical and rightly so, because he knew by experience how unreliable such hearsay could be.

> January 24. Newes was brought to towne that the Emperour is dead; but I beleeve rather it is a fable and geven out of purpose to see how people wold take the matter. Once the ould man is subtill.

The rumor, however, persists but Cocks is still not convinced. On Easter Sunday, March 31, he notes:

> There was reportes geven out the Emperour is dead . . . but I esteeme this ordenary Japon newes, which prove lyes.

But two weeks later visitors confirm the rumor, and Cocks records their news without comment.

> April 12. There came 2 Spaniardes from Edo [Tokyo] this day, and tould me it is comenly reported above that the Emperour is dead.

A few days pass and then he receives contrary information.

> April 17. The King of Crates [the daimyo of Karatsu] man came to vizet me, and said it was reported that the Emperour was very sick with a fall he had from his horce in going a hawkling, so that no man might speak with hym. . . . And towardes night a cavelero sent me word how it was trew the Emperour was alive, and had spoaken to the King of Firando and two other princes only, of purpose to stop the mowthes of those which reported hym to be dead; only it seemed to them he was not halfe well.[1]

These reports are confirmed the following month by Richard Wickham, who writes to Cocks from Kyoto:

> Many report that the Emperour is dead, but the report from most of credit saye he is recovered and in resonabel good health.[2]

But doubts were again revived in June when it was learnt in Hirado that the daimyo had not actually seen Ieyasu during their audience.

> June 8. I was enformed that the King of Firando spake not with the Emperour, but only was permitted to enter into a chamber, where they said he la sick in a littell cabbin covered with paper, Codgkin Dono [Honda Masazumi, who bore the title Kōsuke no suke], the secretary, going into it and telling hym that the Tono of Firando was there to vizet hym, and came out againe, telling hym the Emperour thanked hym and gave hym lycense to retorne to his cuntrey. But they verely beleeve he is dead, and that they keepe it secret; yet it may be a pollecie to see whether any will rise against hym in armes.[3]

In fact Ieyasu was still alive when the Hirado daimyo paid his visit, but the old ruler died shortly afterwards on June 1. The premature rumors are understandable, however, when it is recalled that the death of Hideyoshi eighteen years previously had initially been kept secret for security reasons. It was not until the daimyo reached Hirado that Cocks definitely learnt of Ieyasu's death and he pays a striking tribute to the late ruler's iron strength of character.

---

[1] *Ibid.*, I, pp. 103, 125, 126, 128.   [2] *Ibid.*, II, p. 278.   [3] *Ibid.*, I, p. 141.

June 16. Semi Dono [Shume *Dono*, secretary of the daimyo] sent me word, it was certain that the ould Emperour was dead 26 daies past, and that he saw the place where he was buryed; and that Shongo Sama [Hidetada] did it of purpose, that they might see he was dead. . . . But I do verely beleeve he will sowne rise againe, yf any wars be moved against his sonne within these 3 years.[1]

But national events do not figure greatly in the diary; instead, Cocks is generally content to record the day-to-day business transactions of the English factory and then, almost as an afterthought, he mentions local happenings in a matter-of-fact way. But not even Frois' eloquent accounts of the Christian martyrdoms can rival the starkness of some of the merchant's terse entries showing the low value set on human life and, incidentally, his own compassion.

December 23 [1615]. This day a boy of 16 years ould was cut in peeces for stealing a littell boate and carying it to an other iland. I sent to the kyng [daimyo] to beg his lyfe, which he granted me, and in the meane tyme sent a man after the execusoner to stay a lyttell; but he would not, but put hym to death before the pardon came, cuting hym in many mammocks to try their cattans [*katana*, "swords"] upon hym.

Another case two years later is recorded even more laconically.

August 3 [1617]. This day was a Japon rosted to death, runing rownd about a post, fyre being made about hym. The occation was for staling a small bark of littell or no vallue.[2]

But such grim entries are relatively few and Cocks often refers to convivial events; he describes, for example, the jolly occasion of a housewarming party, which he attended with every sign of enjoyment.

December 28 [1615]. The China Capt. [Li Tan] built or reard a new howse this day, and all the neighbours sent hym presentes, nifon catangue [*nihon katagi*, "Japanese fashion"]. So I sent hym a barill morofack [*morohaku*, a type of sake wine], 2 bottells Spanish wine, a dried salmon, and halfe a Hollands cheese; and after, went my selfe with the nighbours. Where I saw the seremony was used, the master carpenter of the kinge doing it, and was as followeth: First they brought in all the presentes sent and sett them in ranke before the middell post of the howse, and out of eache one took something of the best and offred it at the foote of the post, and powred wyne upon each severall parcell, doing it in greate humilletie and silence, not soe much as a word spoaken all the while it was a doing. But, being ended, they took the remeander of the presentes, and so did eate and drink it with much merth and jesting, drinking themselves drunken all or the most parte. They tould me they beleeved that a new howse, being hallowed in this sort, could not chuse but be happie to hym which dwelled in it, for soe their law taught them, ordayned by holy men in tymes past.

Later that evening Cocks took part in further celebrations, this time English fashion:

The shipps company came to the English howse in a maske, and after plaied Christmas ule games in good sort and merryment.[3]

Cocks also takes note of various religious practices and makes several references to the Buddha, or "Shacca, the greate profet of Japon." He does not have a very clear knowledge of Buddhism, which he frequently confuses with the indigenous cult of Shintō, but he diligently records his impressions after visiting monuments and temples. On his return journey from Edo in 1616, he stopped at Kamakura and went to admire the *Daibutsu*, the great bronze statue of Amida Buddha.

---

[1] *Ibid.*, I, pp. 142–143.   [2] *Ibid.*, I, pp. 91, 291.   [3] *Ibid.*, I, pp. 92–93.

October 18. . . . . But that which I did more admire then all the rest was a mighty idoll of bras, called by them Dibotes, and standeth in a vallie betwixt 2 mountaynes, the howse being quite rotten away, it being set up 480 years past. This idoll is made siting cros legged (telor lyke) and yet in my opinion it is above 20 yardes hie and above 12 yardes from knee to knee. I doe think there may above 30 men stand within the compas of the head. I was within the hollownes of it and it is as large as a greate howse. I doe esteem it to be bigger then that at Roads, which was taken for 1 of the 7 wonders of the world, and, as report goeth, did lade 900 camells with the ruens thereof. But for this, it is thought 3000 horses would nothing neare carry away the copper of this. In fine, it is a wonderfull thinge.[1]

Obviously overwhelmed by the bulk of the great monument, the English merchant exaggerates both its size and age, but his imaginative description is far more attractive than many of the factual accounts to be found in modern guide books. Continuing his journey to Hirado, Cocks passed through Kyoto and went on a sight-seeing tour of the capital. On November 2, he visited the Sanjūsangen-dō, a temple much frequented by foreign tourists to this day, and showed a keen eye for detail when he wrote up his diary that night.

Pl. 39

Pl. 40

And not far from this temple is an other, of very neare 10 skore yardes lenghe, I say ten skore; but it is narow. And in the midest thereof is placed a greate bras Dibotes, (or idoll). And out of the side of it proceed many armes with hands, and in each hand on thing or other, as speares, sword, dagges, spades, arrowes, knyves, frutes, fyshes, fowles, beastes, corne, and many other matters and formes; and out of the head procead many littell heades, and over the great head proceadeth a glory of long bras rayes made lyke to the son beames, as the papostes paynt over the saintes. And on both sids, to the end of the howse, are set 3333 other bras images, standing on foote upon steps, on behind an others back, all apart on from an other, with glories over their heads, armes out of their sids, and littell heades out of the great, as the Dibotes had. I enquired what those handes and heads did signefie; and it was answered that they signefied the good and charetable deeds that those saintes (or holy men) had donne while they were liveing. And it is to be noted that both the Dibotes and all the other 3333 idols were made after an excellent forme neare to the life, and clothed with a gowne (or loose garment) over them, and all gilded over with pure gould, very fresh and glorious to behould.

And just before the Dibotes below were set 3 or 4 roes of other idolls, most of them made after a furious forme, rather lyke divells then men; and behind them all stood two deformed ons, one carying a sack of wynd on his shoulders, and the other a cerkeled wreath or hoope with many knots in it, the one resembling the wyndes, and the other the thunder. In fyne, this temple is the most admerablest thing that ever I saw, and may well be reconed before any of the noted 7 wonders of the world.[2]

Along with other European visitors of his time, Cocks was misinformed about the number of statues of Kannon in the temple, for the seated statue in the middle of the long hall is flanked by only a thousand gilded wooden figures, standing silent and immobile in the dim interior for the past six or seven centuries. Probably the Englishman was told that there were 33,033 statues, for the Kannon Bodhisattva is believed to assume thirty-three different forms. But for the rest his description of this remarkable assembly is surprisingly accurate, and apart from the position of the "3 or 4 roes of other idolls," little has changed in the temple since the merchant's visit on that November afternoon more than three centuries ago.

Cocks' narrative, with its quaint style and erratic spelling according to his taste and fancy, is certainly entertaining for the modern reader remote from the upheavals of the early seven-

---

[1] *Ibid.,* I, p. 194.   [2] *Ibid.,* I, pp. 200–201.

teenth century in Japan. But a close study of his diary and letters reveals a somewhat pathetic figure, lacking in confidence and unsuited for a position of authority, more often than not bewildered and out of his depth in the rough-and-tumble world of Asian commerce. Perhaps if he had paid more attention to general trade policy and had spent less time scrupulously noting down every penny (or rather, tael, mace and candareen) paid out, the affairs of the English factory might have improved. But it is doubtful whether the enterprise would have prospered in those difficult times even under more vigorous direction, and Cocks wrote despairingly to London, "Truly to my hartes greefe I am eavery day more then other out of hope of any good be donne in Japon." In the event, the post was closed down in 1623 and the East India Company left behind uncollected debts totalling the considerable sum of £3,200. Cocks was recalled in disgrace to face charges of negligence and mismanagement. Perhaps it was as well that the honest but incompetent factor died on March 27, 1624, on board the *Ann Royal* as he sailed home to England, and was buried at sea to a salute of guns.

While at court trying to obtain a renewal of trading privileges, Cocks wrote dispiritedly to his troublesome colleague, but "loving frende," William Nealson at Hirado.

> I doe protest unto yow I am sick to see their proceadinges, and canot eate a bit of meate that doth me good, but cast it up as sowne as I have eaten it. God send me well once out of this cuntrey, yf it be His blessed will.[1]

He ends this poignant note with an exclamation that perhaps best sums up his ten years' residence in Japan—"Warry, warry, warry!"

JOÃO RODRIGUES (1562-1633), the Interpreter.

If Frois was the chronicler of stirring events and Cocks the recorder of daily life, João Rodrigues was *par excellence* the exponent of Japanese language and culture. Few of his contemporaries from Europe paid much attention to Japanese culture, and even fewer had either the opportunity or the inclination to study it deeply. Rodrigues not only wrote on the subject with enthusiasm, but showed an appreciation and insight seldom attained by a Westerner either in his time or our own.

João Rodrigues was born about 1562 at Sernancelhe in northern Portugal and sailed to the East while still a boy of twelve or thirteen years of age. He entered the Jesuit Order in Japan and obtained such a proficiency in Japanese that he acted as Valignano's interpreter at the audience granted by Hideyoshi in 1591. From that date onwards he made frequent visits to court, acting as spokesman for the Jesuit missionaries and interpreter for the delegations of Portuguese merchants. After Hideyoshi's death in 1598, Tokugawa Ieyasu continued to favor him and even appointed him as his commercial agent in Nagasaki. Jealousy and resentment on the part of local officials resulted in his exile to Macao in 1610 after living in Japan for thirty-three years, during which time he met many of the leading political and artistic figures of the day.

Rodrigues spent the rest of his life in Macao, from where he made several journeys into the interior of China in order to study the esoteric doctrines of Buddhism. In 1628 he accompanied a military expedition to Peking, and was probably the first European to visit the capitals of both China and Japan. Then, after various colorful adventures, including a dramatic escape from a besieged fort at dead of night, he was formally commended for his services by the Chinese court.

But Rodrigues' claim to fame is based on something far more substantial and durable than these spectacular feats. In addition to his business activities in Japan he found time to publish

---

[1] *Ibid.*, II, pp. 294–295.

Pl. 55 at Nagasaki in 1608 the *Arte da Lingoa de Iapam*, a truly monumental work, for it was the first systematic grammar of the Japanese language. Not only does he describe the spoken and written language in exhaustive and possibly excessive detail, but he includes for good measure fascinating accounts of Japanese poetry, letter writing, and history.

Unlike Frois, Rodrigues did not write a large number of letters and had little or nothing to say about contemporary events. But following the example of Frois, he planned to write a history of the Japanese mission, and the two introductory books of this uncompleted work contain most of his discerning observations on Japanese culture. Rodrigues' literary style and presentation may lack the elegance and method of Frois; but whereas the chronicler was generally content to report the events of Japan and seldom allowed himself the luxury of delving beneath the surface, Rodrigues probed deeper and tried to explain the ethos of Japanese culture. It is in his account of Japanese art that he displays his outstanding talent, and his description of the tea ceremony, flower arrangement, painting, lacquerwork and calligraphy is unrivaled in contemporary European reports. His appreciation of the Japanese artistic temperament is remarkable, and he accurately and sympathetically portrays the elusive feeling of *sabi*, the transcendental loneliness of the *homo viator* in this fleeting world of dew, and the sentiment of *wabi*, the spirit of disciplined and aesthetic frugality in art and life.

Rodrigues was well acquainted with the magnificent palaces and mansions of Kyoto and Sakai, and he sets down his recollections of their interior decoration.

Pl. 42

The walls are lined with paintings executed on many layers of paper like thick parchment, and they are excellently decorated with trees, rivers, springs, animals, birds, lakes, seas, ships, human figures, and scenes from ancient legends, some of them containing soldiers, according to individual taste. Or the four seasons of the year may be represented, each one depicted by whatever blooms in that season. In the part representing spring there will be various kinds of flowers that bloom therein, mist, clouds and other things proper to that time of year. For summer there will be other flowers that bloom in that season and green fruit about to ripen. The autumn season will depict ripe fruit, the leaves of the trees losing their color and falling to the ground, and fields of ripe rice being harvested. In winter there will be the dry leafless trees, for their vitality leaves the branches and gathers in the roots; there will also be snow, and the birds of that season, such as wild duck, cranes, swans and others, which come flying in flocks from Tartary with their leader in front, and other birds moving through the fields. Everything is done to imitate nature so that you seem to be looking at the very things themselves. In the houses of the great lords and nobles these paintings and the doors of the rooms have a background richly painted in gold, and on this gold they depict the scenes in various suitable colors.[1]

But after describing the splendors of such paintings, which reached their highest form in the contemporary Kanō school, Rodrigues notes that "the Japanese are fond of melancholy subjects and colors rather than happy ones, and they seek contemplation and nostalgia in everything." For in addition to the magnificent scenes in gold,

They also depict hermitages of recluses dwelling in the wilderness, as well as valleys, forests, rivers, lakes and seas with boats sailing in the distance. There are eight famous lonely places, called *hakkei* or "eight views," both in Japanese and Chinese tradition, and these scenes are often painted and much admired.

Pl. 50

The first scene is a certain famous place with the clear autumn moon reflected in the water; they go out on autumn nights to gaze at the moon in a sad, nostalgic mood. The second view is of a valley or remote wilderness where a hermitage bell, rung at sunset

---

[1] Ajuda Library, Lisbon: *Jesuitas na Asia*, 49-IV-53, ff. 60v–61.

or at night, is heard sounding softly from afar. Third, rain falling quietly at night in a certain lonely spot. Fourth, a ship sailing back from the distant high seas toward the land. Fifth, the sight of a lovely fair in certain mountains. Sixth, fishing boats returning together from the sea at sunset. Seventh, flocks of wild birds landing with their leader in a certain place. Eighth, snow falling on a high place in the evening or during the night. All this is in keeping with their temperament and makes them feel very nostalgic and quietly lonely.[1]

In Rodrigues' opinion, Japanese culture reaches its finest development in *suki*, the gathering of friends to drink tea, and he devotes no less than five chapters to describing the setting and procedure of this aesthetic pastime. He rightly attributes its inspiration to the monks of the Zen sect; and while showing scant sympathy for the degenerate conduct of many of the Buddhist monks during that period of monastic decline, he admires the dynamic Zen spirit, which has left its imprint on practically every aspect of Japanese culture. He outlines with obvious approval the Zen ideal.

> This art of *suki*, then, is a kind of solitary religion instituted to encourage good customs and moderation. This is in imitation of the hermit philosophers of the Zen sect who dwell in their lonely retreats. Their vocation is not to philosophize with the help of books and treatises written by illustrious masters and doctors, as do the members of other sects. Instead, they give themselves up to contemplating the things of nature, despising and abandoning worldly things. They mortify their passions by means of certain enigmatic and figurative meditations and considerations. Thus from what they see in things themselves they attain by their own efforts to a knowledge of the First Cause; their soul and intellect put aside everything evil and imperfect until they reach the natural perfection and being of the First Cause.[2]

Such an ascetical training, says Rodrigues, forms "a resolute and determined character, without any slackness, indolence, mediocrity or effeminacy." This is a far cry from the sweeping condemnation of Buddhist monks in the accounts of other Europeans of that time.

In a desire to savor the harmony of nature, every man of means possesses a small tea house within the grounds of his mansion. Great care and expense are lavished to make the setting appear as natural as possible, for unlike European gardens with their symmetrical and artificial design, those in Japan are planned to blend and harmonize with nature.

> They search in remote areas for a special type of tree of certain fashion and shape to plant in the garden, for any tree whatsoever will not do. This costs a great deal of money until the trees take root and look as if they had sprung up there quite naturally. The stones with which they pave the path make up one of the main expenses; they are of a certain kind and are sought for in distant places. Although rough and unworked, they look as if they have appeared there quite naturally, and they have a certain grace, beauty and simplicity about them. They buy choice stones at a high price, and among them will be a special one containing a pool of water within a cavity in the rough stone for washing the hands. Suitable ones are found only seldom and are worth a great deal.[3]

Pl. 41

Rodrigues enlarges on this subject and goes on to explain the peculiar attraction of Japanese gardens.

> Everything artificial, refined and pretty must be avoided, for anything not made according to nature causes tedium and boredom in the long run. If you plant two trees of the same size and shape, one in front of the other, they will eventually cause tedium and boredom; the same applies to other things as well. But lack of artificiality and a certain note of

---

[1] *Ibid.*, f. 143v.   [2] *Ibid.*, ff. 131–131v.   [3] *Ibid.*, f. 134v.

naturalness (for example, a tree consisting of various disordered branches pointing this way and that, just as nature intended) is never boring, because experience shows that there is always something new to be found therein. But this cannot be said of artificial things, which look well only at first sight and eventually cause boredom and disgust.[1]

The tea house itself is far different from the gilded halls of Fushimi Castle, and Rodrigues, who had known some of the leading tea masters of the day, describes with great sympathy the ideal meeting place for this ritual.

> This gathering for tea and conversation is not intended for lengthy talk among themselves, but rather to contemplate within their souls with all peace and modesty the things that they see there and thus through their own efforts to understand the mysteries locked therein. In keeping with this, everything used in this ceremony is as rustic, rough, completely unrefined and simple as nature made it, after the style of a solitary and rustic hermitage. Thus the house and the path leading to it, as well as all the utensils employed therein, are all of this kind.

Pl. 51

> So they do not make use of spacious rooms and richly decorated apartments for this gathering as they do in normal social usage, nor do they use costly and delicate china dishes or other rich and choice vessels. Instead the desired effect is gained by a tiny cottage, thatched with straw and reeds, situated within the compound and next to the house in which they dwell. It is fashioned from timber as rough as it came from the forest and one old piece of wood is merely fixed to another. Everything is left in its natural state; there is no artistry nor genteelness apparent, but only natural elegance and age.[2]

Thus from his exile in Macao the elderly missionary tries to express and explain the spirit of Japanese culture. When Valignano comments that a certain tea bowl, costing fourteen thousand ducats, was fit for nothing more than to serve as a water trough in a birdcage, Rodrigues points out its intrinsic beauty and value. When Matteo Ricci remarks that temple bells give out a note of poor quality because they are rung by a hanging log instead of a metal clapper, Rodrigues maintains, and surely rightly, that such bells emit an evocative and mellow sound precisely because of this arrangement.

Writing about the spirit of the tea ceremony, Rodrigues observes,

> Hence they have come to detest any kind of contrivance and elegance, any pretense, hypocrisy and outward embellishment, which they call *keihaku* in their language. . . . Instead, their ideal is to promise little but accomplish much; always to use moderation in everything; finally, to desire to err by default rather than by excess. . . . The more precious the utensils are in themselves and the less they show it, the more suitable they are.[3]

*THE
SOUTHERN
BARBARIANS*

It would be difficult to improve on this summary description of the traditional Japanese canon of taste. Written today by a Westerner, the passage would indicate a commendable understanding and appreciation of an essentially alien culture; to have been written three and a half centuries ago reveals João Rodrigues as a unique interpreter not only of the language but also of the artistic genius of the Japanese people.

---

[1] *Ibid.*, ff. 136v–137.   [2] *Ibid.*, ff. 127v–128.   [3] *Ibid.*, ff. 133–133v.

THE MEETING OF CULTURES

THE
MEETING OF CULTURES

DURING THE FIRST HALF of Japan's century of contact with the West, the Jesuits enjoyed a monopoly in their work of propagating the Christian religion in that country. Later, in the 1590's, other missionaries began to arrive, but the Jesuits still continued to predominate as regards the number of their men and the extent of their work. This was particularly true in the fields of education and culture. As a result it is no exaggeration to say that the Christianity introduced into Japan in the sixteenth century was largely conditioned by the humanist spirit that characterized the Society of Jesus at that time. This humanist outlook stressed the importance and value of the individual man in comparison with material wealth and power.

Arimichi Ebisawa

This attitude was something new in the history of Japanese thought, and inasmuch as it was novel it was liable to be regarded with suspicion by the political authorities. That this development was eventually brought to an abrupt halt should cause no surprise. The foreigners' world view and humanist approach were seen as a potential threat to the security of the state. The European view was considered harmful to the existing social structure and was accordingly repressed.

Another feature of the Jesuit apostolate in Japan was the determined attempt made towards cultural adaptation, and the missionaries paid special attention to the social customs and etiquette of the Japanese people. In this respect their approach differed considerably from the methods employed in the evangelization of South America, where the cultural development of the indigenous peoples was still at a low level. In Japan, as also in China, the Jesuits found a highly sophisticated culture and polity, and they accordingly varied their missionary methods in keeping with the circumstances. This may be particularly noted in the work of Francis Xavier, the founder of the Japanese mission, who in effect determined the character of the apostolate exercised by his successors. Xavier met Yajirō, a Japanese who had left his country a few years earlier, at Malacca in 1547, and learnt from this native of Kagoshima that the Japanese were "a people very curious and desirous to learn new things, both about God and other natural things."[1]

---

[1] Xavier, *Epistolae*, II, p. 10.

After two years of practical experience in Japan, Xavier wrote that the men assigned to the mission should be prepared to suffer hardship and persecution. They were not only to be physically robust, but should also be intellectually equipped if they were to be successful in their work.

It is also necessary that they be learned in order to reply to the many questions which the Japanese ask. It would be very useful if they were good artists as well, and it would not come amiss if they were also good sophists so that they could hold their own in debates with the Japanese. They should know something about the globe, because the Japanese very much like to know about the movements of the heavens, the eclipse of the sun, the waxing and waning of the moon, as well as the origin of rain, snow, hail, thunder, lightning, comets and other natural phenomena. The explanation of these things is very useful in winning over the people.[1]

As may be seen from this and other observations, Xavier was convinced of the necessity of basing the pastoral approach in Japan largely on the cultural and educational level. This policy was for the most part continued by his successors, some of whom noted with admiration that the Japanese were in many respects superior to Europeans. The missionaries studied the cultural values of Japanese society and showed considerable respect for the customs and traditions of the country. Efforts were made to adapt the Europeans' outlook and actions, and to make them conform as closely as possible to Japanese norms. Both the Jesuits' attempts at adaptation and their farsighted educational program met with considerable success.

These educational activities were, in fact, another characteristic of the Society of Jesus in the sixteenth and seventeenth centuries. The fourth part of the Jesuit Constitutions laid down the general guidelines to be followed in the educational policy of the Order. This was later revised in the light of the experience gained in running educational centers in Europe, such as the Roman College and the German College in Rome. In 1599 there was issued the famous *Ratio Studiorum*, a directive providing the basis of Jesuit educational policy in subsequent centuries.

Here again the influence of Christian humanism is very prominent. The curriculum of studies emphasized the importance of liberal arts, but the natural sciences were by no means neglected in the system. Natural science was, in fact, a very important subject in Japan, where a traditional concept of God as a personal creator was completely lacking. Consequently it was more necessary in Japan than in Europe to stress the natural order to be found in the universe in order to introduce the concept of an all-wise creator. Thus the three disciplines of theology, liberal arts and natural sciences were all represented in the Jesuit schools in Japan.

As more than one missionary had occasion to observe, the appointment of Alessandro Valignano as Visitor of the Jesuit mission was certainly providential. He was entrusted with the task of conducting a thorough inspection of the mission and was granted wide powers to effect any changes that he thought might be required. Valignano was Italian (it is interesting to note that both Matteo Ricci in China and Roberto de Nobili in India were also Italians), and he had received a liberal education at Padua University and had later studied at Rome. He was quick to appreciate the need for adaptation to local customs and ways of thought if the mission was to expand and establish itself permanently in Japanese society. This view may perhaps be regarded today as practically self-evident, but in the climate of thought among sixteenth-century Europeans the advantages of cultural assimilation in Asia were not often fully appreciated.

Among the Europeans who notably failed to recognize this need was Francisco Cabral, the Superior of the Jesuit mission in Japan from 1570 to 1580. A zealous and hard-working missionary, Cabral not only disagreed with this policy but took positive steps to prevent its implementation. He viewed the Japanese and their culture with a lack of sympathy and under-

[1] Xavier, *Epistolae*, II, p. 373.

standing. He treated the Japanese members of the Order with undue severity and discriminated against the *dōjuku*, or "lay catechists," attached to the Jesuit churches and residences. He furthermore saw no need for the missionaries to study the Japanese language, which in any case he judged was too difficult for them to learn, and he was quite prepared to let them conduct their ministry through interpreters. That this was a narrow and shortsighted outlook was just as obvious to many of the missionaries then as it is today, and Cabral's policy understandably caused resentment among the Japanese.

Valignano first arrived in the country in 1579. For the first year of his stay he studied the situation closely, held meetings with experienced missionaries and discussed the problem with various Japanese Christians. Cabral was reassigned to Macao and the way was opened for developing the mission more in harmony with the original plans of Xavier. In June, 1580, the Visitor compiled the *Rules for the Superior of Japan*, tracing out the general lines of mission policy and stressing the need for adaptation. At the end of the same year he established a novitiate at Usuki, in Bungo, so that more Japanese recruits could be received into the Order. At about the same time he also founded a college for Jesuit studies at Funai and two boarding schools, or *seminarios*, at Arima in Kyushu and Azuchi near Kyoto.

In direct contrast to the negative policy of Cabral, Valignano insisted that the missionaries should make every effort to learn Japanese well. As he observed, "To speak or write Japanese other than in the accustomed manner is impolite and invites ridicule, just as if we were to speak Latin backwards and with many mistakes."[1] He further recommended that newcomers from Europe should devote at least eighteen months to language studies so that they might obtain a good grasp of Japanese. For the success of such studies textbooks were obviously required, and when Valignano arrived in Japan in 1590 for his second tour of inspection, he brought with him a printing press. This was the first press in Japan to use movable metal type and gave valuable service to the mission for a quarter of a century.

Manuscript aids to language study had in fact been produced by the missionaries long before the press was imported into Japan. Brother Duarte da Silva had produced a simple grammar and dictionary in the 1550's. Following his example Juan Fernandez also compiled a grammar and dictionary in 1564, and these were later revised by Luis Frois. The reforms of Valignano added great impetus to language studies and placed them on an organized basis.

In 1581 Brother Paulo Yōhō taught Japanese to the young Portuguese Jesuits at the college in Funai, and he used a grammar and dictionary based on Frois' edited work. In 1585 yet another dictionary was produced at the Arima school. Once Valignano's press was assembled and various initial difficulties overcome, language books of greater permanence began to appear. In 1595 the press put out the trilingual *Dictionarium Latino-Lusitanicum Ac Iaponicum*, which could be conveniently used by Portuguese and Japanese students alike.

This work prepared the way for the first Japanese dictionary ever to be published, the outstanding *Vocabulario da Lingoa de Iapam*, which appeared at Nagasaki, together with a supplement, in 1604. This Japanese-Portuguese dictionary contains more than thirty thousand entries, and was compiled by a committee of European and Japanese Jesuits. The words are carefully listed, two columns to a page, in alphabetical order. Phrases illustrating the use of a particular term are often quoted and many of these examples were taken from classical works of Japanese literature. The publication of this book marked a major advance in Japanese language studies. In view of the trials which the mission was experiencing during the time of its compilation, the *Vocabulario* was an extraordinary project both in scope and imagination.

The dictionary was followed by João Rodrigues' celebrated *Arte da Lingoa de Iapam*, published at Nagasaki in 1608. This lengthy treatise on the Japanese language runs to 480 pages, and following the pattern of Latin textbooks of the day it sets out the grammar and

Pl. 54

Pl. 55

---

[1] Valignano, *Historia del Principio y Progresso de la Compañia de Jesús en las Indias Orientales*, ed. Josef Wicki, S.J. (Rome: 1944), pp. 152–153.

syntax of Japanese in a thorough but somewhat stylized form. This was the first systematic analysis of the Japanese language and appeared a century before any comparable work was published by the Japanese themselves.

But the *Arte* was more than a grammar, for Rodrigues included sections on correct pronunciation (stressing the elegant usage of Kyoto), regional dialects and colloquial language, so that the missionaries using his book might be able to converse with Kyoto nobles and Kyushu peasants with equal ease. In addition the *Arte* contains further information that was not strictly relevant to language studies but certainly useful to the newcomer from Europe who wished to adapt himself to Japanese life. Rodrigues included short sections on letter-writing, weights and measures, and Japanese history, as well as a brief but comprehensive survey of Japanese poetry, illustrated by numerous examples. Only two or three copies of the *Arte* are known to still exist. Interesting though the book is, it has to be admitted that the grammar is undoubtedly long and diffuse. The author appears to have realized this defect, and in 1620 he published at Macao a revised and slimmer edition of the *Arte*, in which much of the additional information in the earlier work was pruned away. Following the example of Rodrigues, the Dominican friar Diego Collado compiled a more concise Japanese grammar and dictionary, which he published at Rome in 1632.

Rodrigues made a great contribution to Japanese language studies, and the necessary effort put into the production of his *Arte* and of the earlier *Vocabulario* demonstrates the importance that the Jesuit attached to this aspect of cultural adaptation. The value of these works is certainly recognized in Japan today, and a painstaking Japanese translation of Rodrigues' *Arte* has appeared in recent years. These language books have an important place in the history of Japanese-European relations, and they are also a useful source for modern philologists in their study of the grammar and pronunciation of Japanese in the early seventeenth century.

For Valignano, however, language study was merely one aspect, although an important one, of his policy of adaptation. In October, 1581, he wrote a general guide to missionary policy concerning cultural adaptation, and this *Avertimentos e Avisos acerca dos Costumes e Catangues de Jappão* is in many ways the most interesting of all his literary works. The treatise contains only seven chapters but deals with a wide range of topics. Above all it is remarkable for the discernment shown by Valignano within a year or so of his arrival in Japan. With an intuitive insight he issued detailed instructions concerning missionary policy of adaptation. Incorporating into the Portuguese text more than a hundred Japanese terms, he describes the norms of etiquette to be observed by the Jesuits among themselves and towards their guests and visitors. He repeatedly suggests that the missionaries should seek the advice of prudent Japanese on such matters, and he warns his readers always to treat the Japanese with due respect and courtesy. The Jesuits should conduct their church services with reverence and decorum, "just as the bonzes do." He recommends that mission residences should be built in Japanese style, and the depiction of the exterior and interior of Jesuit houses in *Nanban* screens shows that his directions were followed. Every residence should have a tea room, along with an experienced attendant and all necessary utensils; he even lays down that there should be available two or three types of tea, depending on the rank of the guest to be entertained. In a similar way he goes into great detail when dealing with the norms to be followed in the performance of the traditional *sakazuki*, "the ritual drinking of wine."

Valignano was not content that the missionaries should adapt themselves merely as regards housing and external observances, but he also took into account the difference between Japanese and European temperaments. The traditional Japanese custom of conducting important business through an intermediary is strongly recommended. The Jesuits are urged to practice as much as possible the calm decorum of the Japanese, and they are warned against talking loudly or gesticulating wildly. Moreover,

They must likewise take great care not to show impatience, anger or irritation, nor to

DE MISSIONE
LEGATORVM IAPONEN
fium ad Romanam curiam, rebufq; in
Europa, ac toto itinere animaduerfis
DIALOGVS
EX EPHEMERIDE IPSORVM LEGATORVM COL-
LEGTVS, & IN SERMONEM LATINVM VERSVS
ab Eduardo de Sande Sacerdote Societatis
IESV.

In Macaenfi portu Sinici regni in domo
Societatis IESV cum facultate
Ordinarij, & Superiorum.
Anno   1590.

53. Title page of *De Missione Legatorum*, published at Macao in 1590 before the Jesuit press was taken to Japan. The book was composed by Alessandro Valignano and describes, in the form of a dialogue, the visit of the Kyushu ambassadors to Europe.

VOCABVLARIO
DA LINGOA DE IAPAM
com adeclaraçao em Portugues, feito por
ALGVNS PADRES, E IR-
MAÓS DA COMPANHIA
DE IESV.

COM LICENÇA DO ORDINARIO,
& Superiores em Nangafaqui no Collegio de Ia-
PAM DA COMPANHIA DE IESVS
ANNO. M.D.CIII.

54. Title page of *Vocabulario da Lingoa de Iapam*, Nagasaki, 1603; a supplement was issued in 1604. The Japanese-Portuguese dictionary contains 32,000 entries

ARTE DA LINGOA DE IA-
PAM COMPOSTA PELLO
Padre Ioão Rodriguez, Portugues da Copa-
nhia de IESV diuidida em tres
LIVROS.

COM LICENÇA DO ORDI-
NARIO, E SVPERIORES EM
Nangafaqui no Collegio de Iapão da
Companhia de IESV
Anno. 1604.

FSOPONO
FABVLAS.
Latinuo vaxite Nippon no
cuchito nasu mono nari.

IEVS NO COMPANHIANO
Collegio Amacufani voite Superiores no gomen-
qiotoxite coreuo fanni qizamu mono nari.
Goxuxxe yori M.D.L.XXXXIII.

55. Title page of *Arte da Lingoa de Iapam* by João Rodrigues, S.J.; although it bears the date 1604, the work was not published until 1608. This was the first systematic study of the Japanese language to be published. Bodleian Library, Oxford: Arch. B. d.14.

56. Title page of a Japanese translation of *Aesop's Fables*, published by the Jesuit press at Amakusa in 1593. The stories proved very popular and were republished several times in the Tokugawa period.

Seminar. Arimaenfe in Idpone

Sem. Auzuchixamenfe in Idpone

57–58. The seminary at Arima (*left*) and the seminary at Azuchi, on the east bank of Lake Biwa. Both were founded by Alessandro Valignano, S.J., in 1580, but the latter was destroyed only two years later in the disturbances following the assassination of Oda Nobunaga. From Marc'Antonio Ciappi, *Compendio delle Heroiche, et Gloriose Attioni, et Santa Vita di Papa Greg. XIII . . . .*, Rome, 1596.

59. Title page of an abridged and simplified version of the Japanese classic *Heike Monogatari*; this edition was published by the Jesuit press at Amakusa in 1592.

60. Title page of *Sanctos no Gosagueo no Uchi Nuqigaqi* ("Selections from the Acts of the Saints"), a collection of saints' lives, printed in Romanized Japanese and published at Katsusa in 1591. Bodleian Library, Oxford: 8°. Z. 21, Th. Seld.

NIFON NO
COTOBA TO
Hiſtoria uo narai xiran to
FOSSVRV FITO NO TAME-
NI XEVA NI YAVA RAGVETA-
RV FEIQE NO MONOGATARI.

IESVS NO COMPANHIA NO
Collegio Amacuſa ni voite Superieres no go men-
qio to xite core no fan ni qizamu mono nari.
Goxuxxe yon M.D.L.XXXXII.

SANCTOS
NOGOSAGVEONO
VCHINVQIGAQI
quan dai ichi.

FIENNOCVNITACACVNOGVN
IESVSNOCOMPANHIANOCOLLEGIO
Cazzuſa ni voite Superiores no von yuruxi uo co
muri core uo fan to naſu mono nari.Goxuxxe uai
MDLXXXXI.

61. *Virgin and Child.*
Oil on wood; 58 × 36
cm.; Nanban Bunka-
kan, Osaka.

64. *Dolorosa*. Oil on canvas; 52.5 × 40 cm.; Nanban Bunka-kan, Osaka. One of the religious pictures imported into Japan by the missionaries about the beginning of the seventeenth century.

◀ 62. *Virgin and Child (left)*. Oil on wood; Nanban Bunka-kan, Osaka. A European painting, probably of the Primitive Spanish or Italian School, brought to Japan in the sixteenth or seventeenth century to decorate a missionary church.

◀ 63. *Virgin and Child (right)*. Oil on metal; 26.5 × 19.5 cm.; Nanban Bunka-kan, Osaka. Another work of the same subject, imported into Japan by the missionaries. These paintings not only served to decorate the Christian churches throughout the country, but were also used as models by Japanese artists painting in the Western style.

65. *Virgin of the Thumb*. Oil on canvas; 24.5 × 19.6 cm.; Tokyo National Museum. Possibly a later work of the Florentine artist Carlo Dolci (1616– 86), this painting is said to have been brought to Japan in 1708 by the Italian missionary Giovanni Battista Sidotti (1667–1714). Sidotti was arrested on his arrival and died in captivity.

66. *Christ Carrying the Cross* (detail). Oil on metal; Nanban Bunka-kan, Osaka.

67. *The Repentant Magdalen* (detail). Oil on metal; Nanban Bunka-kan, Osaka.

68. *The Mysteries of the Rosary.* Color on paper; 66.7 × 54.5 cm.; formerly in Urakami Cathedral, Nagasaki; destroyed in 1945. The most primitive of the three known Japanese paintings of this subject, the work is obviously inspired by European retables, which often portrayed the same theme. The Joyful, Sorrowful and Glorious Mysteries are depicted, in Japanese fashion, from right to left, starting from the lowest row. The figures in the lower part of the composition represent Saints John the Baptist, Francis of Assisi and Anthony of Padua. This particular work was probably commissioned by Franciscan missionaries, while the other two Japanese paintings illustrating the Rosary were obviously inspired by the Jesuits.

69. *The Mysteries of the Rosary.* 81.6 × 64.8 cm.; Azuma Collection, Osaka. The painting features two Jesuit saints, Ignatius of Loyola and Francis Xavier, and was produced sometime after 1623. The inscription in Portuguese across the center of the painting reads "Praised be the Blessed Sacrament." The sequence of the Mysteries of the Rosary begins at the bottom left-hand corner. Both this and a similar work in Kyoto University (Plate 72) were probably painted by the same artist.

give any sign of any other passion in their speech or countenance, because in the eyes of the Japanese such things greatly detract from the credit and respect in which they are wont to hold the Fathers.[1]

Valignano was obviously not alone among the missionaries to recognize the cultural values of the Japanese. Luis Frois, for example, produced a treatise in which he contrasted different aspects of European and Japanese life and customs. Another missionary, the Italian Organtino Gnecchi-Soldo, enthusiastically praised Japanese culture in his letters to Europe. For many years he worked in Kyoto, and by about 1580 a large and influential Christian community had been built up in the capital. Much of Organtino's personal success was due to his knowledge and practice of social customs and etiquette. In September, 1577, he wrote to Rome:

> We have great hopes of converting all these kingdoms of Miyako [Kyoto], and we wish that you would help us by sending here some good men, because these regions in Japan are like Rome in Europe. Scholarship, learning and culture are held in greater account here than elsewhere. You should not think that they are barbarians, for apart from our religion we ourselves are greatly inferior to them. After I began to learn the language, I realized that no other people in the world were so prudent. Once they have embraced the Faith, I think that there will be no other church to surpass them. Our experience makes us believe that with the help of our liturgical ceremonies millions could be converted. If we had organs, musical instruments and singers, all of Miyako and Sakai would be converted without any doubt within a year.[2]

Two weeks later Organtino was again writing:

> You should not think that these people are barbarians because, apart from the Faith, however prudent we may believe we are, we are great barbarians compared with them. In all truth I confess that I learn from them every day, and I think that there is no other nation in the world with such and so many talents and natural gifts as the Japanese.[3]

It goes without saying that Organtino's admiration was not completely unqualified, but it is obvious that he had acquired a deep appreciation of the life and culture of the Japanese.

Yet another European who studied the cultural heritage of Japan was João Rodrigues. In addition to his famous grammar, he also wrote a history of the Japanese mission, entitled *História da Igreja do Japão*, and in the introduction to this work he describes at length different aspects of Japanese art and culture—the tea ceremony, ritual wine-drinking, painting, calligraphy, flower arrangement and gardens. What is more, he writes about these cultural pursuits not only with much accuracy but also with deep appreciation and sympathy.

Thus Valignano's policy of adaptation in Japan did not go unheeded, and with varying degrees of success the Jesuits tried to accommodate themselves to their surroundings. This they managed to do, at least outwardly. The Spaniard Pedro de Figueroa Maldonado arrived in Japan in 1596 and referred to the Jesuit missionaries, not without a note of disapproval, in the following way:

> They so imitate the Japanese that they wear their clothes, speak their language, eat like them on the floor without cloths, tables or napkins. Nor do they use their hands but eat with a small stick, observing the same ceremonies as the Japanese do themselves. To this end they have compiled a book entitled *The Customs and Ceremonies of Japan*, to be read to the pupils in the seminary.[4]

---

[1] Valignano, *Il Cerimoniale per i Missionari del Giappone*, ed. J. F. Schütte, S.J. (Rome: 1946), p. 290.
[2] Jesuit Archives, Rome: Jap Sin 8 (Ib), f. 178; L. Delplace, S.J., *Le Catholicisme au Japon* (Brussels: 1909), I, pp. 187–188.
[3] Jesuit Archives, Rome: Jap Sin 8 (Ib), ff. 179–179v; Delplace, I, pp. 189–190.
[4] Lorenzo Pérez, O.F.M., *Cartas y Relaciones del Japón* (Madrid: 1916–23), III, p. 255.

But in one important field the Jesuits were not prepared or able to accommodate themselves to any notable extent, and this lay in their liturgy and theological terminology. The latter issue was later to cause much trouble in China, and the missionaries in Japan soon ran up against the problem. In Japanese at that time there existed only Buddhist and Shintō terms to convey religious ideas, and the Jesuits experienced great difficulty in trying to express new and unfamiliar concepts of Christian thought and creed. They were at first inclined to use traditional Japanese terms in their preaching, but because of the meanings associated with such terms it was inevitable that an inexact or downright erroneous understanding was conveyed. By the spring of 1550 Xavier had compiled a simple catechism, which was translated into Japanese by Fernandez and Yajirō. The text has not survived to the present day, but it is known that in this treatise Xavier proved the existence of God and the immortality of the soul by arguing from natural theology.

Not surprisingly, this pioneer effort was far from satisfactory and its inelegant presentation invited ridicule from educated Japanese. But apart from mere stylistic considerations, there were more serious problems of translation. The word "God" was rendered into Japanese by the Buddhist term *Dainichi*. The choice of this term was singularly unfortunate, for it conveyed a totally erroneous idea and made Christianity appear as an offshoot of Buddhism. The translation was later corrected and the Latin word *Deus* was thenceforward employed. The introduction of this foreign terminology, such as *Deus*, "God," and *anima*, "soul," was an unfortunate necessity, but in the circumstances it is difficult to see any alternative if a correct and orthodox expression of Christian doctrine was to be taught in Japan.

So far a brief account has been given of the influence of Japanese culture on the Europeans in Japan. For obvious reasons this influence was most strongly felt by the missionaries, who for the sake of their pastoral work made special efforts to adapt themselves to local conditions. There was, of course, far less need for adaptation in the case of the visiting foreign merchants, but the resident Portuguese and Spanish traders who married Japanese and settled in Nagasaki presumably conformed in some ways to the Japanese way of life. But the cultural influence was a two-way process, and in their turn the Europeans had a considerable influence on the Japanese. The most deeply rooted effect produced by the missionaries was the conversion of thousands of Japanese to the Christian religion, a conversion that for many would radically alter their lives and for an appreciable number would involve hardship and even death. But the European influence in Japan was not confined to the strictly religious sphere, for it made itself felt in various ways.

In the first place mention may be made of the medical care that was offered. After entering the Society of Jesus in Japan, the former merchant and surgeon Luis de Almeida opened a small charity hospital in Bungo in 1557 and thus introduced the techniques of European medicine and surgery. Almeida was later withdrawn from this work, but the knowledge of European surgery spread throughout the country, and in the following century it was augmented by the medical knowledge imported by the Dutch. Towards the end of the sixteenth century the Franciscan friars opened various small hospitals, including two in Kyoto, and cared for lepers and other social outcasts.

Similar works of charity were also performed by Japanese Christians belonging to the Confraternities, or pious associations of devout laymen organized for charitable purposes. In the era of civil wars it was natural that Christianity should offer material as well as spiritual help; even after central government had been restored, there was still a good deal of scope for such work. The most famous Confraternity in the country was located at Nagasaki, and it numbered in its ranks many of the leading citizens. Free medical aid was made available, and leper asylums were established; there were also facilities to care for abandoned babies, orphans, refugees and elderly people. Members of the Confraternity even dug graves and buried the dead; they also made efforts to save prostitutes and free slaves.

The question of slavery in Japan and the movement to abolish this abuse is a particular case in point. Trade in slaves was a common practice, and visiting Europeans often took advantage of the situation and purchased girls at will. Numbers of slaves were also transported abroad. This was obviously a matter of deep concern for the missionaries, who condemned the evil traffic and took measures to halt it. Whenever possible they ransomed slaves and obtained their freedom, or at least arranged that their servitude should be limited to a certain number of years and not continue indefinitely. Appeals were made to the authorities in Europe, and both King Sebastian and King Philip forbade their subjects to deal in Japanese slaves. Many Japanese on being converted to Christianity either freed their slaves or changed their status to that of ordinary servants. Shortly after reaching Japan in 1596, Bishop Pedro Martins issued a prohibition of slavery under pain of ecclesiastical censure, and his policy in this regard was continued by his successor Luis Cerqueira. The slave movement was too well entrenched in the country for the missionaries to obtain anything like complete success in their campaign, but their determined opposition to the evil in Japan foreshadowed the movement of emancipation throughout the world.

A more tangible aspect of European influence in Japan may be found in the educational work of the Jesuits. It is quite possible that even in the earliest days of the mission Xavier was thinking of founding a college in the cultural center of Yamaguchi. There can be no doubt that he showed great interest in the Japanese "universities," as he called them. In reality the establishments to which he referred in his letters were more in the nature of Buddhist seminaries attached to large monasteries, such as Kōya and Hiei. The first missionary venture in education was the foundation of primary schools during the term of office of Cosme de Torres, who was Superior of the mission from 1551 to 1570. Much of the curriculum of these schools was devoted to catechism and the teaching of Christian doctrine. Their establishment was especially numerous in the province of Higo and in other regions of Kyushu, and it has been estimated that by 1580 the number of these schools had risen to two hundred.

The same year 1580 saw a great development in Jesuit educational work in Japan for, as has already been mentioned, Valignano started at that time the two *seminarios*, or "boarding schools," at Azuchi and Arima (the two schools were later amalgamated in 1587) and the college for Jesuit studies at Funai in Bungo. These establishments produced some notable results in the introduction of European art and science into Japan. Incidentally, these educational activities should not be viewed in isolation from their context and must be seen against the background of social and political change that was the taking place in Japan. The Japanese were in a better position than ever before to appreciate objectively their place in the world on account of their increasing contact with European missionaries and merchants. This contact with foreigners was instrumental in fostering a spirit of independence among the middle classes and the new humanist education fully accorded with this development.

Pls. 57, 58

A good deal of information is still available about the boys' colleges, and there are extant documents giving their timetable, curriculum and pupils' reports. In addition to classes devoted to religious instruction, the boys were also taught Latin, Japanese reading and writing, mathematics and singing. There was instruction on the etiquette and social customs of Japan, and for the older boys, classes were given in Latin composition. Pupils with artistic talents received tuition in European painting, engraving and instrumental music. From the time the boys rose at 4:30 in the morning (5:30 in winter) until they retired to rest at 8:00 in the evening, their day was evenly filled with a balance of study and recreation. Wednesday was a half-holiday if there were no other holiday in the week, and swimming was allowed in the lake or river whenever the weather was suitable.

Valignano's plan was for the boys to be "happy and contented" in these colleges and there are many indications that this was generally the case. They were given every encouragement to enjoy their studies, and one of the most effective means to this end was the production of plays. This particular activity was a marked feature of Jesuit education throughout the world and was by no means limited to Japan. The Englishman Peter Mundy witnessed such a play in St. Paul's Church at Macao in 1637, and was much impressed by the performance. The Jesuit pupils in Japan staged similar productions, and when Bishop Martins visited the college, then situated at Arie, in 1596 a special theatrical program was put on in his honor. The production of this particular allegorical work was quite a *tour de force*, for different roles were duly declaimed by the youthful actors in Japanese, Latin and Portuguese, and the onlookers were filled with admiration at the display of precocious talent.

A boy representing "Christianity in Japan" expressed joy at the bishop's arrival, while "Christianity in Kyoto" offered Martins the keys of the city and weapons symbolizing victory. "Christianity in Arima" and "Christianity in Omura" likewise added to the welcome accorded to the distinguished visitor. Then appeared Lucifer, accompanied by evil spirits, and he bitterly complained about the souls that he stood to lose by the bishop's arrival in Japan; he further threatened to cooperate with the bonzes and to lay more snares to entrap the Christians in his wiles. Bonzes thereupon tried to harm a group of virtuous Christians, but they were repulsed and thrown to the ground by the recitation of the Rosary. Angels then conveniently appeared, put the demons to flight, and laid upon an altar a palm of victory and a crown symbolizing reward. The performance came to a close with suitable music played and sung by the pupils.

This play was one of many staged by the boys and doubtless provided entertainment for audience and actors alike. In addition it provided pious instruction and practice in music and languages in a painless and enjoyable way. The following day Martins inspected the classes of Latin, Japanese reading and writing. He visited the workshop where religious pictures were being printed, watched pupils working on oil paintings in European style, and spoke with boys engaged in engraving copper plates. Finally he inspected the ingenious bamboo organ, constructed by the versatile Italian Jesuit, Giovanni Niccolo.

The introduction of Western music into Japan cannot be credited to the teachers at the Jesuit *seminarios*, for in fact European music was performed in the country long before the foundation of the two schools. Possibly the first occasion was as early as 1552, when Torres and his companions celebrated a *missa cantata* in Yamaguchi. From then onwards there are various references to the popularity of sacred music in the mission churches. Singing at Christian services proved a great attraction, and trained choirs, sometimes made up of boys from the Jesuit schools, performed at important ceremonies. In addition to polyphony, Gregorian chant was also introduced. In the *Manuale ad Sacramenta Ecclesiae Ministranda*, printed on the Jesuit press at Nagasaki in 1605, there are entire pages devoted to the music of plain chant to be sung at various ceremonies.

In one of the letters written in 1577 and quoted above, Organtino stresses the importance of sacred music and its power of attracting people to the churches. Not only was vocal music sung at the services but on occasion instrumental music was also provided. Organtino specifically refers to organs, and there is ample evidence to show the attraction felt by the Japanese towards Western instrumental music. In 1581 Nobunaga one day paid a surprise visit to the Azuchi school and noticed a viol and harpsichord during his tour of inspection. At his request Jeronimo Itō played on the harpsichord and another boy on the viol, and both earned Nobunaga's praise for their skill. On their return from Europe ten years later, the young Kyushu delegates performed on the harp, violin, lute and clavichord as a quartet during the audience at Kyoto in March, 1591, and Hideyoshi requested several encores. By that time the Jesuits had imported two organs into the country and a number of Japanese became accomplished players. During the embassy to Europe both Mancio Itō and Michael Chijiwa played on the great organ in Evora cathedral. Years later the talented Brother Luis Shiozuka was both the organist and choirmaster in one of the churches at Nagasaki.

Pl. 43

The spread of Western culture was not confined to the work of the *seminarios* founded by Valignano, important though their contribution undoubtedly was. The college for Jesuit studies, which was founded at the same time as the boys' schools, also played a considerable role, both at Funai in Bungo, where it was originally started, and later at Nagasaki, whither it was eventually transferred. The missionaries found that a knowledge of astronomy was useful in their work, for by this means they were able to argue for the existence of God when discussing religious matters. Not a few people were brought to believe in a personal creator by reference to the natural order found in the universe. About 1560, for example, Kamo-no-Akimasa, a noble belonging to a family that for centuries had provided court astronomers, discussed astronomy with the missionaries and subsequently received baptism together with his family. With the inauguration of the Jesuit college at Funai, it was possible to promote such studies on an organized basis. Valignano encouraged this development, for he himself had been a pupil of Christopher Clavius, the renowned German mathematician who had played a large part in the introduction of the Gregorian calendar.

From 1583 the Jesuit students attended lectures on philosophy given by Pedro Gomez, and ten years later their teacher finished writing a compendium of his course. The first part of this work, entitled *De Sphaera*, dealt with the natural sciences and covered various aspects of Western astronomy—the determining of the calendar, solar and lunar eclipses, the movements of the stars; then followed a treatise on terrestrial science, and this described the globe, the four elements and meteorology. It may be noted that João Rodrigues was studying at the college during this period and he later included a remarkable account of oriental astronomy in his history of the Japanese mission. Rodrigues is also known to have discussed astronomy with famous personalities, such as Tokugawa Ieyasu and Honda Masazumi.

Another former student of Clavius was Carlo Spinola, the future martyr, who arrived in Kyoto in 1605. He is said to have met the shogun Tokugawa Hidetada and various daimyo, and to have refuted Buddhist monks in discussions on astronomy. At that time the Jesuit church in Kyoto possessed a terrestrial globe and various astronomical instruments, and it is recorded that the emperor Go-Yōzei secretly sent a court messenger to the mission residence asking for a demonstration and explanation of the instruments. Toyotomi Hideyori, the son of Hideyoshi, also wanted to see the instruments, and a Jesuit Brother presented them for his inspection. It was about this time that Spinola established an academy of mathematics and science at the Kyoto residence. Unfortunately little is known about this enterprise, and in 1611 the academy was closed and Spinola was transferred to Nagasaki. His scientific interest still continued, however, and acting in conjunction with the Jesuit Giulio Aleni at Macao in February, 1612, he made the first scientific observation of a lunar eclipse in Japan. As a result of this experiment, he was able to calculate the latitude of Nagasaki within a margin of error of less than three minutes.

Western influence in scientific matters was not limited to astronomy, for the Europeans also introduced new knowledge and techniques in the related fields of surveying, geography and navigation. Among the Portuguese who accompanied Valignano to court in 1591 was Ignacio Moreira, who during his two years in Japan practiced his interest in cosmography by taking accurate readings of latitude wherever he traveled; he also made diligent enquiries about the position of other places in order to make a scientific survey of Japan. Some years later Girolamo de Angelis, the first European to visit Ezo (modern Hokkaido), wrote a description of his travels containing valuable information about the remote island and its Ainu natives.

Finally, in this connection mention may be made of the introduction of Western maps and atlases, such as Abraham Ortelius' celebrated *Theatrum Orbis Terrarum*, which revealed to the Japanese for the first time the geography of the world and their country's position and size. This knowledge was quickly assimilated on the artistic level and Japanese painters skillfully

*Pl. 103*produced screens, some of which are still extant, depicting the map of the world. Such screens were influenced not only by the Western atlases imported by the missionaries but also by the world maps produced at this time under the direction of Matteo Ricci in China.

Not unconnected with geography and surveying was the art of navigation, which had greatly developed among the Europeans in the sixteenth century as a result of the long voyages of discovery. The services of Portuguese pilots to navigate Japanese merchant ships *Pl. 105*were in great demand and various contemporary prints of Japanese ships clearly show the presence of Europeans on board. The introduction of Western mining techniques may also be mentioned at this point, and Tokugawa Ieyasu showed special interest in obtaining foreign help to increase the yield of his newly discovered silver mines.

The persecution of the Christian mission and the eventual severance of contact with the outside world brought direct study of European scientific knowledge to an end in Japan. But interest aroused in Western geography, medicine and science still continued, and limited contact was maintained through the Dutch merchants confined on Dejima at Nagasaki. Thus even during the *sakoku*, or closed period, a number of Japanese scholars continued at considerable risk to learn about the technological progress of the West. Because of its associations with Christianity, the title of the so-called *Nanban* school of learning was considered undesirable and so was changed to the Dutch school, for throughout the long period of isolation the Dutch were allowed to continue some restricted trade in Japan. Thus, in a 1718 manual of arcane medical instruction we read, "To avoid persecution from the authorities, our school will call itself for the time being the Dutch School instead of the *Nanban* School."

Perhaps the most remarkable of all the cultural enterprises of the Jesuits in Japan is the impressive collection of books that were printed on their press from the time it was imported by Valignano in 1590 until it was dismantled and shipped back to Macao in 1614. During these twenty-four years the press turned out a stream of publications, some rare copies of which still survive to this day. The large output is all the more surprising when one considers the difficulties under which this work was undertaken. Because of the unstable political situation, the press was moved several times; it first arrived at Nagasaki, but was then removed to Katsuta, and from there to Amakusa, and finally back to Nagasaki. In addition to the upheaval caused by all these transfers, there was also great difficulty at the beginning in obtaining suitable Roman and Japanese type.

It has already been noted that the press was used to produce dictionaries and grammars for European students of the language, but the greater part of its output was devoted to books for Japanese readers. Various books were published for the benefit of the pupils at the Jesuit schools. One such book appeared even before the press arrived in Japan, for Valignano used his enforced two-year stay at Macao before returning to Japan for his second tour of inspection to write a description of the Kyushu envoys' visit to Europe in the form of a dialogue between the young men. This was duly translated into simple Latin by the Jesuit Duarte de Sande and published at Macao in 1590 under the title *De Missione Legatorum Iaponensium*. The book had a twofold purpose, for the Japanese pupils reading the interesting text not only practiced their Latin but also learnt about Europe at the same time. To give further help to these students in the mysteries of Latin composition, the *De Institutione Grammatica*, an abridged version of the widely used grammar first compiled by the Spaniard Manuel Alvarez, was published at Amakusa in 1594. This edition was especially adapted for the use of Japanese students, for references to Japanese literary works were included. For the more advanced students classical Latin texts were printed; although no copy has survived to the present day, it seems certain that an edition of Cicero's speeches was printed sometime before 1593.

But not surprisingly the greater part of the books put out by the press was devoted to works in Japanese dealing with religious topics. Here it may be noted in passing that centuries elapsed after the introduction of Buddhism into Japan before a Japanese Buddhist literature emerged, and this was generally in the form of learned commentaries on the Buddhist scriptures. In contrast, Christian literature, although much of it was not original and consisted of translated work, was disseminated within forty years of the advent of Christianity into Japan.

In about 1591, there appeared the first printed Japanese Christian catechism, entitled *Dochirina Kirishitan* (Christian Doctrine). This was printed in Japanese script, but for the benefit of the European missionaries another work of the same title was produced in Roman transliteration at Amakusa in 1592. A larger edition of this latter work appeared later in 1600. The lives of the apostles and saints, the *Sanctos no Gosagueo no Uchi Nuqigaqi*, was published in Japanese at Katsuta in 1591. This version is known to have been compiled and translated by two talented Japanese Jesuits, Paulo Yōhō and his son Vicente Hōin, both of whom were renowned for their fine literary style. In fact, during this somewhat barren period of Japanese literature these Christian books developed a simple but elegant style that has won widespread praise from Japanese scholars.

Pl. 60

A year later, in 1592, part of Luis de Granada's *Symbolo de la Fe* appeared at Amakusa in Japanese translation, but in Roman script, under the title of *Fides no Doxi*, and this work, also written in elegant literary style, was probably prepared by Yōhō. A Japanese translation of four books from *De Imitatione Christi*, the celebrated spiritual work ascribed to Thomas à Kempis, was published in Roman script in 1596 under the title of *Contemptus Mundi*. This was also printed in Latin at Amakusa in the same year and partly in Japanese script in 1610. Other religious books put out by the press include Ignatius Loyola's *Spiritual Exercises* (Amakusa, 1596); a preparation for confession, printed in cursive Japanese script and entitled *Salvator Mundi* (Nagasaki, 1598); an abridged translation of Luis de Granada's *Guia de Pecadores* (Nagasaki, 1599).

The press also produced various manuals of prayers, devotions, meditations, an account of the Passion and an anthology of the Bible and the Fathers of the Church. Many of these works are characterized by their literary style, and references in contemporary Jesuit letters show that these books were in much demand. One particular work, which unfortunately has not survived to the present time, dealt specifically with the merits of martyrdom and did much to encourage the Christians to remain steadfast during the times of persecution.

In addition to the language textbooks and devotional manuals, the press busily continued to produce a wide variety of works. The publishers even ventured into the field of literature, both Western and Japanese. An example of the former may be found in *Esopo no Fabulas* (Amakusa, 1593), a translated version of seventy-four of Aesop's fables. This work enjoyed considerable popularity in Japan, and as the stories bore no direct connection with Christianity several editions were later brought out by Japanese publishers during the Tokugawa era. Bound together with these fables was the *Feiqe no Monogatari*, an abridged version of the classic *Heike Monogatari* ("The Tale of Heike") written in colloquial Japanese by Brother Fabian. The text could thus be used as a simple reading book by European language-students and Japanese pupils alike. The third part of this volume is made up of the *Kinkushū*, a collection of aphorisms taken from Japanese anthologies and Confucian works. This truly remarkable volume, the only known extant copy of which is preserved in the British Museum, thus had something for everybody—a simplified Japanese classic for Europeans, a translated Western classic for Japanese, and proverbs illustrating the traditional wisdom of the East.

Pl. 56

The *Heike Monogatari* was not the only Japanese literary classic to be edited and printed, for at an unknown date the press brought out a popular abridgement of the fourteenth-century work, the *Taiheiki*. Yet another work dealing with Japanese and Chinese literature was the *Royei Zafitsu* (Nagasaki, 1600), a medley of verse and classical writings. As an aid to reading some of these classical texts, the *Racuyoxu*, a three-part dictionary of Chinese characters, was published at Nagasaki in 1598. Various stories written in colloquial Japanese also appeared at different times, but unfortunately none has survived to the present day. They appear to have been the work of Brother Paulo Yōhō, but little is known about them save for their titles (for example, *Bungo Monogatari*, "The Tale of Bungo," and *Kurofune Monogatari*, "The Tale of the Black Ship") and some textual quotations found in the *Vocabulario* and Rodrigues' *Arte*.

Considering its relatively brief existence of only twenty-four years in Japan, its various enforced transfers from place to place, and the difficulty of obtaining suitable type and of training Japanese printers, the press performed a remarkable service. As has already been noted, it was the first press to use movable metal types in Japan, but it has various other innovations to its credit as well. It was the first in Japan to use copper engravings; it popularized the use of *furigana*, or phonetic letters written by the side of difficult characters; it was an early pioneer in printing *handakuon* marks to facilitate reading. But in addition to these merely technical feats, the press maintained a fine literary style in its books during a notably unproductive period of Japanese literature. Much more could obviously be written about this press, but enough has been said to give some indication of its valuable contribution towards mutual comprehension between Japanese and Europeans.

This brief survey has tried to show that the cultural movement between Japanese and Westerners during the *Nanban* period was a genuine exchange of knowledge, that the Europeans learnt from the Japanese and the Japanese learnt from the Europeans. Furthermore, it is obvious that in many cases this was not merely a superficial interchange, for knowledge of the others' culture was often both wide and profound. That this cultural exchange was not allowed to continue was perhaps in the nature of things inevitable. But while it lasted it was a heartening advance in mutual understanding between men from opposite ends of the world.

A SURVEY OF NANBAN ART

A SURVEY OF NANBAN ART

The Introduction of Western Art

JAPAN'S CONTACTS with foreign countries date back to the very beginning of her recorded history. The influence of Chinese thought was received through Korea from the earliest times and played a major role in the political, religious and cultural formation of the country. Later, during the Nara period (646–794), the cosmopolitan culture of the great T'ang dynasty (618–907) made a further contribution to the development of Japanese civilization. The Shōsō-in Repository at Nara still preserves objects used at the Japanese court during the eighth century, and many of these samples reflect strong Chinese influence. In subsequent ages, during the Sung (960–1279) and Ming (1368–1644) dynasties, the Japanese continued to study and admire Chinese learning. Some Western elements may be discerned in the arts and crafts imported from China; brocade weaving and musical instruments stored in the Shōsō-in show certain Iranian features, while traces of Greek influence may perhaps be noted in some of the ancient Buddhist statues of Japan. But direct contact with Europeans did not occur until the middle of the sixteenth century.

The first Europeans to reach Japan were three Portuguese traders, who landed on the island of Tanegashima off the coast of Kyushu in 1543. The introduction of Western art, however, did not take place immediately, and the earliest recorded instance occurred half a dozen years later when Saint Francis Xavier arrived in Kagoshima, bringing with him some examples of religious paintings. The daimyo of Satsuma, Shimazu Takahisa (1514–71), tried to obtain information about the West and was shown a painting of the Virgin Mary which had been brought from India. The noble greatly admired the picture, and his mother asked for a copy, but as there was nobody at that time capable of making a reproduction, it was impossible to meet her wish.

In a letter about the expansion of the apostolate in Japan, Xavier noted that religious paintings were a very effective means of propagating Christianity among the Japanese. Demand for these works increased, and there are references to a number of such paintings imported into Japan at about this time. It is recorded that Xavier showed an illustrated bible to Ōuchi Yoshitaka (1507–51), daimyo of Yamaguchi, and a painting of the Virgin Mary to Ōtomo Sōrin (1530–87),

Fernando G. Gutiérrez, S.J.

daimyo of Bungo. A portrait of the same subject decorated the chapel of Luis de Almeida's hospital in Bungo, while other religious paintings were displayed in the church at Yamaguchi. The growing demand for such pictures far exceeded the supply from Europe, and the mission authorities realized the need for training Japanese artists to reproduce Western works of religious art.

Two seminaries were founded at Arima and Azuchi by the Jesuit Visitor Alessandro Valignano in 1580 to provide a thorough religious education for the sons of the Christian gentry. Valignano placed considerable emphasis on the importance of these establishments, for he saw in them a means of harmonizing Japanese and Western cultures. In addition to the usual curriculum, the schools also provided tuition in Western music and art, especially painting and engraving. Because of the uncertain political situation, the seminaries were frequently transferred from place to place, and at various times they were established at Nagasaki, Hachirao and Shiki. There was an obvious need for a capable instructor in Western art, and writing in 1581 Francisco Cabral reminded the Jesuit authorities in Rome that a qualified missionary had been promised but had yet to arrive. He pointed out that religious paintings not only helped the devotion of the faithful but also raised Christianity in the esteem of the Japanese in general. According to Cabral, large and beautiful churches were being built throughout the country, but most of them were decorated only with pictures of indifferent quality drawn on paper.

In 1583 Giovanni Niccolo, the European who most influenced the artistic formation of Japanese painters in Western style and technique, arrived at Nagasaki. Born in Naples in 1560, he entered the Society of Jesus at the age of twenty and was duly assigned to the Japanese mission. For many years Niccolo produced religious paintings for the Japanese churches and taught Western art to the students of the Kyushu seminary; as far as is known, none of his own works has survived to the present day. A mission catalogue drawn up in 1592 mentions his work as a painter and instructor, and then adds briefly, "He has other manual skills." Among the other accomplishments of the talented Neapolitan was his skill in constructing organs with bamboo pipes, and ingenious clocks; Ieyasu expressed great delight in 1606 when he was presented with one of his elaborate clocks, which showed not only the time of day but also the movements of the sun and moon.

Details about the instruction in Western art are often mentioned in the missionary letters to Europe. In the annual letter of 1591–92, Luis Frois remarked that the seminary had been transferred once more and that the boys' studies included painting, printing and copper engraving, in addition to the more conventional lessons in Latin and religion. He added that the students produced oil paintings and engravings, which proved extremely useful in decorating the missionary churches. Frois was not alone in expressing admiration for the high quality of this work. The students reproduced some of the paintings brought back from Europe by the young Kyushu ambassadors in 1590, and some missionaries were apparently unable to distinguish between the original works and the copies. In other letters from missionaries there are frequent comments on the students' ability to assimilate the new artistic techniques. But, writing in 1599, Pedro Gomez pointed out that despite their undoubted imitative skill the students lacked creative originality when it came to producing their own work.

According to the mission catalogues, Niccolo was still teaching painting at Nagasaki up to the year 1614, and so it is certain that the school of painting continued until the expulsion of the missionaries in that year. But this does not mean that the practice of Western art in Japan came to an end at that time and died out at the very beginning of the Tokugawa persecution. There are various extant examples of works in the Western style that were produced after this date. The portrait of Saint Francis Xavier and *The Mysteries of the Rosary* were certainly painted after 1623, while the battle flags used at Shimabara in 1638 were obviously inspired by Western design and probably produced during the persecution. Some of these works may have been smuggled in from Macao, where Niccolo continued teaching Western art until at least 1623, while others were probably painted in secret by artists who remained in Japan.

Most of the artists who painted in the Western style were trained at the Kyushu seminary, and the names of some of them have been preserved. Leonardo Kimura was born in 1574 at Nagasaki, worked there as a painter at All Saints' Church and was martyred in the same city in 1619. Luis Shiozuka was also a native of Nagasaki and studied at the seminary in 1588; he later became a Jesuit and worked as a painter. Mancio Taichiku was born in 1574 at Uto in Higo, entered the Society of Jesus in 1607 and was occupied with painting until his death eight years later. Other Jesuit painters were Mancio João and Thadeu, both from Usuki in Bungo, and Pedro João from Kuchinotsu. The best known name, however, is that of Brother Jacobo Niwa, who was born of a Chinese father and a Japanese mother in 1579. He left Japan in 1601 and went to Macao, where he produced a painting of the Assumption for Saint Paul's Church. He afterwards worked in the interior of China and was of considerable assistance to Matteo Ricci in Peking; he was still painting at Macao as late as 1635. Finally, the names of some Japanese laymen who most probably studied under Niccolo are known. Ikushima Saburōzaemon was a native of Nagasaki, but apparently none of his works has survived until the present time. The artist called Nobukata has been more fortunate, and several paintings bearing his seal are still preserved. Yamada Emonsaku was another pupil of Niccolo; during the Shimabara uprising he was incarcerated in a dungeon of Hara Castle under sentence of death for treachery but was released by the victorious Tokugawa troops.

Although Japanese artists certainly knew and practiced the technique of oil painting, they usually continued to employ their traditional pigments; this is especially true of the paintings in which they depicted Western scenes. The style of their work is of the greatest interest, for they were able, with varying degrees of success, to combine the vitality of the contemporary Kanō school of Japanese painting with the style and technique introduced from the West. Despite the European influence, the clarity and composition characteristic of the Kanō school are evident in many of their works. If this combining of Western technique and Japanese style had not been interrupted and had been allowed to reach greater maturity, there would undoubtedly have risen one of the most fascinating schools in the universal history of painting. But, in the event, the new fashion had no time to develop fully and reach perfection, and on the whole the art of the so-called Christian century of Japan lacks both depth and personality.

Nanban Art

The term *Nanban* art is generally applied to works that were in any way influenced by or connected with the Europeans during this period. *Nanban* literally means "Southern Barbarian" and was originally derived from the Chinese concept that all foreigners were barbarians in comparison with the enlightened civilization of China. The Europeans reached Japan from the south and were consequently called Southern Barbarians. Of all the forms of *Nanban* art, paintings occupy the most important place, and the term *Nanban-ga* refers to Japanese paintings related in some way to Western art. In general *Nanban* art was produced in Japan under European influence during the century of contact with the West, but by extension the term is also used to designate European works that were imported into the country and influenced the native artists of the period.

Nanban paintings may be divided into two categories. To the first belong the works either introduced by the missionaries or executed under their direction, and as a result this type of painting is usually religious in theme. Although such paintings were relatively numerous and formed a large part of the output of the *Nanban* school, most of them were later destroyed in the anti-Christian persecutions and only a few survive to this day. In the second category are found the works of local Japanese artists who employed traditional techniques to depict on screens the customs and dress of Europeans. Some portray Europeans conversing, reading or playing musical instruments against a classical Western background. Another type of work shows European knights preparing to fight their Moorish adversaries or engaged in battle. There are also screens on which are illustrated views of some of the better-known European cities, such as Lisbon, Rome and Seville. In a separate and perhaps the most fascinating group may be included the *Nanban byōbu*, or screens on which the artists portrayed the arrival of the great Portuguese trading ship, or *nao*, at Nagasaki and the welcoming scenes at the port. The works belonging to this second category are of particular interest, for they show the meeting between two distinct cultures and vividly illustrate the impressions that the Japanese formed of the Europeans from the distant and exotic West.

Paintings of Religious Subjects

Owing to their religious and educational value, European paintings were imported into Japan in considerable numbers by the missionaries. Some were used to decorate churches, while others were donated to individual Japanese as gifts. Despite the quantity imported, however, there were never enough to satisfy the demand, and in 1584 Frois noted that fifty thousand such paintings were needed to help evangelical work in Japan. He added that a certain missionary had started out from Europe with five thousand pictures, but so great was the demand from Christians en route, especially at Macao, that he had hardly any left by the time he finally reached Japan. As has already been pointed out, this constant demand and insufficient supply necessitated the production of such works in Japan itself. Very few of the religious paintings that were imported during this period have survived to the present day, and the European origin of some of them cannot definitely be established in every case, since the skill of the Japanese artists in copying these works is well known. But first of all we may make a brief survey of some of the paintings that appear to have certainly been brought from Europe, and in this way it will be possible to determine which of the European schools influenced the formation of the Western style of painting in Japan.

Virgin and Child (Pl. 70) is certainly one of the European works brought to Japan at this time. It belongs to the Italian school and was probably produced in a Venice studio toward the end of the sixteenth or at the beginning of the seventeenth century. The paintings taken to Japan were obviously not the finest works of art that Europe had to offer, and many of the pictures introduced by the missionaries were of poor quality. In addition to the obvious financial difficulties involved, first-class works could not be obtained in the required large numbers. This *Virgin and Child* is one of the best of the imported paintings; its rich color, delicate composition and intimacy are characteristic of the better examples of the Venetian school and can be easily appreciated.

The *Dolorosa* (Pl. 64) was discovered some forty years ago in the possession of an Echizen family together with some ancient lithographs used for catechetical instruction. Various paintings based on this *Dolorosa* were produced in Japan, most of which were exact replicas, but in some cases a few original details have been added by the artists. This type of picture was also brought to Japan by the missionary Giovanni Battista Sidotti, who arrived from Manila in 1708; the actual painting brought by this priest is probably the *Virgin of the Thumb* (Pl. 65), now preserved in Tokyo National Museum. The painting was kept for years in a government building at Nagasaki before being added to the national collection in Tokyo. The work appears to be by the Florentine artist Carlo Dolci (1616–86), and the Japanese would have been impressed by the tenderness that the painter managed to impart to the face. There is yet another painting of the *Dolorosa* in the Okuda Collection, but this belongs to the Spanish School and was probably brought to Japan toward the end of the Keichō period (1596–1614). The figure is depicted with clasped hands and a sword through the heart, and the portrait is framed by curtains held back by cherubs. The work is a reproduction of a Spanish retable and clearly shows the characteristics of the best Spanish painting of that time by combining a realism of the figure with a profound idealization. The face has a youthful, innocent expression and yet displays a mellow grief. Such portrayal of human sentiment and feeling was not common in the traditional Buddhist-inspired art of Japan, and the humanism of Christian art was one of the features most imitated by Japanese painters when they produced Western-style pictures.

Another work also related to the Spanish school of painting is an oil painting on canvas of *Saint Peter* (Pl. 75). Until comparatively recently this picture was kept in a Buddhist temple at Funabashi in Chiba Prefecture, where it was revered as a Buddhist portrait. The saint is shown carrying the traditional keys in his left hand and reading a book held in his right. The elongated figure, the thin delicate hands, and the color of the mantle and tunic are all reminiscent of the school of El Greco (1541–1614). The painting is certainly not one of the illustrious artist's own works, but it may have been produced by a painter connected with his school. The elongation of the figure to express an intense spirituality is not unknown in Eastern tradition and may be found in famous works of sculpture such as the statue of the Kudara Kannon at Hōryū-ji near Nara. Similar paintings of other Christian saints, for example, Saint Laurence, Saint Stephen and Saint Vincent, are preserved in the National Museum at Tokyo.

Another well known religious work brought to Japan at this time is *The Veil of Veronica* (Pl. 71). Frois mentions in one of his letters that Valignano had presented a picture of *The Holy Face of Christ* to the family of Shibata Katsuie as a decoration for the chapel of his mansion. Shibata was an influential figure in the administration of Oda Nobunaga, and Frois saw and admired the painting during a visit to his mansion. Whether or not Shibata's painting is the same as *The Veil of Veronica* is not known, but it is quite possible that the two pictures are identical. In the present work the restrained sentiment and clarity of expression of the face are characteristic of the Flemish school, which was much in vogue at the time in Europe.

In the course of time it was natural that Japanese artists of the *Nanban* school should become dissatisfied with mere copying of imported paintings and should wish to produce more original work in accordance with their own inspiration. The degree of their success in combining Western style with Oriental inspiration may be seen in their pictures, for they created a type of work that was entirely new to Japanese artistic tradition, especially as regards theme. The undoubted Western influence under which they worked still left plenty of scope for personal interpretation, and they began to produce their own work on cloth, paper, tablets and copper plates. In general, Japanese painters of religious subjects necessarily relied on European models, since there was no precedent of Christian themes in their own traditional painting. The genre painters were not so circumscribed in this respect, and they provide far better examples of the fusion of styles and themes.

Of the works painted on wooden tablets, two examples of the same subject may be briefly mentioned. In the first *Virgin and Child* (Pl. 61), the Virgin has her hands clasped in prayer, while the Child lies in her lap. The simplicity of design and clarity of line make the work appear more like an engraving than an oil painting. Both faces show extreme refinement, and there is a deep religious sense about the painting. In the background may be seen a landscape divided into two unequal parts with all the characteristic detail of European tradition. This form of landscape undoubtedly attracted the Japanese artists who studied the paintings of the Flemish school. Another painting of the same subject (Pl. 62) has the Child being held in the left arm while the mother's right hand joins his hands. The background is obscure and there is no landscape visible. The inspiration of the painting, with the small-proportioned angel kneeling before the principal figures and the large golden haloes, is strongly reminiscent of the Primitive Spanish and Italian Schools of the Renaissance, and also suggests the Russian icons of the Byzantine tradition. The same theme was also represented on metal plates; the subject was the most frequent and popular among the religious works of Japanese artists and in this, of course, they were merely following the tradition of European painters.

NANBAN

ART

In *Virgin and Child* (Pl. 63), the Virgin holds the Child to her face and the two faces are united in an expression of tenderness. Here again this portrayal of sentiment in religious iconography evidently attracted the attention of the Japanese. This particular painting was probably inspired by works of the Spanish school of the sixteenth and seventeenth centuries. Two other works on copper plates may also be mentioned. In *Christ Carrying the Cross* (Pl. 66), Christ is depicted carrying the cross on his right shoulder; the facial expression is hard and the head is turned to the left in a somewhat unnatural manner. This particular theme was constantly repeated in contemporary Spanish paintings, and it is obvious that the Japanese painters were influenced by this school. The color of Christ's tunic in this work is also reminiscent of the same school. Yet another painting on copper is the *Repentant Magdalen* (Pl. 67). The saint is portrayed resting against a rock and contemplating a crucifix placed to one side. The composition leaves much to be desired, especially as regards the figure of the saint and the landscape that serves as a background. Apart from some details in the center of the painting, the work appears to have been left unfinished. Both Magdalen's strong facial expression and the ray of light appearing in the sky remind one of the baroque school of Spanish painting; in addition, this was a favorite theme for Spanish painters, and the general handling of the picture shows various characteristics of their school.

The later paintings, on which the Japanese artists were able to leave a more distinct imprint of their own personality are of greater interest than the early reproductions of European works. Among these may be numbered three paintings illustrating the fifteen mysteries of the rosary; all of these works are far more original than the paintings described above, and the composition, coloring and technique of traditional Japanese painting are more freely utilized in the depiction of a Christian theme. They show that the artists had learned to unite their individual technique with Christian spirituality, and in so doing they produced a new type of religious painting in Japan. The artists evidently had sufficient confidence in their own inspiration to employ their traditional materials and techniques; all three pictures are painted on paper with the customary Japanese pigments. The chromatic richness of the painting in Kyoto University is also traditional, and the artistic style of some of its details reminds one of scenes in the *emaki-mono*, or "picture scrolls," produced during the finest periods of Japanese painting. The mysteries of the Redemption, particularly in the works at Kyoto and Osaka, are painted with the same ease, spontaneity and narrative technique to be found in *emaki-mono*. But to these traditional qualities have been added Western techniques in the use of light and perspective. In this way the works show a happy union of tradition and technique, which resulted in paintings aesthetically far more attractive than the earlier reproductions.

The Mysteries of the Rosary (Pl. 68), formerly preserved at Urakami Cathedral but destroyed by bombing in 1945, is the most rudimentary and probably the earliest of the three paintings in question. The Joyful, Sorrowful and Glorious Mysteries are depicted, in Japanese fashion, from right to left, starting from the bottom row. Beneath them are portrayed the figures of three saints, of whom two are Franciscan, probably Saint Francis and Saint Anthony, while the third appears to be Saint John the Baptist. These large figures are not placed in the center of the composition, as in the case of the other two pictures. These other two works were, in fact, probably painted by the same artist, since they show many similarities, but the Urakami painting is quite distinct in various respects. It is possible that the artist who produced this latter work had been instructed by the Franciscan friars, since two of the saints appearing in the lower part of the painting belong to the Order of Saint Francis; alternatively he may have been commissioned by the friars to produce this particular work for use in catechetical instruction. The remote origin of all three works may probably be traced to the retables of the churches in Europe, especially in Spain. These retables generally present a synopsis of the Redemption expressed in painted or sculptured figures representing each mystery, while in the center of the composition is usually depicted the principal figure of

70. *Virgin and Child*. Oil on metal; 21.8 × 16.6 cm.; Tokyo National Museum. A work of the Spanish School imported into Japan in the latter part of the sixteenth or the early seventeenth century. The rough brushwork of the Virgin's shoulder suggests that the painting has been inexpertly worked over at some time.

71. *The Veil of Veronica*. Oil on metal; 40.4 × 32.4
cm.; Tokyo National Museum. A painting of the
Flemish School, which was stored away in a government office at Nagasaki before eventually being presented to the Tokyo museum. The painting may
have once belonged to the sixteenth-century daimyo
Shibata Katsuie.

72. *The Mysteries of the Rosary.* Color on paper; 75 × 63 cm.; Kyoto University. Saints Ignatius and Francis Xavier are portrayed in the lower foreground, together with Saints Matthias and Lucy. As the two Jesuit saints were canonized only in 1623, the painting was executed probably several years after this date at the very earliest. The depiction of the Mysteries of the Rosary around the sides and across the top of the painting is particularly skillful. During the anti-Christian persecution in Japan, the picture was hidden inside a bamboo cylinder and was discovered only in 1930.

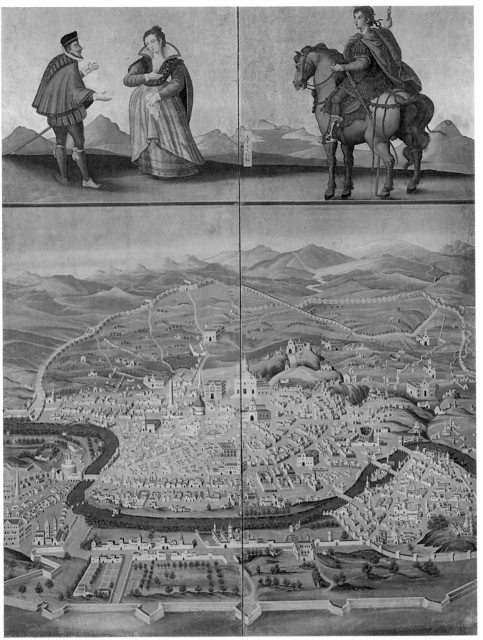

73. Rome. Detail from an eight-panel screen, *Four Great Cities of the West*; color on paper; Kobe Municipal Museum of Nanban Art. Many of the landmarks featured in this painting, based on a European plan of the city, are easily identifiable. The Jesuit Church of the Gesù stands prominently in the centre background, with the Roman College to the left behind the green-domed Pantheon. On the right-hand side of the painting can be seen the Coloseum near the north bank of the Tiber, while to the far left, on the near side of the river, is Castel Sant'Angelo, with the nearby obelisk of Saint Peter's Square just visible.

74. Lisbon. Detail from an eight-panel screen, *Four Great Cities of the West*; color on paper; Kobe Municipal Museum of Nanban Art. The other cities featured on this fine screen are Rome, Madrid and Constantinople. This depiction of Lisbon, copied from a European work by a Japanese artist who had never seen the city, would have been of special interest

in Japan, for it was from this port that the Portuguese ships began the two-year voyage to Nagasaki. The figures at the top of the screen represent the inhabitants of the cities featured below. It has been recently shown that the mounted figure in this painting is based on a European portrait of the Emperor Vespasian.

75. *Saint Peter*. Oil on canvas; 119 × 69 cm.; Nanban Bunka-kan, Osaka. The portrait belongs to the Spanish school of painting and was taken to Japan in the sixteenth or seventeenth century. For many years the painting was preserved in the temple of Kakuō in Funabashi, Chiba Prefecture, and was venerated as a portrait of a Buddhist saint.

76. *Crusaders and Mussulmen.* A four-panel screen, formerly a wall painting; color on paper; 166.2 × 468 cm.; Kobe Municipal Museum of Nanban Art. These mounted warriors were painted by an unknown Japanese artist about 1590. The work displays considerable skill in Western painting techniques, but the use of perspective is faulty and the overall effect of the composition is somewhat overpowering.

77. *Woman Playing the Guitar* (*see overleaf*), by the Japanese painter Nobukata about 1590. Color on paper, mounted as a *kakemono*; 55.5×37.3 cm.; Yamato Bunkakan, Nara. Europeans playing musical instruments were a popular subject for Japanese artists painting in Western style, and similar figures may be found in various other works of this period (*see* Pl. 86).

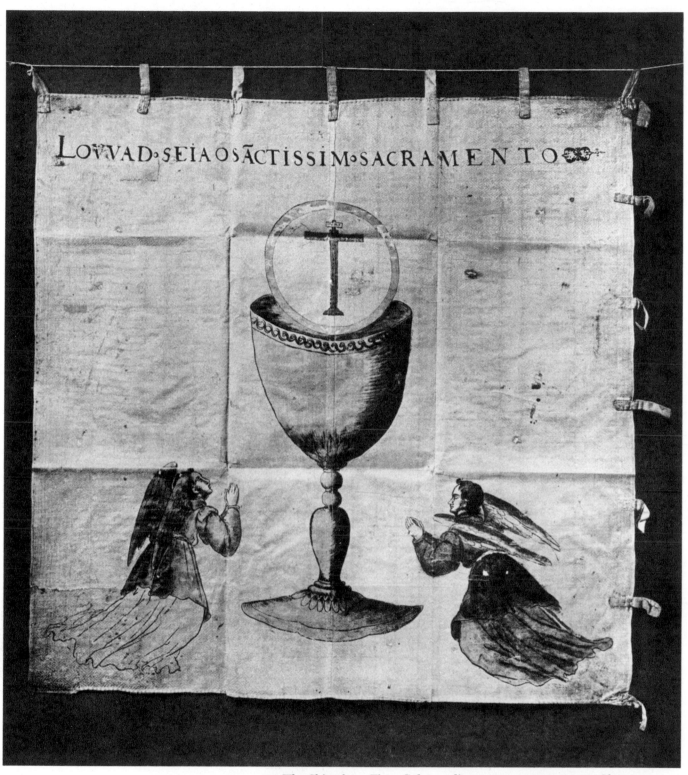

78. The Shimabara Flag. Color on linen; 108.6 × 108.6 cm.; Okuyama Binshi Collection. This flag was used by Christians in the Shimabara Rebellion, 1637–38; the Portuguese inscription reads "Praised be the Blessed Sacrament."

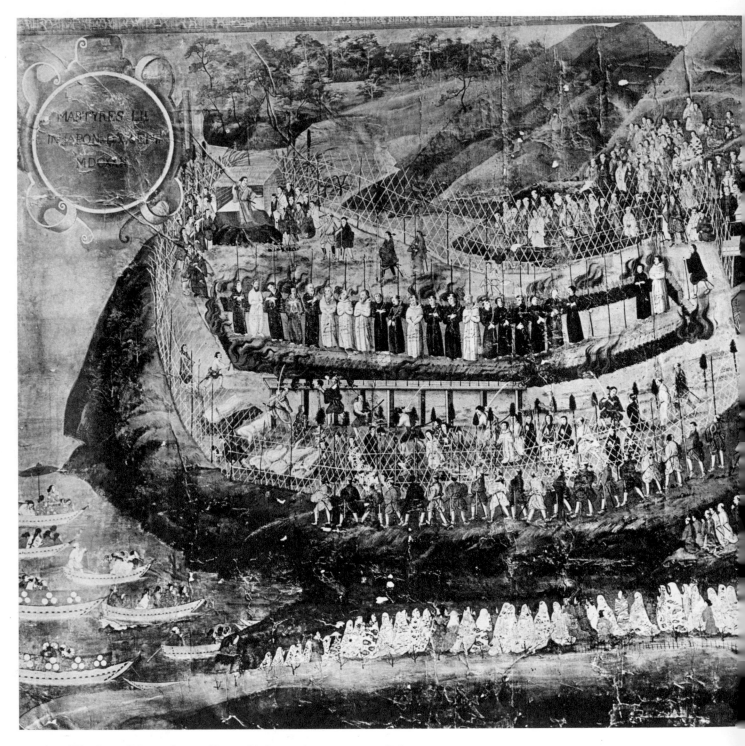

79. *The Great Martyrdom at Nagasaki*, September 10, 1622. Color on paper; 108.5 × 157.5 cm.; Church of the Gesù, Rome. This mass martyrdom is extensively described in contemporary missionary reports, and the unknown Japanese artist has reproduced the scene in exact detail. Some fifty Christians, both European and Japanese, were put to death on this occasion; twenty-five died at the stake, while the rest were beheaded. The figure at the fifth stake from the left is the Italian Jesuit Carlo Spinola, who lectured on European mathematics and astronomy in Kyoto at the beginning of the seventeenth century. Three Christians broke away from the fires (hence the three unoccupied stakes in the picture), but were forced to return. A crowd of about 30,000 people witnessed the martyrdom, and the artist has correctly included various Portuguese among the onlookers. At that time the sea extended further inland and the execution site occupied a small peninsula jutting into the bay.

80. Portrait of the Buddhist monk Nikkyō (1552–1608), by the Japanese artist Nobukata. Color on paper; 112×60 cm.; Seiren-ji, Hyōgo Prefecture. The three Japanese inscriptions from left to right are the date of Nikkyō's death, the prayer of the Nichiren Buddhist sect and the name of the monk. The seal of Nobukata may be seen on the right-hand side.

82. *Two Young Nobles*. Detail of a painting by an unknown Japanese artist; color on paper; Nanban Bunka-kan, Osaka. The awkwardly posed figures were copied by a Japanese artist from a European painting. A similar work, signed by Nobukata, is preserved in Kobe Municipal Museum of Nanban Art.

81. *Portrait of a Western Woman*. Color on paper; 84 × 37.5 cm.; Nanban Bunka-kan, Osaka. The Japanese artist has represented his subject in a somewhat feeble, static way, but he was only reproducing figures from pictures imported into Japan from the West. In all probability he had never seen a European woman.

83–84. Monk and priest reading books. Color on paper; details from paintings in Nanban Bunka-kan, Osaka. This was another favorite theme of Japanese artists painting in the Western style and was often repeated with some slight variations. A practically identical figure of the priest who is reading to the young boy may be found in a screen in the Yabumoto Collection, Osaka.

85–86. *Social Customs of Foreigners.* A pair of six-panel screens; color on paper; 93 × 302 cm.; Hosokawa Collection, Tokyo. The unnatural grouping of the figures and the faulty perspective of the background would have been amply compensated for in Japanese eyes by the strange robes and scenery of the exotic West.

87–88. *Social Customs of Foreigners.* Details from a pair of six-panel screens; color on paper; 84×268 cm.; Nanban Bunka-kan, Osaka. A pair of screens depicting a European pastoral scene and a boar hunt. The buildings both in this screen and the Hosokawa screen (Plates 85–86) were obviously copied from the same European painting.

Christ or a patron saint. But whatever the genesis of this Urakami picture, the painter evidently possessed sufficient skill and personality to produce a genuine work of art illustrating the principal Christian truths.

The painting now in the Azuma Collection at Osaka (Pl. 69) was discovered in 1920, and, although depicting the same theme, it has a far different composition. The mysteries are distributed around the central figures, with the Joyful Mysteries running up the left-hand side, the sorrowful across the top, and the glorious down the right-hand side. The central portion is divided into two parts: in the upper division the Virgin and Child are portrayed between hanging curtains, while in the lower part Saint Ignatius Loyola, the founder of the Jesuit Order, and Saint Francis Xavier are shown venerating the Eucharist, represented by a host and chalice, below which is found the Jesuit emblem IHS (*Iesus Hominum Salvator*). Across the top of the lower section runs an inscription in Portuguese, "Praised be the Blessed Sacrament." Beneath the two saints is written in Latin, "S.[anctus] P.[ater] Ignatius. S. P. Franciscus Xaverius. Societatius Iesus"; the artist made a slip in the spelling and should have written, of course, *Societatis*. The artist has made no attempt to integrate the two central parts of the work, and it is most probable that he copied them from two different pictures. Nevertheless this painting is far superior to the Urakami example in composition and execution. The figure of the Virgin in the center has badly deteriorated and has almost disappeared; fortunately this is not true of the Child, who carries a sphere of the world in his left hand while giving a blessing with his right. The mysteries around the sides are painted with greater ease and inspiration than those in the Urakami picture and some of them are depicted in an extremely skillful manner; the Nativity, for example, is quite extraordinary and is reminiscent of the style of the Primitive Spanish School. In general the assimilation of the theme and the way in which the traditional materials are handled are wholly admirable.

The best preserved of the three paintings is to be found at Kyoto University (Pl. 72). The work was discovered as recently as 1930, hidden in the thatched roof of an old house; it had been rolled up within a bamboo cylinder for several centuries, but was still in excellent condition. The fact that this is a later work than the Urakami painting enables us to note the development and perfection of the Japanese artists in their representation of Christian themes. In comparison with the earlier paintings of the same century, the application of color in this work is most original and is somewhat similar to the technique practiced in the production of *emaki-mono*. As in the Azuma painting at Osaka, an attempt has been made to employ the techniques of perspective and chiaroscuro in this picture. The distribution of the mysteries and the grouping of the central figures are the same as in the former work, but the figures of Saint Matthias and Saint Lucy have been added somewhat awkwardly in the lower section; the names of these saints were written in different colored lettering, probably after the work was completed. The general artistic quality of the picture, however, is more advanced than in the previous examples, and this superiority may be especially noted in the drawing of the faces of the principal figures and of the Virgin's delicate hands, particularly the left one holding a flower. The depiction of the mysteries is more or less identical with that of the previous work, but is marked with a greater dynamic sense. The composition of some of the scenes has been slightly changed; in the Nativity, for example, the Virgin is seen kneeling to the right of the Child, whereas in the Azuma picture she is depicted on his left. But there need be no hesitation in ascribing both paintings to the same artist; the fact that Saint Ignatius and Saint Francis Xavier are portrayed suggests that he was trained in the Jesuit seminary.

Closely connected with these pictures featuring the Mysteries of the Rosary is the portrait of Saint Francis Xavier (Pl. 2), which may have been painted by a Japanese artist in Macao about 1623. It was natural that the Jesuits and their students should continue to produce religious paintings in their exile, and the post-1614 mission catalogues specifically mention that Niccolo, Thadeu, Mancio João and Niwa carried on their artistic work in Macao. This particular portrait, painted in color on paper, is typically Japanese in its material and style; only the subject is Western. The handling of the theme is also Japanese, especially in the background where a mystical vision breaks through the darkness; this is characteristic of the Kanō school, which often depicted visions against such a golden background. The details of Xavier's face remind one of the portrait of the same saint in the two rosary pictures at Kyoto and Osaka, and the same artist may well have painted all three works. In this portrait Xavier is depicted in ecstasy, and from his mouth issue the words *Satis est, Domine, satis est* ("Enough, Lord, enough"), which he is known to have exclaimed in moments of intense prayer. His facial expression reflects the mystical experience that he was undergoing, while a vision of a crucifix surrounded by angels appears from the background. From the aesthetic point of view the hands are obviously the weakest element in the composition; they are clumsy and awkwardly out of place, and the artist was not able to depict them naturally. There are, incidentally, many examples of Japanese portraits in which the artist's efforts have been totally spent in depicting the facial expression of the subject, leaving the hands somewhat neglected in the overall composition.

In the Jesuit Church of the Gesù at Rome there are two paintings, both by Japanese artists of the seventeenth century, illustrating scenes of martyrdom in contemporary Japan. The first depicts *The Great Martyrdom of Nagasaki* (Pl. 79), which took place on September 10, 1622, when more than fifty Christians—European and Japanese—were decapitated or burned at the stake, while the second is a composite painting of the Jesuit martyrs who suffered death between 1597 and 1633. In both these works the artists have depicted scenes of great breadth with extraordinary richness of detail. This is particularly true of the first painting, in which the victims are seen enclosed within a bamboo stockade on the hillside. Outside the barrier are the crowds gathered to witness the event, and many of the onlookers are kneeling in prayer as the martyrs are put to death. Some men dressed in European clothing, presumably Portuguese merchants, are shown in the upper right-hand corner, while long rows of armed guards keep watch to prevent any disturbance or rescue attempt. There is a great sense of composition in both these works, reminiscent of Kanō school paintings, although Western influence can be discerned in the use of perspective on the different levels on which the scene is depicted. In *The Great Martyrdom of Nagasaki*, however, the perspective owes more to oriental than Western inspiration. The spectator looks down upon the scene from above, and the artist continues to develop the theme from this overhead viewpoint. The hills and trees in the landscape are clearly oriental in inspiration, but the dark tones employed are closer to Western tradition; possibly the Japanese artist preferred to describe the scene in this somber manner to emphasize and bring out the horror and suffering in the events portrayed.

The Shimabara flag (Pl. 78) was used in the rebellion that took place in 1637–38 and shows that Japanese artists continued to work in the Western style for a considerable time after the outbreak of persecution. The flag is made of white linen, upon which is painted a chalice and host, symbolic of the Eucharist, with two attendant angels in attitudes of prayer. Across the top runs the inscription in Portuguese, "Praised be the Blessed Sacrament"; loops are attached along the top and right-hand side so that the flag could be hung from a castle wall or flown from a mast. The drawing is simple, almost lineal, with the figures sketched in ink, although the artist has added some shading according to the normal technique employed in water coloring. This shading is certainly Western in style and gives the figures greater depth than is normally found in oriental paintings. Above all, the worshiping angels are painted with great agility. The dynamic sense of line and the shading of the figures recall European engravings produced in the fifteenth century. But the artist may well have received some inspiration from traditional Japanese painting, such as the figure in *Bodhisattva Seated upon a Cloud*, a tinted painting executed on hemp during the Nara period and preserved in the Shōsō-in Repository. It is also possible to appreciate in this Shimabara work the dynamic technique of ink tracing, which was later developed to such a high degree of excellence. The technique is generally used to give a sensation of movement, and this effect has been successfully achieved by the seventeenth-century Japanese artist in his depiction of the angels, apparently flying towards the chalice.

The flag is said to have been the standard of the rebel leader Amakusa Shirō, and some authorities have attributed the work to Yamada Emonsaku, who, as already mentioned, was present in Hara Castle during the uprising. Together with the flag a document is preserved stating that the banner was captured by members of the Nabeshima family and that they were given special permission to retain the trophy despite the general prohibition against the possession of objects related to Christianity.

For want of a better category into which they may be fitted, portraits of the Zen patriarch Bodhidharma and other Buddhist personalities may be conveniently included in this section dealing with religious paintings executed by Japanese artists in the European manner. There are several extant works painted in a semi-Western style of portrait technique and depicting oriental figures. One of the best of these is *Bodhidharma* by the painter Nobukata, while another portrait (Pl. 80) by the same artist features Nikkyō, a Buddhist monk of the Nichiren sect. This fusion of Western technique with a strictly oriental theme is not common, and its originality presents considerable interest. It seems that Japanese artists wished to employ modern Western techniques even when portraying oriental subjects; this is particularly the case after the expulsion of the missionaries in 1614, when the public portrayal of Christian subjects or themes was strictly forbidden.

Paintings of Secular Subjects

These works can be classified under the general heading of genre paintings produced by Japanese artists during the century of contact with the West. Such paintings served as a means of spreading knowledge of Western life and culture, and fortunately a comparatively large number has been preserved. An examination of these works shows which details of European life caught the attention of the Japanese and also what type of Western paintings were best known to the native artists. It is hardly surprising that the very best examples of Western art did not generally find their way to Japan, and as a result Japanese painters were not influenced by works of the highest quality. But this disadvantage did not prevent them from creating a new style by combining aesthetic details from the West with those of the Japanese tradition. As has been noted, Japanese artists felt freer to express their own inspiration in these genre paintings than in religious works, and they thus provide a tantalizing glimpse of the possibilities that could be reached in this new composite style. This does not mean that when producing genre paintings the artists did not copy Western pictures, since it is known that many of the paintings brought back by the young Kyushu ambassadors were either copied or closely imitated in Japan. Some of these paintings, incidentally, are specifically mentioned in contemporary records: there was a portrait of the Duchess of Tuscany, Bianca Capello, by Alessandro Allori; a self-portrait of Vicenzo Gonzaga, heir to the Duke of Mantua; and a painting of the funeral of the Emperor Charles V.

But while copying the European originals the Japanese artists did not slavishly reproduce every single detail but felt free to adapt the subject as they saw fit and to interpret certain details according to their own inspiration. Their originality was often necessarily exercised by the enlarging of the Western paintings when they were reproduced on screens, since the works brought from Europe were generally small in size owing to lack of space on the merchant ships. The artists' originality was further expressed by their use of traditional materials and techniques, for Japanese pigments were commonly used instead of the thicker and more consistent oil. Japanese brushes also have a greater flexibility than those of Europe, for they can produce faster tracing and express details in a more dynamic manner. All of this goes to make Japanese genre painting executed in this style far more interesting from the artistic point of view than the paintings illustrating religious themes.

Among the various categories into which these genre paintings may be divided is the type portraying European figures. An example may be seen in *Portrait of a Western Woman* (Pl. 81), a painting of color on paper. The artist has depicted a woman of rather feeble aspect as she emerges from behind some curtains; the general posture of the figure is somewhat artificial and unsatisfactory. But the interest of the work lies in the depiction of figures and costumes of Renaissance style, subjects that most attracted the attention of contemporary Japanese artists, who must have experienced considerable difficulty in portraying figures so different from those of their own tradition. It should also be borne in mind that the artist had probably never personally seen a European woman and was obliged to rely completely on imported portraits. Another painting belonging to this class is *Two Young Nobles* (Pl. 82). The facial expressions and postures of the two youths are also feeble and affected, but the picture's interest is found in the inclusion of a landscape background typical of contemporary European pictures. There is some attempt to use perspective in the Western style, although the faintly sketched mountains in the far distance appear to owe their inspiration more to oriental tradition.

A favorite theme of Japanese artists was to portray Europeans reading from books. There are pictures showing a hermit or priest reading, while others depict men and women intent on their books. Among the first type is a picture (Pl. 83) of a solitary monk, seated on a rock and reading a book; another painting (Pl. 84) shows a priest reading aloud from a book to a youth, who is gesturing with his left hand and perhaps drawing attention to a particular passage. In the last painting a landscape may be discerned in the background, and the artist has done his best to demonstrate the Western technique of perspective. In both pictures, in fact, the landscape is more interesting than the figures in the foreground, since the depiction of the men is poor and lacking in naturalness.

Another activity often represented in these genre paintings is the playing of musical instruments, and such works purportedly illustrated the social customs of the West, which the Japanese found so intriguing. It is probable that such pictures were commissioned by wealthy patrons who wished to decorate their mansions with exotic paintings. *Woman Playing the Guitar* (Pl. 77) is a painting in the form of a *kakemono*, or "hanging picture," and was produced by Nobukata about 1590. There is still extant a very similar painting—or perhaps a copy—with a landscape, which this work completely lacks; however, Nobukata's painting is far superior and more deft in manner, and the mature style of this artist can be appreciated by a comparison of the two works. The two themes of Western people reading books and playing musical instruments are occasionally combined on large six-panel screens. The pair of screens *Social Customs of Foreigners* (Pls. 85, 86) shows groups of Westerners engaged in conversation, playing musical instruments, reading a book and tending sheep. The figures are seen against a background in which the artist has included views of the countryside, mountains, bays and towns in an apparent effort to depict practically all the different types of landscape included in the paintings imported into Japan. The result is not wholly satisfactory, for there is a certain crowding and artificial note in the composition. The artists were perhaps a little overwhelmed by the novelty of the Western paintings reaching Japan in such abundance, and they often tried to unite indiscriminately, but not without ingenuity, all the features of the imported works. The coloring of this particular painting is as rich as the chromatic brilliance of the grand screens produced by the pictorial artists during the Momoyama period (1573–1615), and the materials employed were the same as those used in traditional Japanese works. The artist has attempted to present a perspective interpretation in the Western manner and on the whole he has been successful. The general style and composition are reminiscent of European paintings produced in the latter half of the Renaissance period, and the artist appears to have copied the affected and feeble-looking gestures of the figures from this source.

In another pair of six-panel screens representing *Social Customs of Foreigners*, the first (Pl. 87) has a section depicting a marine landscape with ships sailing in the distance. The center of the screen is dominated by a Western-style building, not unlike the building seen in the previous screen; the perspective of the circular tower at the rear appears incorrect, and the edifice is noticeably tilted. To the right are shown people conversing and playing instruments; again various points of similarity with the previous screen may be noted, making it quite probable that the same artist produced both works. In the second screen of this pair (Pl. 88), a boar hunt is in progress, while to the right groups of people converse or walk along the road leading to the hills in the background. The work as a whole reflects a totally unreal, bucolic atmosphere, which clearly demonstrates the exotic concept that the Japanese had formed of life in the West. In all likelihood the source of inspiration of these screens was drawn from separate European engravings and combined into one large original work.

The Kobe Municipal Museum of Nanban Art preserves a similar pair of six-panel screens also painted on paper with traditional Japanese pigments. In the background may be seen mountains and the sea, but the principal interest is in the Western figures depicted prominently in the foreground. Once more people are shown conversing, playing instruments and sleeping, but their distribution is unnatural and forced. This lack of realism, both as regards the figures and the background, may perhaps not be due to lack of artistic skill but may well be meant to depict the strange and distant scenes so totally foreign to the Japanese tradition. An original note is struck by the introduction of a Japanese woman wearing a kimono in the center of the second screen, and the seated figure to the left is looking up from his book and gazing at her. This may have been intended as a symbol of the encounter between East and West or of the fusion then taking place between European and oriental styles of painting.

There is a second group of Western-style paintings illustrating secular subjects, and these portray Christian nobles confronting or actually fighting Moorish adversaries. In this category may be found a screen, *Crusaders and Mussulmen* (Pl. 76), painted in color on paper. The screen is made up of only four panels instead of the customary six, and the paintings originally decorated some *fusuma*, or "sliding doors," of a chamber in Wakamatsu Castle. It is thought that it was painted about 1590 by a Japanese artist trained in the Jesuit seminary. In comparison with the scenes depicting foreigners' social customs, these screens possess a distinctly higher artistic quality. This superiority is possibly due to the fact that the artist has limited himself to portraying the Western figures as the only new element in the work and has disregarded everything else in order to follow the best style of Japanese decorative art. Little attempt has been made to show the landscape in any detail; the background is painted in a rich golden color, and the foreground is shown in a darker color representing the ground on which the horses are stamping. The figures obviously represent Westerners, as may be seen from their robes and weapons; the warrior on the extreme left carries a great sword on which is stamped the Roman monogram SNPQR (*Senatus Populusque Romanus*). The horses have the grandeur seen in Chinese paintings of the T'ang dynasty, which were occasionally reproduced by Japanese artists. The same sense of vigor and movement so ably communicated by Chinese artists is found here in these equestrian figures painted by a Japanese artist in the Western style. The chromatic richness of the work is in the best tradition of Japanese decorative art. It is obvious that the intention to use the Western techniques of perspective and chiaroscuro is far less pronounced in this painting than in others already described, but the success achieved by the painter in combining elements of European and oriental art in the one work indicates the breadth of his talent.

Another pair of screens (Pl. 89) has the same theme of four mounted warriors, but in this case the figures are not confronting each other in fighting stances. It has been suggested that the two African nobles are meant to portray Ethiopian kings, while various conjectures have been made regarding the identity of the European knights. There is considerable similarity between these screens and the previous one, and the terrace on which the figures are depicted is the same in both works. But this pair has been executed in a far less able manner; the perspective of the terrace is unnatural, and the horses have been painted in a somewhat static manner lacking in vitality. It is interesting to note that the Imperial Household possesses an eight-panel screen that depicts eight practically identical mounted warriors, grouped in the same four pairs. The treatment of the horses, incidentally, has obviously been influenced by the sixteenth-century Spanish and Portuguese schools, and these in turn were influenced by the Italian School of the previous century. In these paintings these influences have been united with the oriental, especially Chinese, tradition. The names of two painters of the fifteenth-century Italian School, the Florentine Tommaso Masaccio (1401–28) and Paolo Uccello (1397–1475), immediately come to mind in this regard. Uccello, in particular, depicted his horses in a monumental style and for this purpose employed the technique of considerable foreshortening; this is particularly noticeable in three of his battle paintings, which once belonged to the Medici family, and can be admired today in museums at Florence, Paris and London. This foreshortening of Uccello's horses appears to have influenced Japanese painters, especially the artist responsible for this pair of screens.

One of the most splendid examples of Japanese decorative painting in the Western style is undoubtedly the six-panel screen, *The Battle of Lepanto* (Pl. 90). The battle took place on October 7, 1571, and was, of course, a naval engagement, but the artist has conveniently transferred the conflict to dry land. Mounted warriors, foot soldiers, elephants and ships have all been painted in the most brilliant colors; once more the Roman monograph SPQR is to be seen on the banners and flags of the ships and soldiers. At the far left, Philip II, dressed as a Roman emperor, sits on a throne in his chariot and impassively surveys the tumultuous scene before him. The screen is reminiscent of the paintings in a chamber of the Escorial called the Room of Battles, which was decorated by Italian artists. There can be no doubt that examples of their style reached Japan and served as models for the battle scenes painted during this period. Despite this Western influence and theme, however, the artist has painted the clouds in the upper background according to traditional Japanese fashion.

Yet another type of painting depicts views of well-known cities in the West. Such paintings generally provide a bird's-eye view of each city and sometimes include figures of men and women representing the inhabitants of each particular place. *Twelve Cities* (Pl. 91) is painted on paper and divided into two parts. The left-hand portion shows a map of the northern hemisphere, surrounded by plans of the six cities of Lisbon, Venice, Bergen, Ankara, Mexico and Goa; in the other half the artist has depicted the southern hemisphere, along with the plans of Aden, Stockholm, Antwerp, Hamburg, Seville and Genoa. The artist has carefully distinguished the characteristic details of each city, and provides the spectator with a bird's-eye view that is half-map and half-landscape.

Another work in this category is a fine eight-panel screen (Pls. 73, 74) illustrating *Four Great Cities of the West*, again painted in color on paper. Each city covers two panels while in the upper part are seen representative citizens of each place. The work is artistically far superior to the previous screen in Osaka. The views are more complete and detailed, and the portrayal of the citizens has a novel and ingenious appeal. From left to right the cities depicted are Lisbon, Madrid, Rome and Constantinople; typical views of each place are clearly shown, together with a suitable landscape. The picture of Lisbon is extremely interesting (Pl. 74), for, as well as featuring easily recognizable landmarks of the city, the painter has included different types of ships of that time anchored in the harbor. The chromatic richness of the work is quite extraordinary, and the screen presents a brilliantly decorative appearance. The screen mentioned above in the collection of the Imperial Household not only depicts eight horsemen but also includes identical, but reduced, pictures of these cities in the same order.

To a certain extent this type of work may perhaps be related to the intervention of Alessandro Valignano, for in several letters he expressed his appreciation of such painted screens. He particularly admired the screen depicting the city and castle of Azuchi and sent the painting as a gift to the pope; it is also recorded that while in Macao he ordered a map of China to be painted on a screen as another gift to the pope. He further proposed that views of Rome and other European capitals should be painted in Europe after the fashion of Japanese *byōbu*. It is possible that his suggestion was duly followed, and that paintings of European cities were sent to Japan and there served as models for local artists.

Closely connected with these works are the screens on which are depicted maps of the entire world drawn in accordance with the geographical knowledge of the time. Such paintings usually have a greater cartographical interest than artistic merit, although they certainly do not lack skill and attraction. In general these *mapa mundi* are illustrated with great richness of color against a blue background; ships ploughing through the seas and disporting dolphins are added to break up the scientific rigidity of the work (Pl. 103). Contemporary European documents affirm that Japanese artists had great ability in accurately reproducing maps of the world and of different countries. The Japanese had obviously a great deal to learn from the maps and engravings imported from the West, but at the same time European cartographers were able to improve their own maps of Asia by carefully studying the Japanese maps of Japan and China that were sent back by the missionaries. While visiting Padua in July, 1585, the young Kyushu ambassadors were presented by Melchior Guilandinus with a copy of Abraham Ortelius' celebrated atlas, *Theatrum Orbis Terrarum*, which they carried back to Japan. This volume probably served as a basis for many of the world maps painted on screens during this period. It may also be noted in passing that the same benefactor in Padua also presented the embassy with a three-volume work illustrating the cities of the world. Although the title of this work is not given in contemporary accounts, the book was most probably Georg Braun's *Civitates Orbis Terrarum*, published in Cologne in 1572; certainly the view of Lisbon on Japanese screens is very similar to the illustration of the same city in Braun's work.

Nanban Screens

The final group of paintings to be considered can best be entitled *Nanban byōbu*, or "Southern Barbarian screens", and for the most part they depict the arrival of the great Portuguese ships at Nagasaki and the ensuing scenes of welcome. These paintings form the most original group within the limits of the *Nanban* school, for they interpret European and Japanese relations in a distinct and quite unmistakable way. About sixty of these screens are known to exist, and some of them are preserved outside Japan. Their popularity clearly demonstrates the interest of the seventeenth-century Japanese in everything related to the exotic customs and dress of the foreigners from the West. Moreover, these works were also popular among European merchants, and several were bought or received as gifts from the Japanese. Although Western influence can be discerned in these pictures, the materials employed and the pictorial technique were entirely traditional. Most of the paintings are unsigned, but their style shows that *NANBAN* practically all the best examples were produced by artists of the Kanō school in the second *ART* half of the Momoyama period. A few of the artists are known by name. The screen in the Kobe Municipal Museum of Nanban Art is signed by Kanō Naizen (1570–1616), and he also appears to have painted the screen in the National Museum of Antique Art at Lisbon. The screen in the Suntory Art Museum, Tokyo, is attributed to Kanō Sanraku (1559–1635), while the Nanban Bunka-kan, Osaka, possesses another which is the work of Kanō Mitsunobu (1561–1608). In other screens small details appear, which seem characteristic of one particular artist, but such indications are generally insufficient to attribute the work with any degree of certainty.

The precise period in which these screens were produced is not known, and various dates have been suggested, but both internal and external evidence points to the period between

1590 and 1630. The return of the Kyushu ambassadors in 1590 aroused great interest in things European, and this event may well have begun the demand for screens depicting the arrival of the *Nanban* ship. In 1614, however, Christianity was proscribed, and the screens that show neither missionaries nor churches were presumably painted after this date. Furthermore, the paintings generally depict the great Portuguese carrack, or *nao*, but this ship was replaced in 1618 by fleets of smaller and faster galliots in an attempt to break the Dutch blockade. It may be safely presumed, then, that most of the best-known screens were painted during the Keichō period lasting from 1596 to 1614.

The *Nanban byōbu* were usually produced as pairs of six-panel screens and they can be roughly classified according to their content. The standard type shows the great ship in harbor on the left-hand side, while missionaries and Japanese are seen on the right coming forward to greet the Portuguese captain-major and his retinue. A map of the world is occasionally included in the composition, and the foreigners may sometimes be seen trading with the Japanese. In another type of screen the artist portrays the merchants leaving a foreign port, presumably Goa, and arriving at Nagasaki. But whatever the composition of the screen, the Portuguese *nao* invariably appears prominently and is shown in considerable detail.

The artists did not attempt to reproduce the scene in rigorous detail either as regards the place or the event. They tended to concentrate on the decorative value of the screens and emphasized the elements that would have been unfamiliar to most Japanese; thus the exaggerated height of the foreigners and the bagginess of their *bombacha* pantaloons are regular features of these works. Care was taken to include all the foreign items that would most interest the Japanese. The great ship is placed well to the fore; figures on board are clearly shown and negro sailors can be seen gaily performing acrobatics in the rigging. The exotic animals, such as tigers, deer, monkeys and caged birds, which were imported to serve as gifts to the Japanese authorities, are also featured prominently. As a result the *Nanban byōbu* are extraordinarily attractive to both Japanese and foreigners alike, and they contain great social, historical and artistic interest.

From the artistic point of view these *byōbu* belong to the best of Japanese decorative painting and illustrate the high level reached in screen production during the Momoyama and Edo periods. The screens are made of paper stuck upon a wooden framework; only the traditional pigments were used to paint the scenes. The characteristics of the Kanō school are most noticeable, for the screens possess clarity of composition, chromatic richness and a uniform gold background; no influence of Western perspective or chiaroscuro can be observed. Only the original theme distinguishes these screens from the more conventional products of the Kanō and other Japanese schools. Although artists of the Tosa and Sumiyoshi schools apparently produced some *Nanban* screens, it was the Kanō painters who most distinguished themselves in this type of work. The Kanō was probably the only school that made a real effort to assimilate Western culture so as to inject new life and vitality into Japan's long pictorial history. In the words of a modern critic:

> It is most interesting to speculate that European culture was probably the impetus to that process in which the Kanō school put off the old and became a school of gorgeous wall painting, taking into itself also other elements of the *yamato-e* school. The contact of the two cultures, however, was to be severed before its tremendous possibilities could be realized.[1]

The central object of interest in most of the *Nanban* screens is undoubtedly the Portuguese ship. The *nao do trato*, which plied between Lisbon, Goa, Macao and Nagasaki, was known to the Japanese as the *kurofune*, the "black ship," or *Nanban bune*, the "*Nanban* ship." It was a

---

[1] Miki Tamon, *The Influence of Western Culture on Japanese Art*, in *Monumenta Nipponica*, XIX (1964), p. 388.

89. Two mounted kings. Detail from a pair of four-panel screens;
color on paper; Fujii Collection, Hyōgo Prefecture. As in the case of
the screen in Kobe Municipal Museum of Nanban Art (Plate 76),
this pair shows four mounted kings, two Europeans and two Africans,
but in this composition the figures are stationary. Despite the color
and the grandeur of the work, the Japanese artist was not entirely
successful either in the depiction of the horses or in the perspective of
the terrace.

90. *The Battle of Lepanto.* A six-panel screen; color on
paper; 153 × 362.5 cm.; Murayama Collection, Hyōgo
Prefecture. The battle of Lepanto took place on October 7,
1571, and the Japanese artist has here transferred the naval
engagement onto dry land. The screen is painted in brilliant color and is unlike any other extant work of Japanese
artists painting in Western style. In a chariot on the left-
hand side sits "The King of Rome," copied from a portrait
of Philip II of Spain. Many of the standards carried by the
Christian soldiers bear the monogram of Rome, SPQR.

91. *Twelve Cities.* A four-panel screen; color on paper; 143.2 × 234 cm.; Nanban Bunka-kan, Osaka. On
the left-hand side are shown the northern hemisphere
of the globe and the cities of Lisbon, Venice, Bergen,
Ankara, Mexico and Goa; on the right-hand side are
the southern hemisphere and the cities of Aden,
Stockholm, Antwerp, Hamburg, Seville and Genoa.
The paintings were copied from European books of
maps and city views.

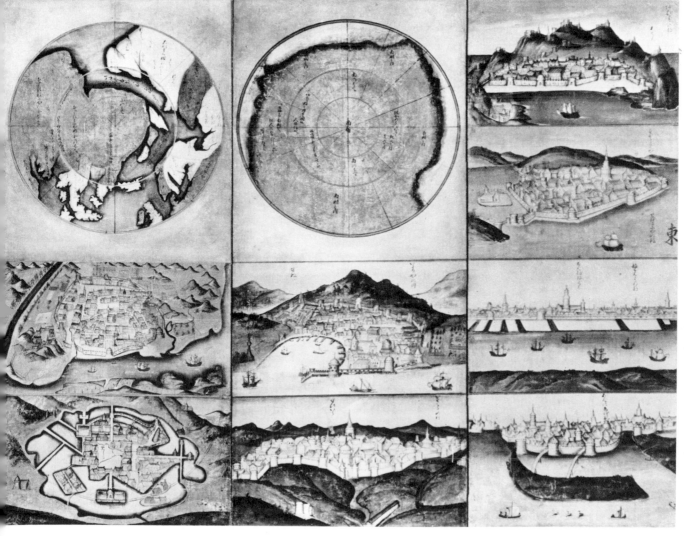

92–93. Europeans watching kabuki. Details from a horizontal scroll; color on paper; Tokugawa Reimei-kai Collection, Nagoya. Two Europeans can be seen at the rear of the crowd watching the kabuki performance. One actress wears a rosary around her neck; such was the craze for things European in the last decade of the sixteenth century that even non-Christian Japanese sometimes wore rosaries.

94. The departure of the *Nanban* ship for Japan. One of a pair of six-panel *Nanban* screens, signed by Kanō Naizen (1570–1616); color on paper; 154.5 × 363.2 cm.; Kobe Municipal Museum of Nanban Art. The artist shows a Portuguese ship leaving a foreign port.

95. The *Nanban* ship at Nagasaki. Detail from a pair of six-panel *Nanban* screens, signed by Kanō Naizen (1570–1616); color on paper; Kobe Municipal Museum of Nanban Art. Kanō here shows the great Portuguese carrack in Nagasaki harbor. The depiction of the alarming acrobatic feats of the crew in the rigging is traditional and may be seen in pictures of Japanese ships. In the foreground the merchants' slaves carry exotic gifts intended for Japanese officials.

96. The procession of the captain-major in Nagasaki. A six-panel *Nanban* screen; color on paper; 156 × 330 cm.; Tōshōdai-ji, Nara. Although various details are different, the general composition of this screen is practically identical with that of one of the *Nanban* screens in Kobe Municipal Museum of Nanban Art. For added interest the artist has rather awkwardly included a plan of the northern hemisphere, possibly to illustrate the voyage from Lisbon to Nagasaki.

97. The procession of the captain-major. Detail from a pair of six-panel *Nanban* screens, color on paper; 178.3 × 332.7 cm.; M.H. de Young Memorial Museum, San Francisco. The composition of the picture is somewhat uneven and there is a certain stiffness about the figures, although they are not without interest. It seems obvious that the artist was not so skilled as some other *Nanban* screen painters, such as Kanō Naizen.

98. Lacquer box. Lacquer on wood, with inlaid mother-of-pearl; 27.2 × 23 × 21.3 cm; Powers Collection, New York. This superb *jūbako*, or "nest of boxes," features in its decoration *Nanban* foreigners aboard a junk.

99–100. Portuguese merchants in Nagasaki. A pair of six-panel *Nanban* screens, attributed to Kanō Mitsunobu; color on paper; 163.5×362 cm.; Nanban Bunka-kan, Osaka. An exceptionally fine pair of *Nanban* screens as regards both color and composition. The artist has painted the scene from close-up and as a result a great deal of interesting detail can be seen clearly. His accurate portrayal of scenes inside the Jesuit residence shows that he was familiar with the life of the missionaries. The second screen follows directly on from the first, so that in effect the artist has produced a twelve-panel picture.

102. The procession of the merchants. One of a pair of
six-panel *Nanban* screens; color on paper; 155.8 × 334.5
cm.; Imperial Household Agency.

101. The arrival of the Portuguese ship at Nagasaki. One of a pair of six-panel *Nanban* screens; color on paper; 182 × 371 cm.; Suntory Art Museum, Tokyo. A work of the Kanō school with various interesting details. But on the whole this and the following screen (Pl. 102) are somewhat overcrowded with figures and there is a certain lack of dexterity in the handling of the theme.

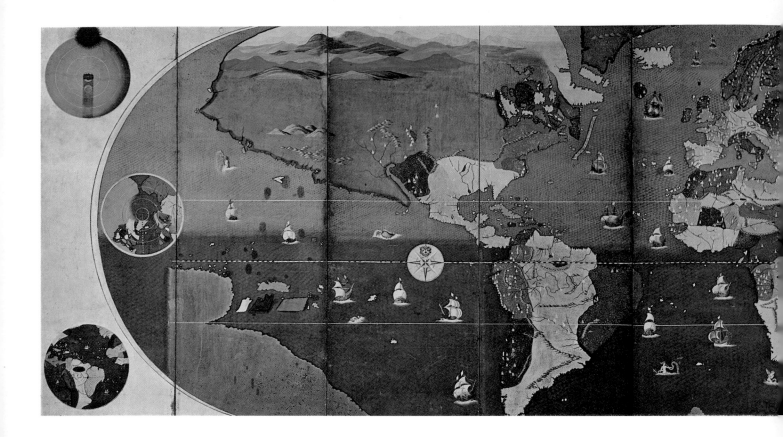

104. Japanese portrait of an Iberian merchant. Detail from a six-panel *Nanban* screen; private collection, Portugal.

190

105. A red-seal ship with European passengers. Painted wooden tablet; Kiyomizu-dera, Kyoto. In the early Tokugawa period Japanese ships sailing abroad were obliged to obtain a patent stamped with the red seal of the shogun; hence such ships were called *go-shuin bune*, or "red-seal ships." This wooden tablet, dated 1634, was presented to Kiyomizu Temple for the prosperous voyage to Annam (North Vietnam) of a ship belonging to the merchant house of Sumikura in Kyoto. A number of Europeans can be seen on deck, while one, very possibly the pilot, is seated within the cabin.

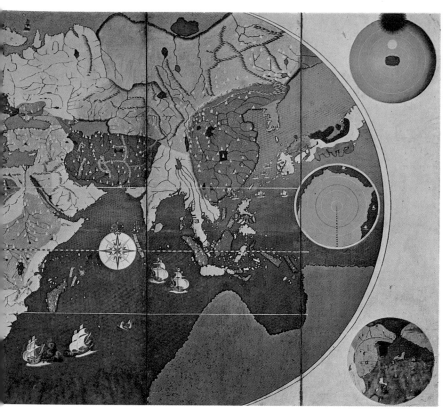

103. *Map of the World.* An eight-panel screen; color on paper; 158.7 × 477.7 cm.; Kobe Municipal Museum of Nanban Art. The Europeans introduced into Japan a knowledge of world geography, and the Japanese artist may well have copied this world map from the books brought back by the Kyushu ambassadors on their return from Europe in 1590. In accordance with contemporary geographical knowledge, Europe, Africa, South America, East and South Asia are depicted fairly accurately, while considerable guesswork has been used in drawing North America, northern Asia and Australia. The size of Japan has been obviously exaggerated. This is one of a pair of screens, the second being *Four Great Cities of the West.*

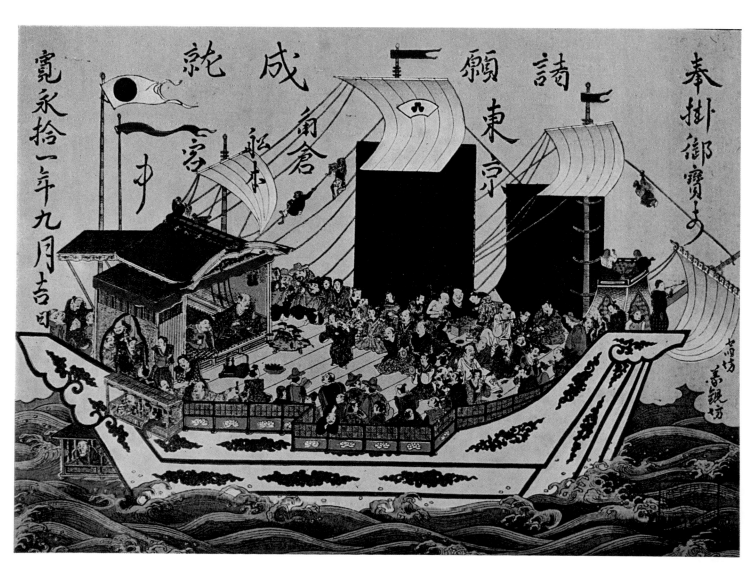

106. Maria Kannon statue. Porcelain; height 32 cm.; Kirishitan Bunko, Sophia University, Tokyo. Maria Kannon are statues of the Buddhist deity Kannon that were secretly revered by Japanese Christians in persecution times as images of Our Lady. This particular example is of Chinese origin and for many generations belonged to a Christian family at Saki-tsu, Amakusa Islands.

107. European-style bell, bearing the *Kyūmon* ("Nine Balls") crest of the Hosokawa family. Height 80cm., diameter 70 cm., weight 200 kg.; Nanban Bunka-kan, Osaka. The bell was presented by the Hosokawa family to the daimyo Mori Tadamasa (1570–1634) in 1616 on the occasion of the completion of his castle at Tsuyama.

108. Metal *tsuba*, or "sword guard," decorated with crosses (*upper plate*). Signed Myoju (Umetada Myoju, 1558–1632); 7.5 × 7.8 cm.; Nanban Bunka-kan, Osaka. As well as often being a highly decorated part of the sword, the *tsuba* helped to give the weapon its correct balance.

109. Metal *tsuba* with cross (*lower plate*). Made by Myōchin Nobuie (1496–1564); diameter 9.5 cm.; Nanban Bunka-kan, Osaka.

110. Metal stirrups, with inlaid decoration of instruments of the Passion. Height 23 cm., length 27 cm., width 12.5 cm.; Nanban Bunka-kan, Osaka. The Cock can be seen on the stirrup on the left, while the other is decorated with the Crown of Thorns and Veronica's Veil.

Domina nostra S MARIA (cui ab antiquitate cognomen) cuius imago in summa
... dum Ferdinandus tertius Hyspalim expugnarit in pariete depicta inuenta
... Senora Del Antigua ... en Sem Jap 159

111. *Virgin and Child.* Engraved print on paper; 22 × 14.5 cm.; Ōura
Cathedral, Nagasaki. This print is based on the famous mural painting
Nuestra Señora de Antigua in Seville Cathedral. According to the
Latin inscription at the foot of the picture, the print was produced at
the Jesuit seminary in Japan in 1597. At that time the school was
situated at Arie in Kyushu.

112. Our Lady of the Rosary *fumi-e*. 18.5 × 13.6 cm.; Tokyo National Museum. The ceremony of *e-fumi*, or treading on these religious plaques, is illustrated in plate 23. This and the *fumi-e* below (Pl. 113), together with the paintings shown in plates 70 and 71, were stored away for a long time in Nagasaki and were brought up to Tokyo in 1874.

113. Ecce Homo *fumi-e*. 19 × 13 cm.; Tokyo National Museum.

114. Lacquered saddle, probably belonging to Ōtomo Yoshishige (1530–87). Kyoto University. The main point of interest of this red lacquered saddle is the monogram FRCO. Ōtomo Yoshishige, daimyo of Bungo, was baptized as Francisco in 1578 and later used a seal with exactly the same monogram.

115. *Inrō* with *Nanban* decoration (*left*). Lacquer on wood; signed Tsuchida Sō-etsu; 8.5×5 cm.; Nanban Bunka-kan, Osaka. An *inrō* is a small seal case, divided into compartments and often exquisitely carved, and was usually suspended from the owner's sash. The *netsuke*, or "toggle" (decorated in this example with a dragon), prevented the cord from slipping through the sash, while the *ojime*, or "bead," was used to tighten the two cords and keep the *inrō* closed.

116. *Inrō* with cross and swastikas (*right*). Lacquer on wood; signed Tamura Ryūeki; 7.5×4.8 cm.; Nanban Bunka-kan, Osaka.

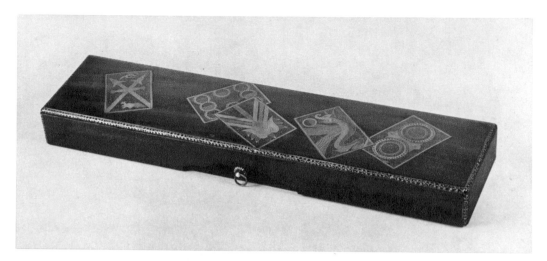

117. Box for playing cards. Lacquer on wood; Powers Collection, New York. Playing cards, introduced by the Europeans and still called *karuta* in Japanese, were extremely popular in Japan in the last quarter of the sixteenth century.

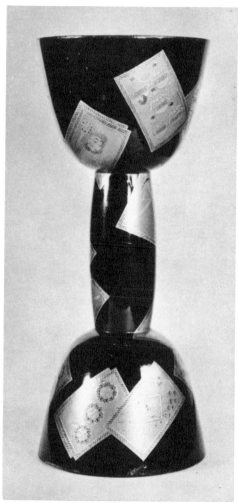

118. Lacquered drum with card motif. Lacquer on wood, with gold *maki-e* decoration; height 25.2 cm., diameter 10.2 cm.; Nanban Bunka-kan, Osaka. This type of musical instrument was accurately described by Richard Cocks, who wrote, "Their Musique is little Tabers, made great at both ends, and smal in the middest, like to an Houre-glasse, they beating on the end with one hand, and straine the cords which goe about it, with the other, which maketh it to sound great or small as they list."

119. Host box, bearing the Jesuit monogram IHS. Lacquer on wood, with motif of ivy worked in gold; height 9.3 cm., diameter 11.1 cm.; Nanban Bunka-kan, Osaka.

120. Tea bowl decorated with cross. Height 10 cm., diameter at mouth 10 cm.; Nanban Bunka-kan, Osaka. Some of the Christian daimyo were masters of the tea ceremony, and Alessandro Valignano encouraged the Jesuit missionaries to practice the art. As a result there are still extant today various tea bowls bearing Christian insignia.

121. Tea bowl decorated with cross. Height 8.6 cm., diameter of mouth 12 × 11.2 cm.; Nanban Bunka-kan, Osaka.

198

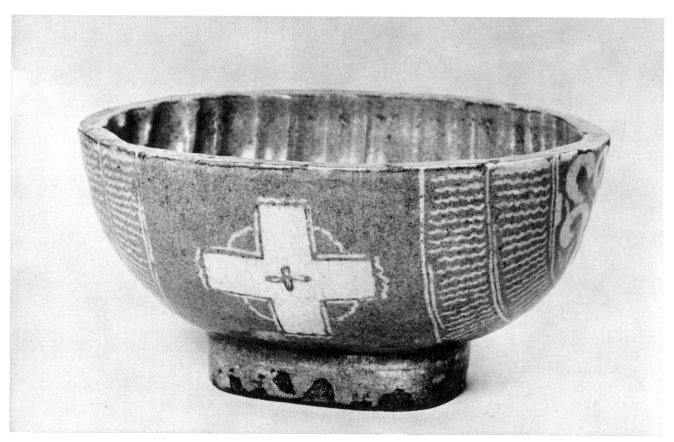

122. Bowl decorated with cross. Height 9.5 cm., diameter of rim 20×15.8 cm.; Nanban Bunka-kan, Osaka.

123. Bowl decorated with cross. Height 20 cm., diameter of mouth 31.5×30 cm.; Nanban Bunka-kan, Osaka.

124. Candlestick. Height 24 cm.; Nanban Bunka-kan, Osaka. This
amusing figure is wearing the baggy *bombacha* type of trousers, so
often featured in the *Nanban* screens.

three–deck carrack of between one thousand and sixteen hundred tons, an enormous size for those days, and the admiration of the Japanese at such an imposing sight is not surprising. One can well imagine the excitement felt by the European and Japanese citizens of Nagasaki when news of the ship's impending arrival was received, and João Rodrigues in his Japanese grammar published in 1608 quotes the phrase *Yarayara medetaya, Nanbanbune ga tsukimashita* —"Rejoice! the *Nanban* ship has arrived!" So great was the impression caused by the *nao* that the depiction of the ship often takes up half the screen; sometimes in fact the ship is shown twice in a pair of screens, once as she sails from Goa and the second time as she lies at anchor in Nagasaki harbor.

Although the scenes on land in most of the screens are fairly similar in content, they all contain different details illustrating various aspects of the encounter between the Europeans and Japanese. They show the colorful dress of the Portuguese merchants and the religious habits of the Jesuit and Franciscan missionaries; the screens, in fact, are about the only source of information about the dress worn at that time by the Portuguese in the Far East. The pictures also demonstrate the European influence on Japanese costume, for some of the Naga-saki citizens are depicted wearing an adapted form of *bombacha*, or baggy trousers tied tightly at the waist and ankles. The missionary churches and residences are shown in some detail, and it can be noted that they were built according to Japanese style with some additional Western features. The accurate depiction of not only the exterior but also the interior of these buildings suggests that the painters were familiar with the missionaries' lives, and it is quite possible that some of the artists had studied at the Jesuit seminary. The name of at least one Christian painter of the Kanō school, Pedro Kanō, is mentioned in contemporary letters.

The pair of six-panel screens in the possession of the Imperial Household was presented to the royal collection by the Tokugawa family at the beginning of the Meiji period (1868–1912), and it bears all the characteristics of the Kanō school. As usual the first of the pair shows the arrival of the ship at Nagasaki, while in the second (Pl. 102), the procession of the captain-major has just reached the gate of the Jesuit residence. In the upper right-hand cor-ner, figures can be seen in a chapel kneeling around a picture of Christ. Various details have been included to add to the interest of the work; some Japanese, wearing Portuguese-style clothing, are standing in shop doorways looking on at the colorful spectacle, although the arrival of the Europeans does not appear to have distracted the attention of the two ladies playing a game of dice. In general the work tends to be overcrowded with too many figures, and as a result a rather unnatural impression is given. Perhaps this was the first time the artist had painted a *Nanban* screen, and he lacked the necessary experience to produce a more satisfactory composition, for he appears to have introduced into this one work practically all the general characteristics of this type of screen.

The pair of screens at Kobe is signed by Kanō Naizen and is a more polished work. In the first screen (Pl. 94) the great ship is seen leaving Goa, while various Portuguese dignitaries gather at the harbor to watch the departure. The usual negro attendants carrying large parasols are shown, and even a placid-looking elephant, bearing a Portuguese official in a decorated howdah, has been included. The ornate buildings are depicted in half-Indian and half-Chinese style, since the artist was presumably unfamiliar with Goa and hence somewhat vague about the details of the architecture to be found there. In the second screen (Pl. 95) the same ship is now safely in Nagasaki harbor, with its sailed furled as the captain-major leads the imposing procession to the mission residence. Behind him march the colorfully dressed Portuguese, and servants carry a caged tiger and lead a prancing white horse. A group of Jesuit priests and novices, as well as two friars and an elderly *dojuku*, or "catechist," are waiting to greet the disembarking Portuguese (Pl. 21). On a higher plane can be seen a chapel in which a priest is celebrating Mass (Pl. 16), and to the left a glimpse of the interior of the Jesuit resi-dence is given. The division between the chapel in the higher plane and the missionaries in the lower is filled as usual by clouds and pine trees in accordance with the style of the Kanō school. The composition of the work is well thought out and the chromatic quality is quite extraordinary. The bright colors stand out splendidly against the gold background and provide a fine decorative element. A pair of *Nanban* screens preserved at Lisbon also bears the stamp of Kanō Naizen and have a practically identical composition—Goa in the first screen (with an extra elephant added) and the procession at Nagasaki in the second.

The screens in the Suntory Art Museum, Tokyo, are of special interest, for they display various features not to be found in other works of this type. In the first screen (Pl. 101) there is a detailed depiction of the Japanese port, with the usual church, residence and shops; Japanese and Europeans are gathered near the quay, where merchandise is being unloaded from a small lighter. The work is generally lacking in naturalness and the figures of the missionaries appear somewhat stiff, but the artist has shown considerable ingenuity in uniting so many elements into such a small space. In the second screen, by way of exception, the *nao* does not appear. Instead, richly dressed Portuguese are seated on a terrace, while a type of horse race, called *cana*, is being run on the near side of what appears to be a canal; some clerical figures view the spectacle from the bridge over the canal and the gateway on the right. The odd hybrid style of architecture, the exotic peacocks and willow tree show that a foreign city is being represented and the general indications point to China. But had the artist had Macao in mind he would have surely featured buildings in pure Chinese style, with which he would have been familiar from oriental paintings, so the presumption once more is that the picture is meant to show a scene from the city of Goa. As regards the identity of the artist, the name of Kanō Sanraku has been suggested, but the attribution is not certain.

The screens at Osaka (Pls. 99, 100) belonged to an old Sakai family and came to light only in 1962. The style of the painting is quite exquisite, and the pictures are a very fine example of *Nanban byōbu*. Although the customary theme of ship and procession is depicted, two special features may be noted. In the first place, the scenes on the two screens are continuous, and the artist has in effect produced a twelve-panel picture. Secondly, these scenes are viewed from close-up, and, as a result, far more detail can be observed than usual. The ship is shown prominently as its depiction is generously spread over no less than four panels, instead of the more usual two or three. Sailors clamber up the mast and rigging, while others are occupied in manning the two lighters and unloading crates of luggage and merchandise onto the shore. A particularly pleasing effect is obtained by the realistic portrayal of the strong waves, which makes the efforts of a sailor to keep the lighter steady as goods are lowered from the ship seem both necessary and difficult. In many *Nanban* screens the sea is shown in a static and lifeless way, and only a faint spray may be seen breaking against the bows of the ship; here, on the contrary, the boisterous waves give a real feeling of motion and energy.

In the second screen the captain-major, accompanied by negro slaves carrying not only a large parasol but also a typical *Nanban* chair, is being greeted by Jesuit and Franciscan missionaries. The citizens of the port peep curiously through doorways and lattices at the resplendent sight, while a bespectacled Jesuit beams myopically in welcome. The principal subject of this screen is undoubtedly the encounter between the newly arrived merchants and the resident missionaries on the main street, but details of great interest may be noted in the mission residence depicted on a higher plane and separated from the activities below by the conventional cloud. In the upper story of a pagodalike building surmounted by a cross a priest is instructing a young man as a novice enters the room carrying a bowl. In the chapel to the right a Japanese is making his confession to a priest, while four other figures kneel before an altar; two men wearing Portuguese dress squat on the balcony, and nearby a Japanese kisses the hand of a friar. Apparently the artist was perfectly familiar with the missionaries and the activities that took place within their residences. This splendid screen can be definitely attributed to Kanō Mitsunobu, and was therefore painted during the Keichō era.

Non-pictorial Art

During the period of contact with the West, but especially in the last decade of the sixteenth century, various customs and features of European life became very popular in Japan. Writing in September, 1594, the Jesuit Francisco Pasio noted that Hideyoshi and his courtiers would often wear Portuguese dress and even carry a rosary; some non-Christians took this fashion for things European a step further and learnt the *Pater Noster* and *Ave Maria* by heart in order to recite the prayers in public as a sort of fashionable talisman. An example of this short-lived craze may be seen in the picture of an open-air stage (Pl. 92), where the principal actress clearly wears a rosary dangling from her neck. Two Europeans, almost certainly Portuguese (Pl. 93), may be seen among the group of spectators, who are portrayed with no little ingenuity and humor. Two members of the audience are smoking pipes, yet another custom introduced from the West.

This foreign influence inspired Japanese artists to decorate their work, whether in ceramics, lacquer or metal, with Christian and European designs. Such decoration, however, was not introduced exclusively for the sake of fashion and novelty. Many converts desired to possess objects decorated with Christian motifs, which could be used in their daily lives. These could be displayed openly while the missionaries were free to work in Japan, but were perforce hidden away after Christianity had been proscribed by the Tokugawa authorities. As a result numerous pieces of ceramic and lacquer ware decorated with crosses and other Christian symbols have survived to this day. There were also other objects, such as bells, reliquaries and host boxes, which were made for specific use in the mission churches and chapels. Some of these pieces were probably manufactured in Europe, but many were undoubtedly produced by Japanese artists, inspired by European imports and the work of the students trained in the Jesuit seminaries.

Metalwork

During the century of contact with the West special importance was attached to engravings on copper plates by which religious pictures could be easily and cheaply reproduced. The missionaries had an urgent need to multiply such pictures for use in the instruction of catechumens, and engraved pictures could obviously be turned out more quickly than copies painted by hand. The technique of metal engraving was one of the subjects taught at the seminary, and the students' ability won high praise in the Jesuit letters. Some of the engravings have survived to the present day, and they amply demonstrate the skill that the Japanese achieved in this specialized art. The engraving *Virgin and Child* (Pl. 111) was made from a copper plate, and is probably the best example of this type of work to be produced in Japan at that time. A Latin inscription at the bottom states that the engraving was made in 1597 at the Jesuit seminary, which was then temporarily situated at Arie in the Shimabara peninsula. This particular copy of the engraving was found in Manila in the last century and brought back to Japan. As the inscription explains, the work is a reproduction of the famous mural decoration *Nuestra Señora de Antigua* in Seville Cathedral; the Spanish picture was the object of much pious devotion, and it is not surprising that copies found their way to Japan. There are other examples of this type of art, such as *Christ and Saint Joseph*, but it is not always possible to prove that they are the work of Japanese artists. But the engravings that decorate the frontispiece of some of the books produced by the Jesuit press in Japan were almost certainly made by local artists.

During the missionary century, many Japanese of the military class were converted and received baptism, and as a consequence Christian or Western emblems may be found on the armor and weapons produced during this period. The part of the sword that was most highly decorated was the *tsuba*, or "guard," and metalsmiths employed various designs, which differed in each period of Japanese art. Decoration of the *tsuba* attained a special prominence towards the end of the Muromachi period (1333–1573), and thus this trend coincided with the early part of the mission period. There are still extant many *tsuba* bearing Christian symbols, such as the cross, and Western designs (Pls. 108, 109). It must be borne in mind, however, that the cross is one of the most elementary forms possible of decoration, and it is not always easy to know definitely whether a cross on a *tsuba* is a genuine Christian symbol or merely a decorative device of no particular religious significance.

Christian emblems may be found on other parts of a warrior's equipment, and they sometimes figure prominently on suits of armor. Gamō Genzaimon Satonari, one of the principal retainers of the Christian daimyo Gamō Ujisato (1556–95), possessed a suit of armor (preserved in the Nanban Bunka-kan, Osaka) that features two large crosses painted in red lacquer, one on the front of the helmet and the other on the back of the corselet. Even more conclusive Christian symbols are to be found on a pair of ornate metal stirrups (Pl. 110), which are decorated with a motif of the Passion—column, nails, hammer and thorns, skillfully applied with gold and bronze encrustment. It is truly an interesting work in which the artist-craftsman has combined devotional and artistic expression. Another example of the same theme has been found engraved along the barrel of a Japanese arquebus manufactured during the same period.

Among the metal objects connected with the mission in Japan are some bronze bells intended for use in Christian churches. There are three of these extant, and all are in good condition. One of them was cast in 1612 for use in the hospital of Saint James, as its inscription clearly indicates. Another is kept in the Buddhist temple of Myōshin-ji at Kyoto and bears the Jesuit emblem IHS and the date 1577; the bell is said to have belonged to the Jesuit church in the capital, and the inscribed date is certainly consistent with this tradition, but the only definite information available states that the bell was at one time in Satsuma and was later transferred to a temple in Sendai. A third example (Pl. 107) is known as the Hosokawa bell, and is decorated with the *Kyūmon* crest of nine balls and a spiraling vegetal border around the rim. The bell belongs to the type called *asagao*, or "morning glory," as its shape is supposed to resemble that flower. It was presented by the Hosokawa family in 1616 to Mori Tadamasa to commemorate the completion of his castle, but later passed into the possession of the Matsudaira family.

Another kind of metalwork that may be included in the general category of *Nanban* productions consists of *fumi-e*, a term that literally means "treading pictures" (Pls. 24, 112, 113). These were cast metal plaques bearing a picture of Christ or the Virgin Mary and were employed by the Tokugawa authorities to discover secret Christians. The actual plaque was sometimes placed in the middle of a wooden tablet, and citizens were periodically required to trample on the figure as a sign of rejection of Christianity. Many of these *fumi-e* are still preserved, and in some cases the relief has been worn smooth through constant use. The plaques illustrate examples of Ecce Homo, Pietà and the Rosary, and undoubtedly show a certain ability in the art of metalwork, but on the whole they have a greater historical and religious value than artistic.

Lacquer Ware

Lacquer ware has a long tradition in the Orient, and it is not surprising that lacquered objects bearing decorative motifs in *Nanban* style were produced in some quantity during the period under examination. There was considerable demand for such pieces, since they were used for religious purposes in churches or carefully preserved by Christian families; in addition, many of these pieces were probably bought merely because *Nanban* decoration was particularly fashionable at the time. In most cases the *maki-e* technique of lacquering was employed in the manufacture of these articles. The decoration was painted on the lacquered surface, powdered with gold, silver or other metals, and occasionally inlay and incrustation were used. At its simplest, the the effect is gained by the metallic powder being sprinkled onto the lacquer while it is still wet; after it has dried, a further coat of lacquer may be applied over the decoration, and a high polish given to the finished product. A most decorative and handsome effect was obtained, and the quality of Japanese lacquering was unrivaled.

The host box shown here (Pl. 119) was discovered at Hagi in Yamaguchi Prefecture and is now preserved at Osaka. The lid bears the Jesuit emblem, surrounded by the customary circle of rays of light and tongues of fire. The sides of the box are decorated with a motif of ivy branches worked in gold by the *maki-e* process. There are similar boxes preserved in Tokyo National Museum, in the Tokugawa collection at Mito and in the Itsuō Museum at Ikeda in Okayama Prefecture.

Also to be found in the Osaka collection is a pair of seal boxes (Pls. 115, 116) which were used to contain seals engraved with the owner's name and were attached to the sash of the kimono by the cords. The first is decorated with flowered crosses and the ancient oriental *manji*, or "swastica," sign; a box with similar decorative motifs is preserved in Atami Museum. The second of these seal boxes is decorated with two *Nanban* figures and bears the name of Tsuchida Sōetsu. A lacquered saddle (Pl. 119), preserved at Kyoto University, also dates from this period and is of special interest as it clearly bears the letters FRCO. Since this was the monogram used by Ōtomo Sōrin, who received the name Francisco at his baptism in 1578, the saddle was probably commissioned for his personal use. The drum with card decoration (Pl. 118) is coated with lacquer and bears a decorative motif in gold *maki-e* featuring the type of playing cards called *unsun*. Western cards were introduced into Japan by the Europeans, and from these the Japanese produced packs of cards of various types, such as *unsun*, *tensho* and *sunkun*. The drum appears to date from the Tenshō era (1573–91), at which time this form of decoration was considered very smart and fashionable. The lacquered card box (Pl. 117) is also decorated with a design of *unsun* cards.

Ceramics

The mission century coincided with the Momoyama period (1573–1615), when the tea ceremony reached its highest point of development. Valignano laid great stress on the need for missionaries to appreciate this pastime and ordered that every major Jesuit residence should possess a fully equipped tea room where the ceremony could be performed with all due decorum to honor distinguished visitors. Some of the more experienced missionaries knew a great deal about this subject, and João Rodrigues wrote knowledgeably about the conventions and purpose of the ceremony in his *História da Igreja do Japão*. Moreover, some of the leading Christians were renowned for their skill and perception in this aesthetic pastime; in particular, Takayama Ukon distinguished himself in his discernment of the aesthetic values related to the art, and no less than three of the seven famous disciples of the celebrated master Sen no Rikyū (1520–91) were Christian.

Various tea utensils bearing Christian symbols are still preserved from this period, and examples of such *chawan*, or "tea bowls," may be found in the Osaka collection. One (Pl. 121) is made in the *oribe-yaki* style and bears a single white cross against a black background as its only decoration. Another (Pl. 120) is an example of the *raku-yaki* style, one of the most typical in the tradition of Japanese tea ceremony ceramics. It bears a tall elongated cross as its sole decoration and possesses great sober beauty in accordance with the Japanese *shibui* aesthetic.

But Western decoration was not confined only to tea utensils, and other ceramic pieces bearing Christian symbols were produced. Another example of ceramic work decorated with a cross is a bowl (Pl. 123), which is probably a product of the Hagi kilns located at the town of that name in Yamaguchi Prefecture. A center of Korean ceramic work was founded in this city, and most of its products bear a characteristic pale color. This particular bowl was discovered at Kyoto. Another bowl (Pl. 122), an exotic creation with thick sides, may have been used as a vase, and is decorated with a prominent cross and rays of light.

The field of *Nanban* art, taken in its widest sense, is so large and fascinating that entire volumes could be, and in fact have been, written about the different aspects of European influence on Japanese culture. In this chapter, however, only a rapid survey of some of the more prominent features of this movement has been possible, and references to related objects (such as Maria Kannon statues and Christian *dōrō*, or "stone lanterns") have had to be omitted. Instead of concentrating on a few particular topics, this essay has tried to present a comprehensive account of the main areas of Japanese art in which European influence was most productive and fruitful. But this influence should not be overestimated, and a specialized account runs the risk of giving the impression that the European impact was overwhelming and all-pervading. Such an extreme view is, of course, exaggerated and far from the truth. For every one *Nanban byōbu* painted during this period, dozens of other screens depicting traditional themes were produced by Japanese artists; for every *tsuba* decorated with a cross, thousands of others were manufactured bearing no relation to Christianity or the West in either design or decoration.

Nevertheless, the European impact was considerable, and the fashion for things Western, at least among the upper classes, reached extraordinary lengths in the last decade of the sixteenth century. Much of this passing enthusiasm was prompted by the return of the Kyushu ambassadors in 1590, with their illustrated books and paintings and their personal reminiscences about the splendor of Renaissance Europe. The same embassy aroused enthusiasm and interest in Europe, but nothing more; the fashion for things European in Japan was not paralleled by a commensurate demand in Europe for things Japanese. It is interesting and instructive to ponder on the reason why the reverse relationship was later to obtain between China and Europe.

It is also interesting and not entirely fruitless to speculate on the probable course of development that Japanese art might have taken if the Europeans had been allowed to remain and work freely in the country. The intemperate enthusiasm for the West would have doubtless subsided to more moderate levels, but the union of artistic techniques and aesthetic concepts might well have matured to produce a unique contribution, neither totally oriental nor totally European, but truly cosmopolitan, combining the best that East and West had to offer. Such might have been the happy outcome in ideal circumstances, but in fact this promising development was not allowed to continue. Perhaps the time was not yet ripe for such imaginative cooperation between peoples of radically different cultures. But a study of the art influenced by the arrival of the Southern Barbarians in Japan provides an intriguing glimpse of an enterprise, which, even if not wholly successful, managed for a time to transcend national and cultural boundaries.

BIBLIOGRAPHY

INDEX

BIBLIOGRAPHY

(For further titles of relevant books and articles, see Laures, *Kirishitan Bunko*, and Matsuda, *Nichi-Ō Kōshō-shi Bunken Mokuroku*.)

Anesaki Masaharu. *A Concordance to the History of Kirishitan Missions*. Proceedings of the Imperial Academy, VI (Supplement), Tokyo, 1930.

Boxer, C. R. "Some Aspects of Portuguese Influence in Japan, 1542–1640," in *Transactions and Proceedings of the Japan Society*, XXXIII, London, 1936.
———. "Padre João Rodriguez Tçuzzu, S.J., and His Japanese Grammars of 1604 and 1620," in *Miscelânea de filologia, literatura e história cultural à memória de Francisco Adolfo Coelho*, II, Lisbon, 1950.
———. *The Great Ship from Amacon. Annals of Macao and the Old Japan Trade, 1555–1640*, Lisbon, 1963.
———. *The Christian Century in Japan, 1549–1650*, Berkeley, 1967.

Cartas que los Padres y Hermanos de la Compañía de Jesus que andan en los Reynos de Japon escrivieron . . . , Alcalá, 1575.
Cartas que os Padres e Irmãos da Companhia de Jesus Escreverão dos Reynos de Iapão e China . . . , Evora, 1598.
Cieslik, S. J., Hubert. "Early Jesuit Missionaries in Japan," in *The Missionary Bulletin*, VIII–X, Tokyo, 1954–56.
———. *Hoku-hō Tanken-ki* ("Records of Exploration of the Northern Regions"), Tokyo, 1961.
———. "The Training of a Japanese Clergy in the 17th Century," in Joseph Roggendorf, S.J., ed., *Studies in Japanese Culture*, Tokyo, 1963.
Cocks, Richard. *The Diary of Richard Cocks, 1615–1622*, 2 vols., ed. N. Murakami, Tokyo, 1899.
Cooper, S. J., Michael, ed., *They Came to Japan: An Anthology of European Reports on Japan, 1543–1640*, Berkeley and London, 1965.
Costa Carneiro, José de. "Notas sobre a iconografia dos portugueses no Japão nos séculos XVI e XVII," in *Boletim da Sociedade Luso-Japonesa*, I, Tokyo, 1929.

Dahlgren, E. W. "Les débuts de la Cartographie du Japon," in *Archives d'Études Orientales*, IV, Upsala, 1911.
Delplace, S.J., Louis. *Le Catholicisme au Japon*, 2 vols., Malines and Brussels, 1909–10.
Doi Tadao. "Das Sprachstudium der Gesellschaft Jesu in Japan im 16. und 17. Jahrhundert," in *Monumenta Nipponica*, II, Tokyo, 1939.
———. *Kirishitan Bunken-kō* ("*Kirishitan* Literature"), Tokyo, 1963. *See also* Rodrigues.

Ebisawa Arimichi. *Kirishitan Shakai Katsudō oyobi Nanban Igaku* ("*Kirishitan* Social Work and *Nanban* Medicine"), Tokyo, 1944.

————. *Yōgaku, Engeki Jisho. Kirishitan no Ongaku to Engeki* ("*Kirishitan* Music and Drama"), Tokyo, 1947.

————. *Nanban Gakutō no Kenkyū* ("Research into *Nanban* Studies"), Tokyo, 1958.

————. "The Jesuits and Their Cultural Activities in the Far East," in *Cahiers d' Histoire Mondiale*, V, Paris, 1959.

Frois, S.J., Luis. *Die Geschichte Japans, 1549–1578*, eds., Georg Schurhammer, S. J., & E. A. Voretzsch, Leipzig, 1926.

————. *Segunda Parte da Historia de Japam, 1578–1582*, eds. J. A. Abranches Pinto & Y. Okamoto, Tokyo, 1938.

————. *La Première Ambassade du Japon en Europe, 1582–1592*, eds., J. A. Abranches Pinto, Y. Okamoto & Henri Bernard, S. J. (*Monumenta Nipponica* Monograph, No. 6), Tokyo, 1942.

————. *Kulturgegensätze Europa-Japan, 1585. Tratado em que se contem muito sustina- e abreviadamente algumas contradições e diferenças de custumes . . .* , ed. J. F. Schütte, S. J. (*Monumenta Nipponica* Monograph, No. 15), Tokyo, 1955.

Guerreiro, S. J., Fernão. *Relação anual das Coisas que fizeram os Padres da Companhia de Jesus nas suas Missões . . .* , 3 vols., ed. Artur Viegas, Coimbra, 1930–42.

Guzman, S. J., Luis de. *Historia de las Misiones que han hecho los Religiosos de la Compañía de de Iesus . . .* , Alcalá, 1601.

Haas, Hans. *Geschichte des Christentums in Japan*, 2 vols., Tokyo, 1902–1904.

Hartmann, O.S.A., Arnulf. *The Augustinians in Seventeenth Century Japan*, Ontario, 1965.

Jennes, C.I.C.M., Joseph. *A History of the Catholic Church in Japan*, Tokyo, 1959.

Kaempfer, Engelbert. *The History of Japan . . .* , *1690–1692*, 3 vols., Glasgow, 1906.

Kirishitan Kenkyū ("*Kirishitan* Studies"), I-XIII, Tokyo, 1942–70.

Lach, Donald. *Asia in the Making of Europe*, I, Chicago, 1965.

Laures, S.J., Johannes. *Nobunaga und das Christentum* (*Monumenta Nipponica* Monograph, No. 10), Tokyo, 1950.

————. *The Catholic Church in Japan: A Short History*, Tokyo, 1954.

————. *Kirishitan Bunko* ("*Kirishitan* Library") (*Monumenta Nipponica* Monograph, No. 5), 3rd ed., Tokyo, 1957.

Matsuda Ki-ichi. *Kirishitan Kenkyū* ("*Kirishitan* Studies"), Osaka, 1953.

————. *Nichi-Ō Kōshō-shi Bunken Mokuroku* ("Catalogue of Studies on the Historial Relations between Japan and Europe"), Tokyo, 1965.

————. *Nanban Shiryō no Kenkyū* ("Studies in *Nanban* Historical Materials"), Tokyo, 1967.

McCall, J. E. "Early Jesuit Art in the Far East," in *Artibus Asiae*, X-XI, Dresden, 1947–48.

Miki Tamon. "The Influence of Western Culture on Japanese Art," in *Monumenta Nipponica*, XIX, Tokyo, 1964.

Nachod, Oskar. *Die Beziehungen der Niederländischen Ostindischen Kompagnie zu Japan im siebzehnten Jahrhundert*, Leipzig, 1897.

Nishimura Tei. *Nanban Bijutsu* ("*Nanban* Art"), Tokyo, 1958.

Okamoto Yoshitomo. *Jūroku-seiki Nichi-Ō Kōtsū-shi* ("History of Japanese-European Relations in the 16th Century"), Tokyo, 1936.

————. *Outline of Nanban Art*, Tokyo, 1949.

————. *Nanban Byōbu-kō* ("Research into *Nanban* Screens"), Tokyo, 1955.

————. *Toyotomi Hideyoshi—Nanbanjin no Kiroku ni Yoru* ("Toyotomi Hideyoshi, According to the Records of the Europeans"), Tokyo, 1963.

Pacheco, S.J., Diego. *Mártires en Nagasaki*, Bilbao, 1961.

Pagès, Léon. *Histoire de la Religion Chrétienne au Japon depuis 1598 jusqu'à 1651*, 2 vols., Paris, 1869–70.

Pérez, O.F.M., Lorenzo. *Cartas y Relaciones del Japón*, 3 vols., Madrid, 1916–23.

———. *Fray Jerónimo de Jesús, Restaurador de las Misiones del Japón, Sus Cartas y Relaciones*, Madrid, 1923.

Purchas, Samuel. *Purchas His Pilgrimes in Japan*, ed. Cyril Wild, Kobe, 1939.

Ribadeneira, O.F.M., Marcelo de. *Historia de las Islas del Archipiélago . . .*, ed. J. de Legísima, O.F.M., Madrid, 1947.

Roberts, P. G. *The First Englishman in Japan*, London, 1956.

Rodrigues, S.J., João. *Arte da Lingoa de Iapam . . .* , Nagasaki, 1608 (Japanese translation: *Nihon Daibunten*, ed. Tadao Doi, Tokyo, 1955).

———. *Arte Breve da Lingoa Japoa . . .* , Macao, 1620.

Rodrigues, S.J., João. *História da Igreja do Japão*, 2 vols., ed. J. A. Abranches Pinto, Macao, 1954–56 (Japanese translation: *Nihon Kyōkai-shi*, 2 vols., ed. Tadao Doi, Tokyo, 1967–70).

Sakamoto Mitsuru et al. *Nanban Bijutsu to Yōfūga* (*"Nanban* Art and Western-style Painting"), Tokyo, 1970.

Sansom, G. B. *Japan, A Short Cultural History*, London, 1952.

———. *A History of Japan to 1334*, London, 1958.

———. *A History of Japan, 1334–1615*, London, 1961.

Saris, John. *The Voyage of Captain John Saris to Japan, 1613*, ed. Ernest Satow, London, 1890.

Satow, Ernest. *The Jesuit Mission Press in Japan 1591–1610*, London, 1888.

Schilling, O.F.M., Dorotheus. *Das Schulwesen der Jesuiten in Japan 1551–1614*, Münster, 1931.

———. *Os Portugueses e a introdução da medicina no Japão*, Coimbra, 1937.

Schurhammer, S.J., Georg. *Das kirchliche Sprachproblem in der japanischen Jesuitenmission des 16. und 17. Jahrhunderts*, Tokyo, 1928.

———. *Gesammelte Studien*, II, *Orientalia*, Lisbon & Rome, 1963.
(The following articles in this volume are of special interest:
"P. Johann Rodrigues Tçuzzu als Geschichtschreiber Japans"
"Die Jesuitenmissionare des 16. und 17. Jahrhunderts und ihr Einfluss auf die japanische Malerei"
"P. Luis Frois, S.I., ein Missionshistoriker des 16. Jahrhunderts in Indien und Japan"
"O descobrimento do Japão pelos Portugueses no ano de 1543")

———. *Franz Xaver. Sein Leben und seine Zeit*, Freiburg, I–, 1959–   .

Schütte, S.J., Josef Franz. *Valignanos Missionsgrundsätze für Japan*, 2 vols., Rome, 1951–58.

———. *Introductio ad Historiam Societatis Jesu in Japonia*, Rome, 1968.

Teleki, Paul. *Atlas zur Geschichte der Kartographie der japanischen Inseln*, Budapest, 1909.

Uyttenbroeck, O.F.M., Thomas. *Early Franciscans in Japan*, Himeji, 1959.

Valignano, S.J., Alessandro. *Historia del Principio y Progresso de la Compañía de Jesús en las Indias Orientales, 1542–1564*, ed. J. Wicki, S.J., Rome, 1944.

———. *Il Cerimoniale per i Missionari del Giappone. Advertimentos e avisos acerca dos costumes e catangues de Jappão*, ed. J. F. Schütte, S.J., Rome, 1946.

———. *Sumario de las Cosas del Japón, 1583 . . .* , ed. José Luis Alvarez-Taladriz (*Monumenta Nipponica* Monograph, No. 9), Tokyo, 1954.

Vocabulario da Lingoa de Iapam com a declaração em Portugues, feito por alguns Padres, e Irmãos da Companhia de Iesu, Nagasaki, 1603–1604 (facsimile edition also published in Tokyo in 1960).

Xavier, S.J., Francisco. *Epistolae S. Francisci Xaverii*, 2 vols., eds. G. Schurhammer, S.J., & J. Wicki, S.J., Rome, 1944–45.

INDEX

214